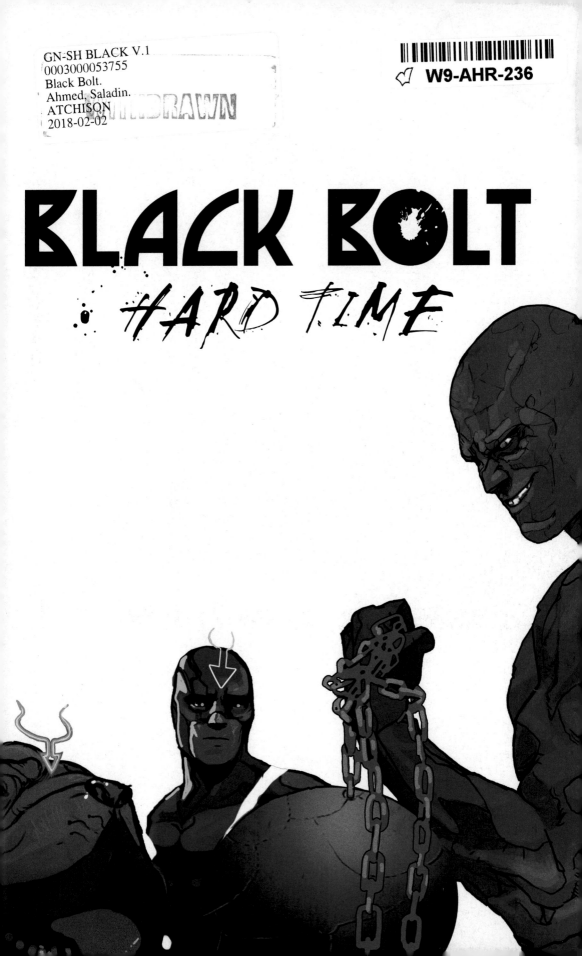

BLACK BOLT
HARD TIME

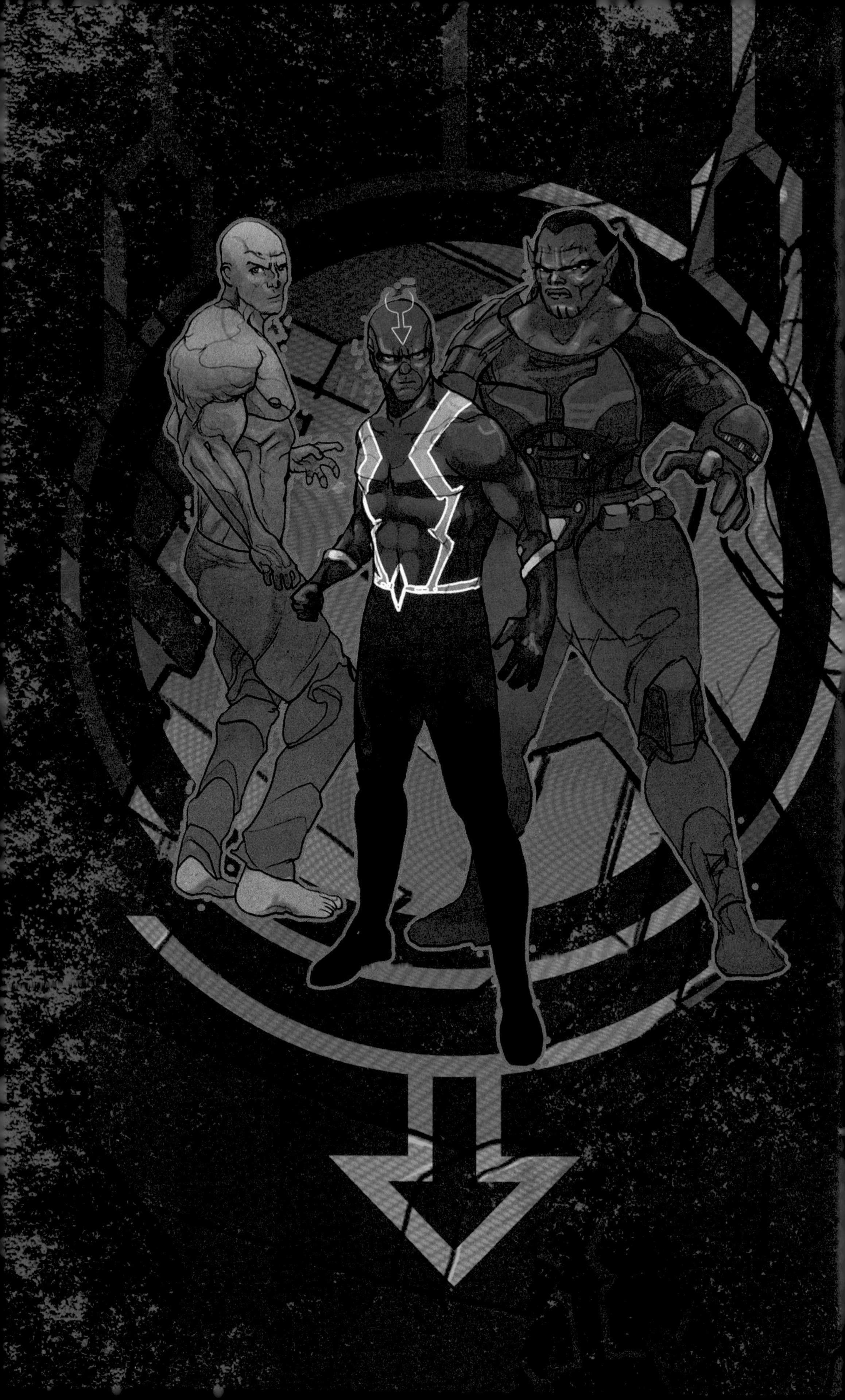

BLACK BOLT
HARD TIME

SALADIN AHMED
WRITER

CHRISTIAN WARD
WITH **FRAZER IRVING** [#5]
ARTIST

VC's CLAYTON COWLES
LETTERER

CHRISTIAN WARD
COVER ART

CHARLES BEACHAM
ASSISTANT EDITOR

SARAH BRUNSTAD
ASSOCIATE EDITOR

WIL MOSS
EDITOR

TOM BREVOORT
EXECUTIVE EDITOR

BLACK BOLT CREATED BY **STAN LEE & JACK KIRBY**

COLLECTION EDITOR **JENNIFER GRÜNWALD** ▪ ASSISTANT EDITOR **CAITLIN O'CONNELL**
ASSOCIATE MANAGING EDITOR **KATERI WOODY** ▪ EDITOR, SPECIAL PROJECTS **MARK D. BEAZLEY**
VP PRODUCTION & SPECIAL PROJECTS **JEFF YOUNGQUIST** ▪ SVP PRINT, SALES & MARKETING **DAVID GABRIEL**
BOOK DESIGNER **JAY BOWEN**

EDITOR IN CHIEF **AXEL ALONSO** ▪ CHIEF CREATIVE OFFICER **JOE QUESADA**
PRESIDENT **DAN BUCKLEY** ▪ EXECUTIVE PRODUCER **ALAN FINE**

BLACK BOLT VOL. 1: HARD TIME. Contains material originally published in magazine form as BLACK BOLT #1-6. First printing 2017. ISBN# 978-1-302-90732-7. Published by MARVEL WORLDWIDE, INC., a subsidiary of MARVEL ENTERTAINMENT, LLC. OFFICE OF PUBLICATION: 135 West 50th Street, New York, NY 10020. Copyright © 2017 MARVEL No similarity between any of the names, characters, persons, and/or institutions in this magazine with those of any living or dead person or institution is intended, and any such similarity which may exist is purely coincidental. **Printed in the U.S.A.** DAN BUCKLEY, President, Marvel Entertainment; JOE QUESADA, Chief Creative Officer; TOM BREVOORT, SVP of Publishing; DAVID BOGART, SVP of Business Affairs & Operations, Publishing & Partnership; C.B. CEBULSKI, VP of Brand Management & Development, Asia; DAVID GABRIEL, SVP of Sales & Marketing, Publishing; JEFF YOUNGQUIST, VP of Production & Special Projects; DAN CARR, Executive Director of Publishing Technology; ALEX MORALES, Director of Publishing Operations; SUSAN CRESPI, Production Manager; STAN LEE, Chairman Emeritus. For information regarding advertising in Marvel Comics or on Marvel.com, please contact Vit DeBellis, Integrated Sales Manager, at vdebellis@marvel.com. For Marvel subscription inquiries, please call 888-511-5480. **Manufactured between 10/13/2017 and 11/13/2017 by QUAD/GRAPHICS WASECA, WASECA, MN, USA.**

10 9 8 7 6 5 4 3 2 1

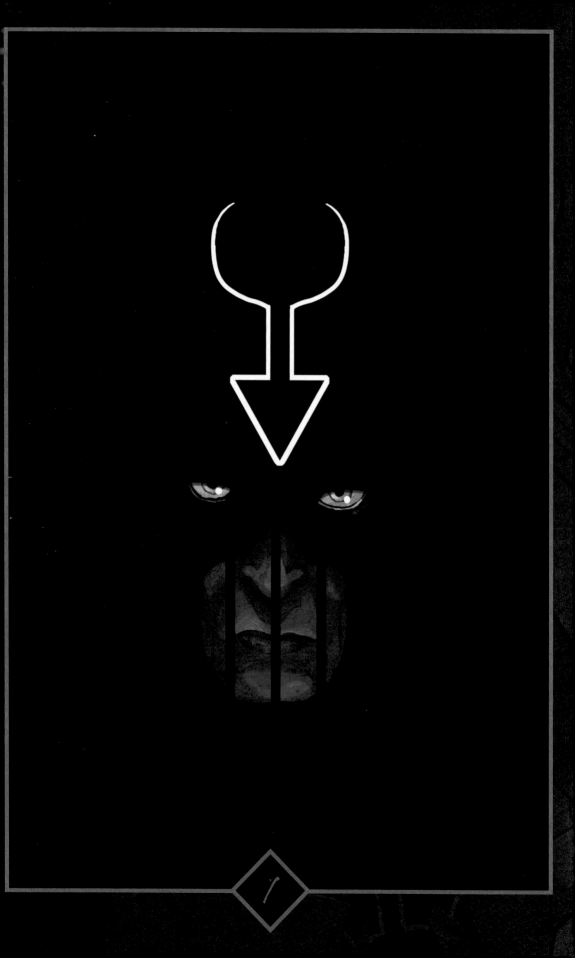

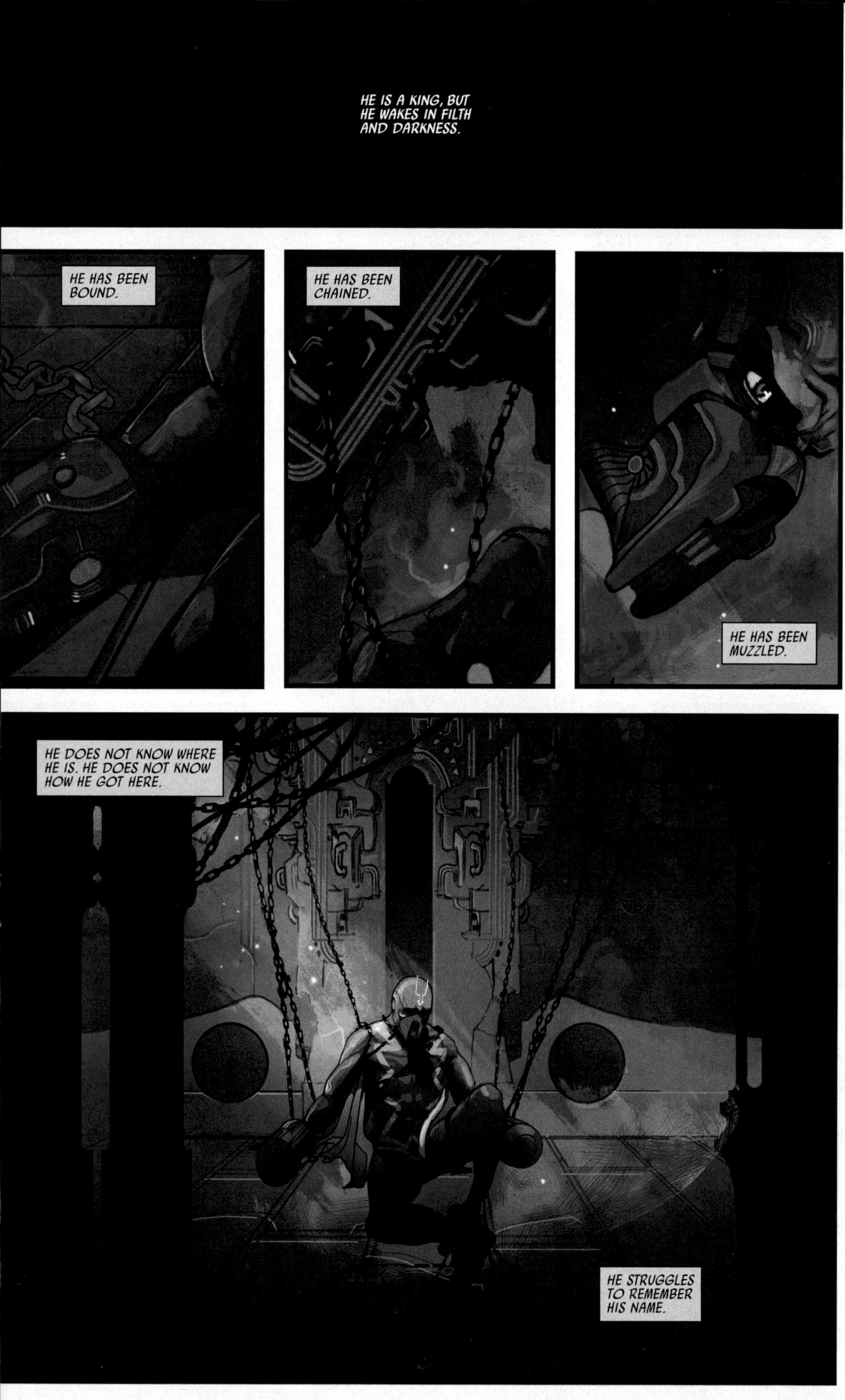
HE IS A KING, BUT HE WAKES IN FILTH AND DARKNESS.
HE HAS BEEN BOUND.
HE HAS BEEN CHAINED.
HE HAS BEEN MUZZLED.
HE DOES NOT KNOW WHERE HE IS. HE DOES NOT KNOW HOW HE GOT HERE.
HE STRUGGLES TO REMEMBER HIS NAME.

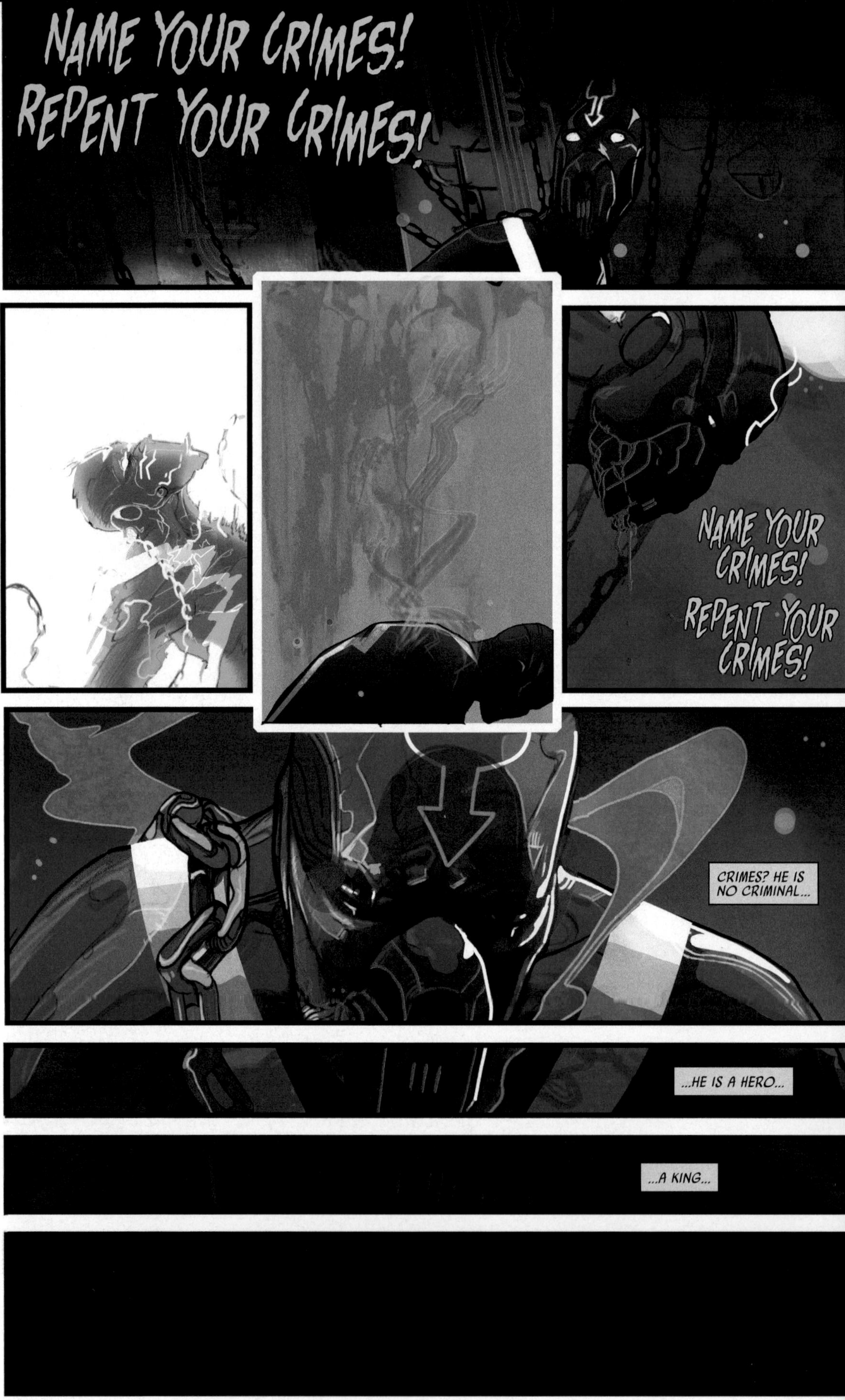
NAME YOUR CRIMES!
REPENT YOUR CRIMES!
NAME YOUR CRIMES!
REPENT YOUR CRIMES!
CRIMES? HE IS NO CRIMINAL...
...HE IS A HERO...
...A KING...

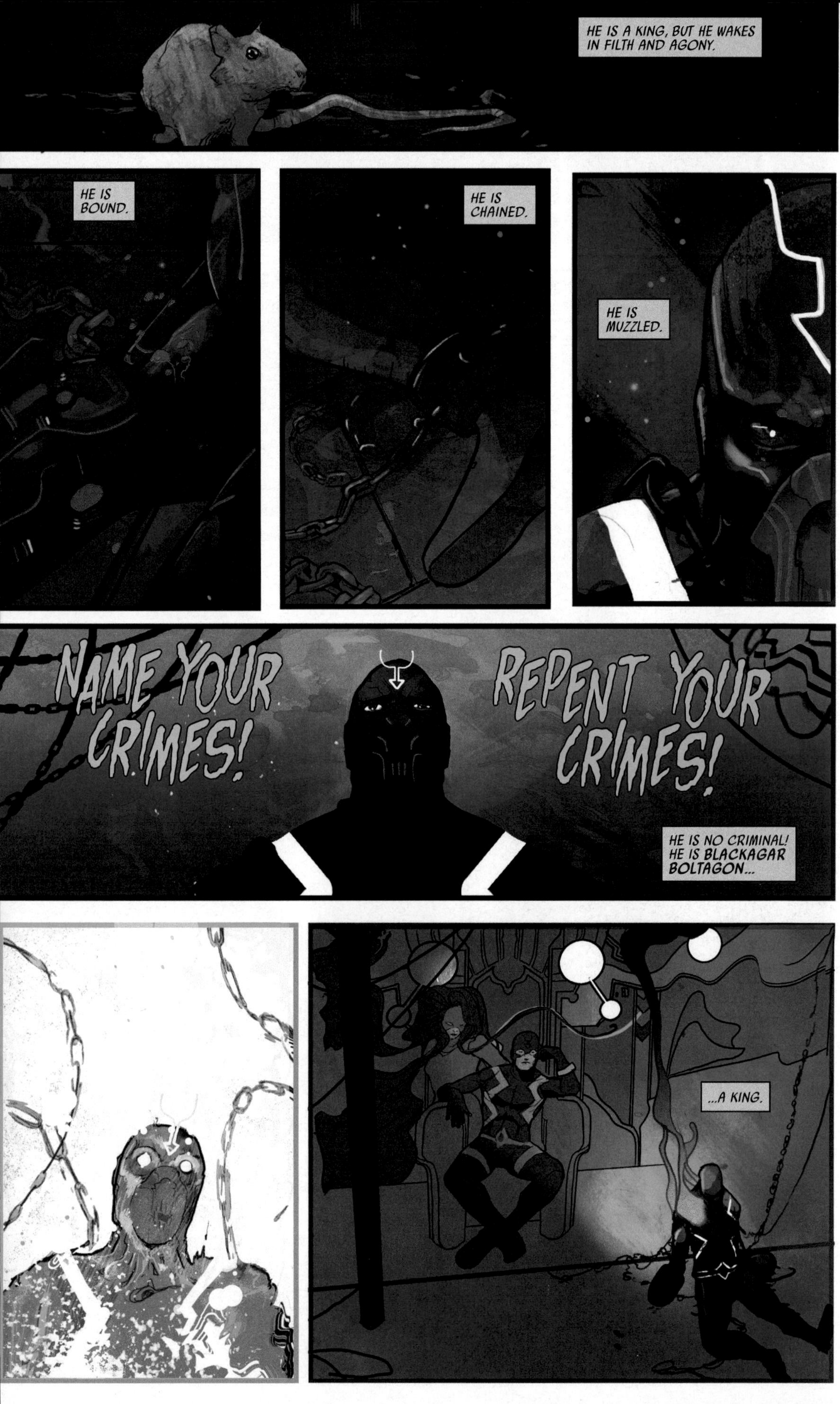

HE IS A KING, BUT HE WAKES IN FILTH AND AGONY.
HE IS BOUND.
HE IS CHAINED.
HE IS MUZZLED.
NAME YOUR CRIMES!
REPENT YOUR CRIMES!
HE IS NO CRIMINAL! HE IS BLACKAGAR BOLTAGON...
...A KING.

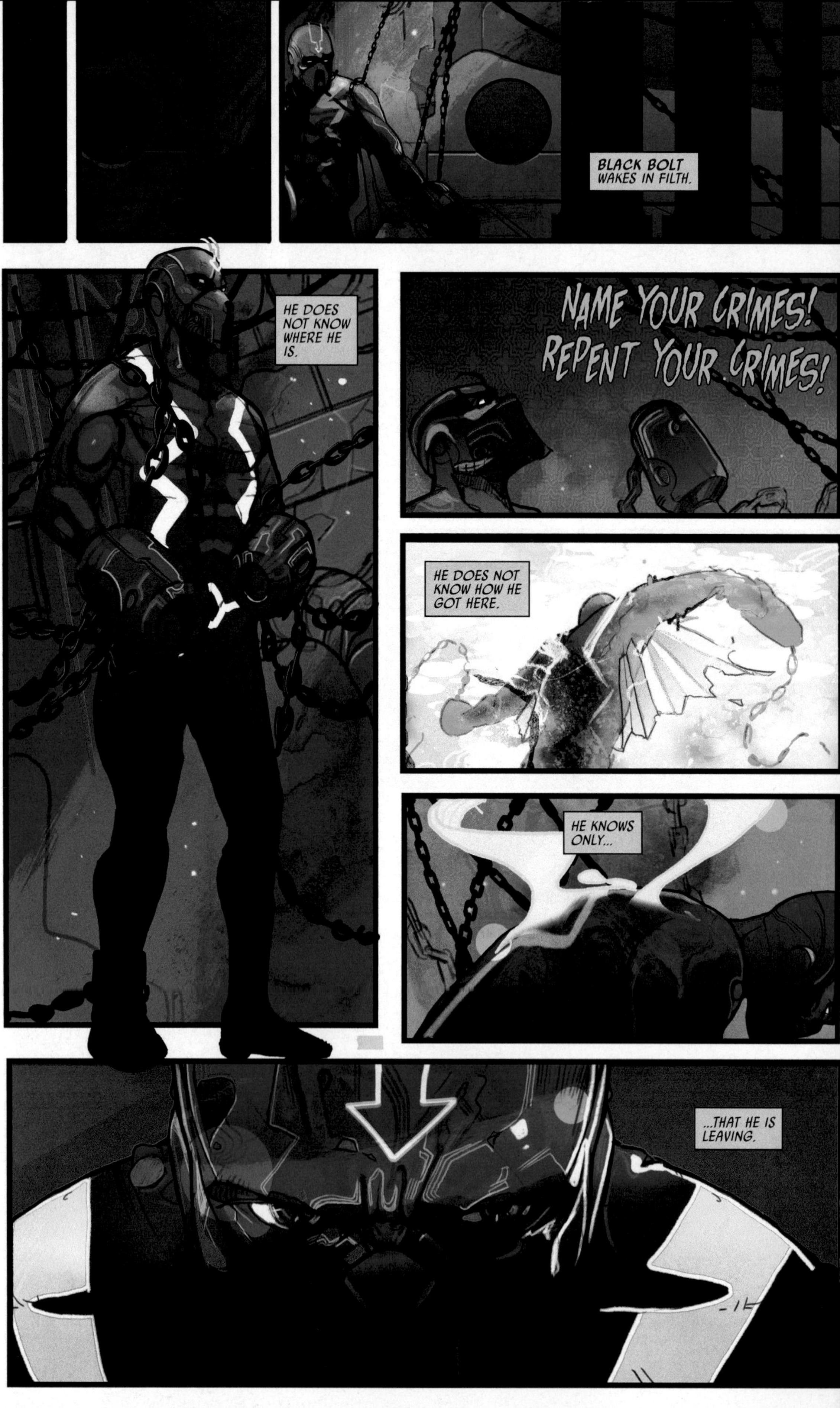
BLACK BOLT WAKES IN FILTH.
HE DOES NOT KNOW WHERE HE IS.
NAME YOUR CRIMES! REPENT YOUR CRIMES!
HE DOES NOT KNOW HOW HE GOT HERE.
HE KNOWS ONLY...
...THAT HE IS LEAVING.

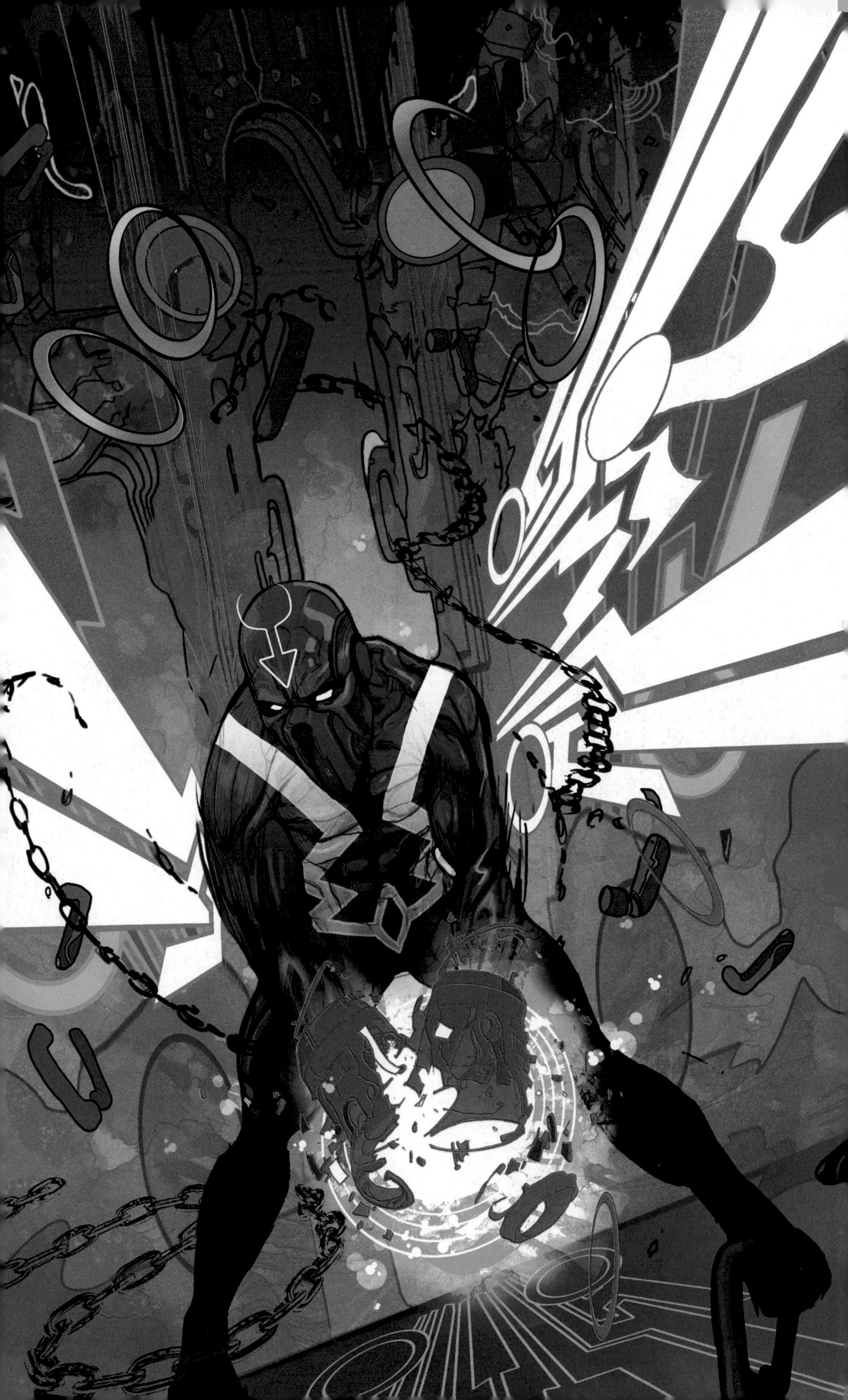

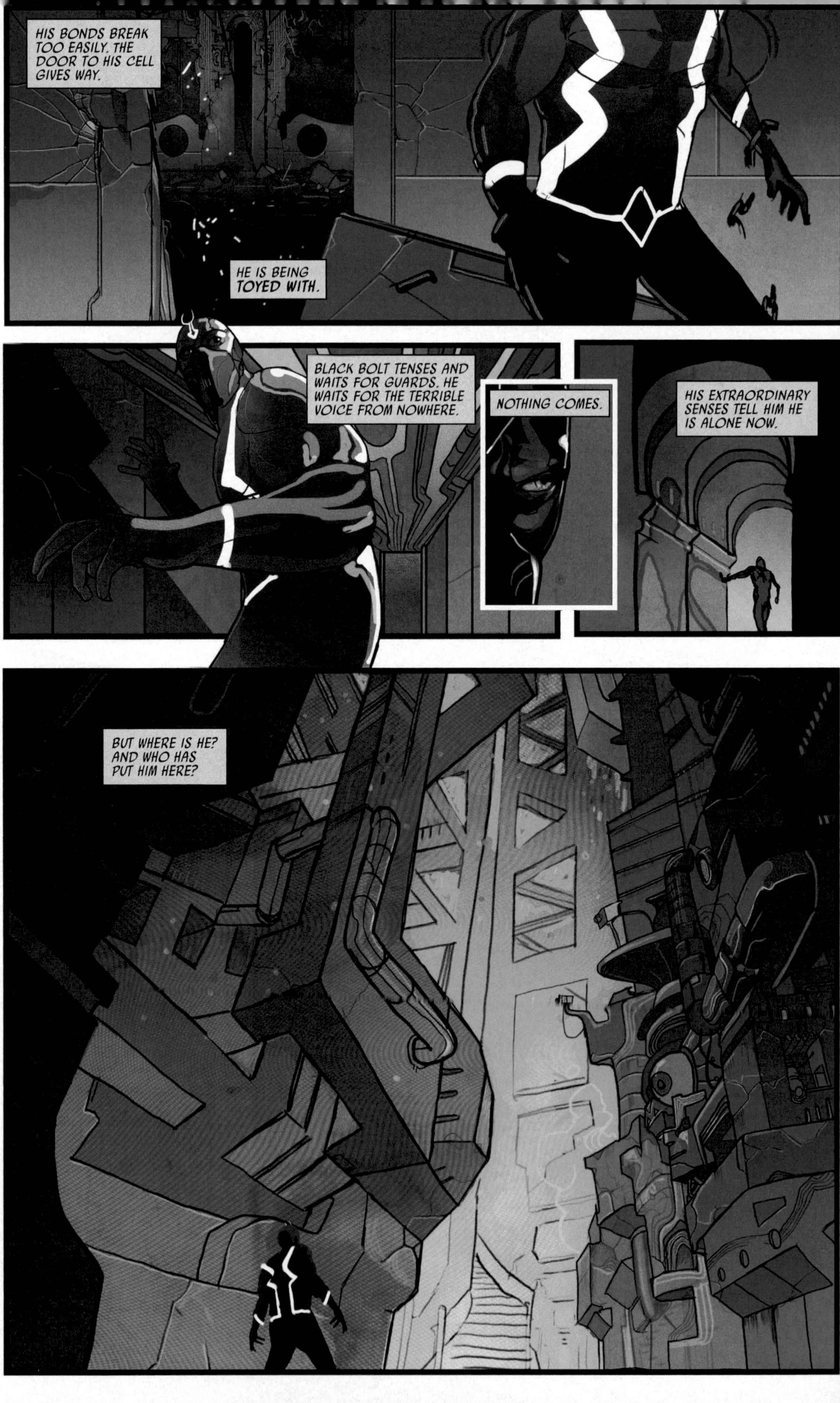
HIS BONDS BREAK TOO EASILY. THE DOOR TO HIS CELL GIVES WAY.
HE IS BEING TOYED WITH.
BLACK BOLT TENSES AND WAITS FOR GUARDS. HE WAITS FOR THE TERRIBLE VOICE FROM NOWHERE.
NOTHING COMES.
HIS EXTRAORDINARY SENSES TELL HIM HE IS ALONE NOW.
BUT WHERE IS HE? AND WHO HAS PUT HIM HERE?

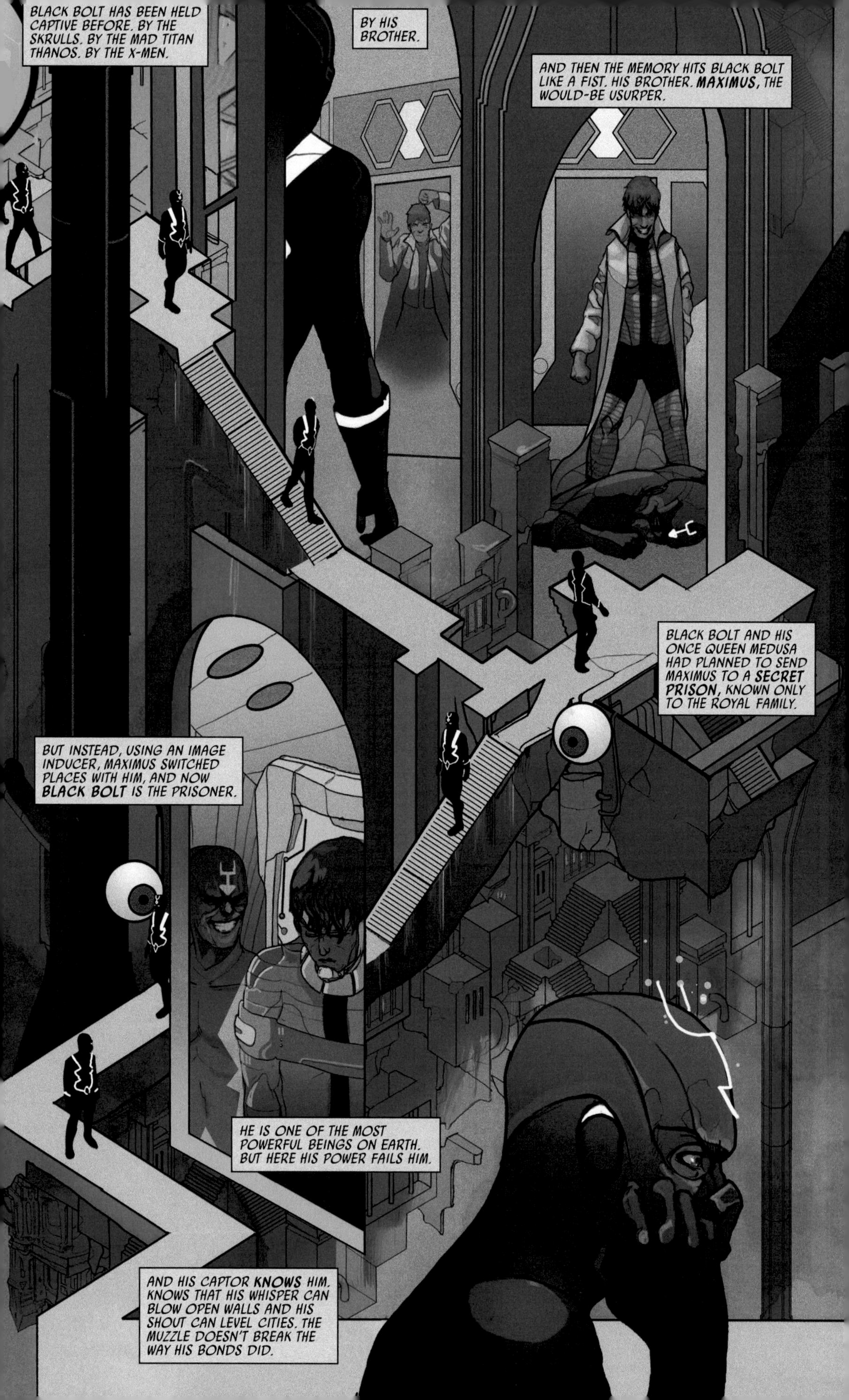
BLACK BOLT HAS BEEN HELD CAPTIVE BEFORE. BY THE SKRULLS. BY THE MAD TITAN THANOS. BY THE X-MEN.
BY HIS BROTHER.
AND THEN THE MEMORY HITS BLACK BOLT LIKE A FIST. HIS BROTHER. MAXIMUS, THE WOULD-BE USURPER.
BLACK BOLT AND HIS ONCE QUEEN MEDUSA HAD PLANNED TO SEND MAXIMUS TO A SECRET PRISON, KNOWN ONLY TO THE ROYAL FAMILY.
BUT INSTEAD, USING AN IMAGE INDUCER, MAXIMUS SWITCHED PLACES WITH HIM, AND NOW BLACK BOLT IS THE PRISONER.
HE IS ONE OF THE MOST POWERFUL BEINGS ON EARTH. BUT HERE HIS POWER FAILS HIM.
AND HIS CAPTOR KNOWS HIM. KNOWS THAT HIS WHISPER CAN BLOW OPEN WALLS AND HIS SHOUT CAN LEVEL CITIES. THE MUZZLE DOESN'T BREAK THE WAY HIS BONDS DID.

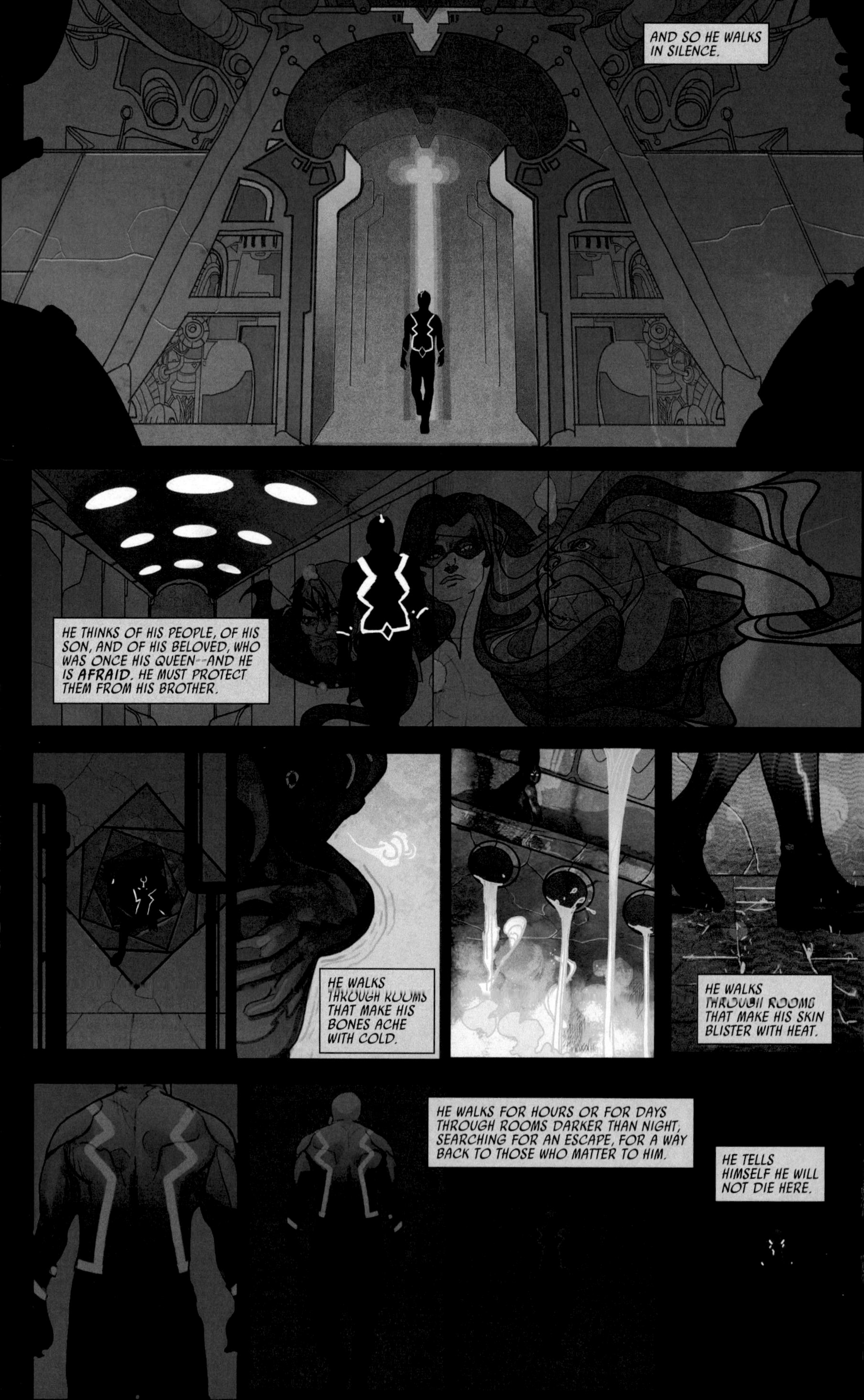
AND SO HE WALKS IN SILENCE.
HE THINKS OF HIS PEOPLE, OF HIS SON, AND OF HIS BELOVED, WHO WAS ONCE HIS QUEEN--AND HE IS **AFRAID**. HE MUST PROTECT THEM FROM HIS BROTHER.
HE WALKS THROUGH ROOMS THAT MAKE HIS BONES ACHE WITH COLD.
HE WALKS THROUGH ROOMS THAT MAKE HIS SKIN BLISTER WITH HEAT.
HE WALKS FOR HOURS OR FOR DAYS THROUGH ROOMS DARKER THAN NIGHT, SEARCHING FOR AN ESCAPE, FOR A WAY BACK TO THOSE WHO MATTER TO HIM.
HE TELLS HIMSELF HE WILL NOT DIE HERE.

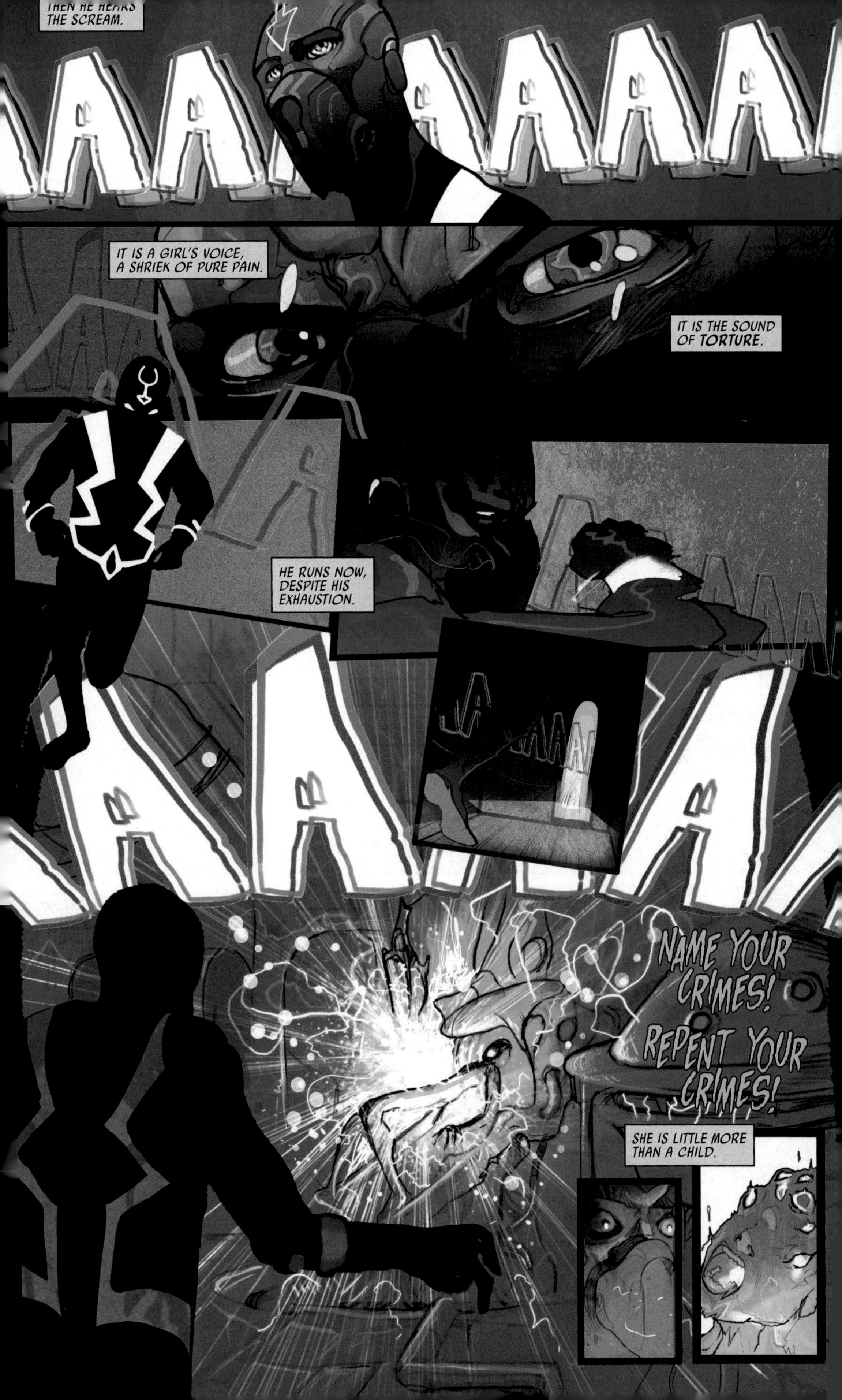

THEN HE HEARS THE SCREAM.
AAAAAAAA
IT IS A GIRL'S VOICE, A SHRIEK OF PURE PAIN.
IT IS THE SOUND OF TORTURE.
HE RUNS NOW, DESPITE HIS EXHAUSTION.
AAAAAAAA
NAME YOUR CRIMES!
REPENT YOUR CRIMES!
SHE IS LITTLE MORE THAN A CHILD.

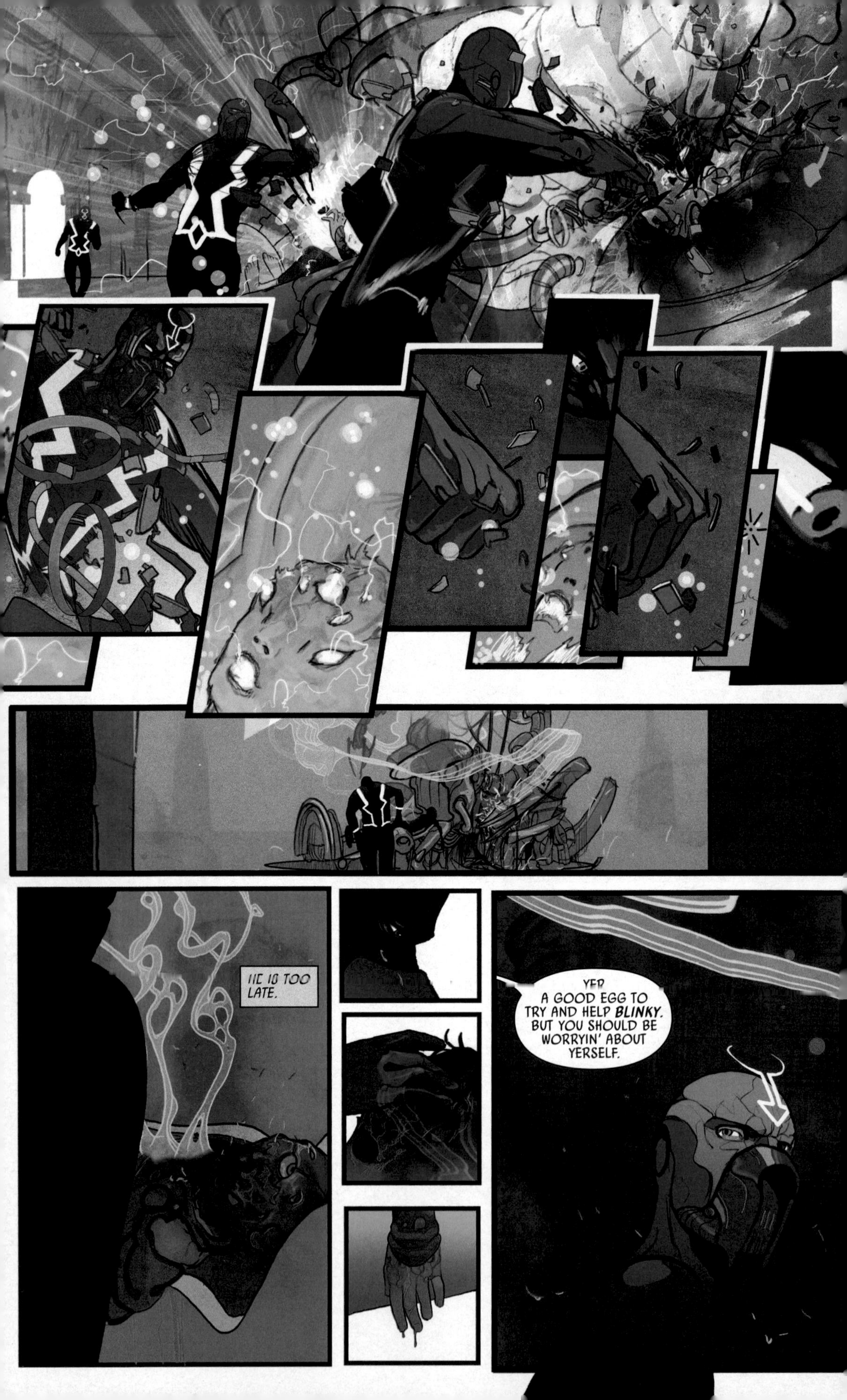
HE IS TOO LATE.
YER A GOOD EGG TO TRY AND HELP BLINKY. BUT YOU SHOULD BE WORRYIN' ABOUT YERSELF.

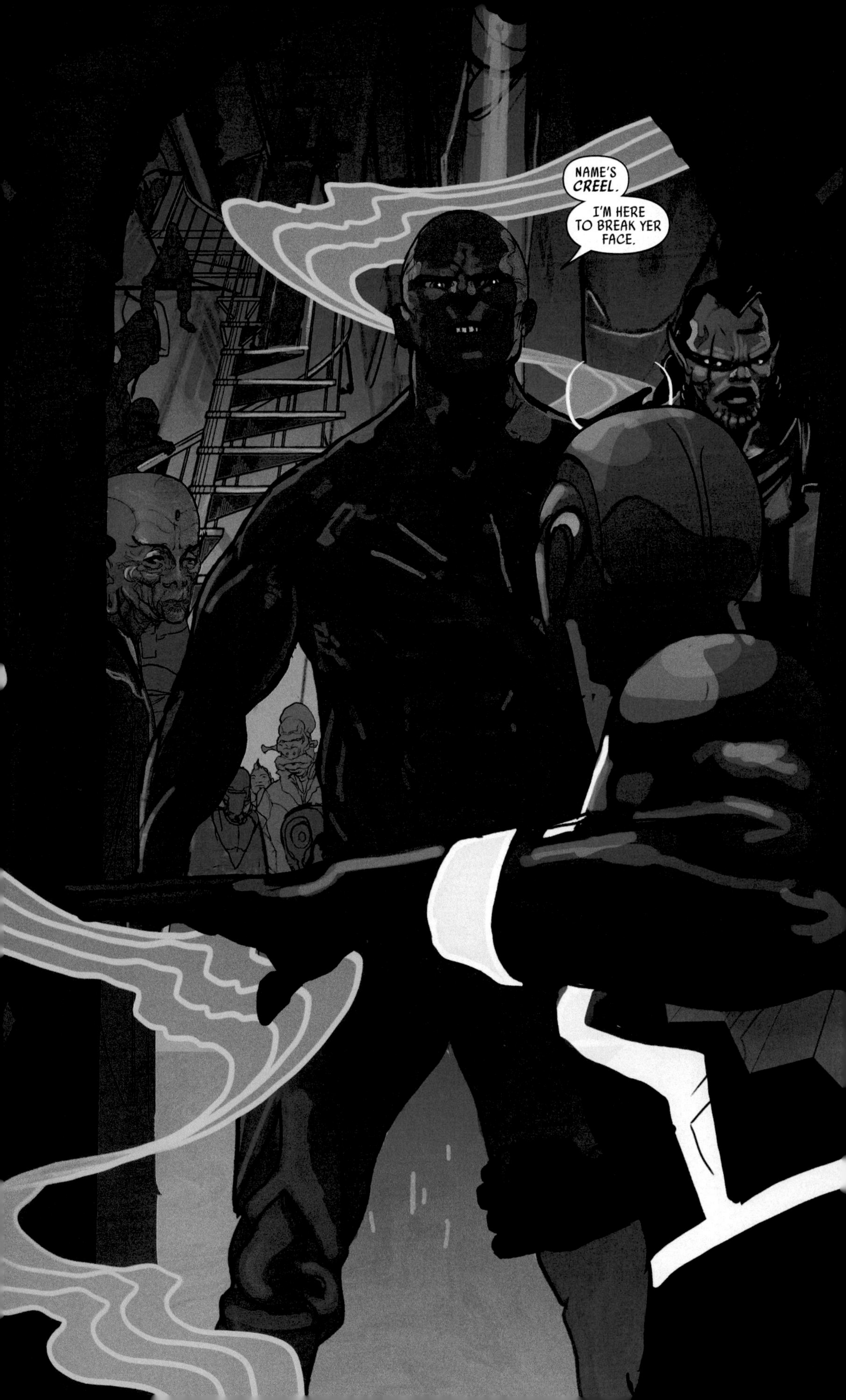
NAME'S CREEL.
I'M HERE TO BREAK YER FACE.

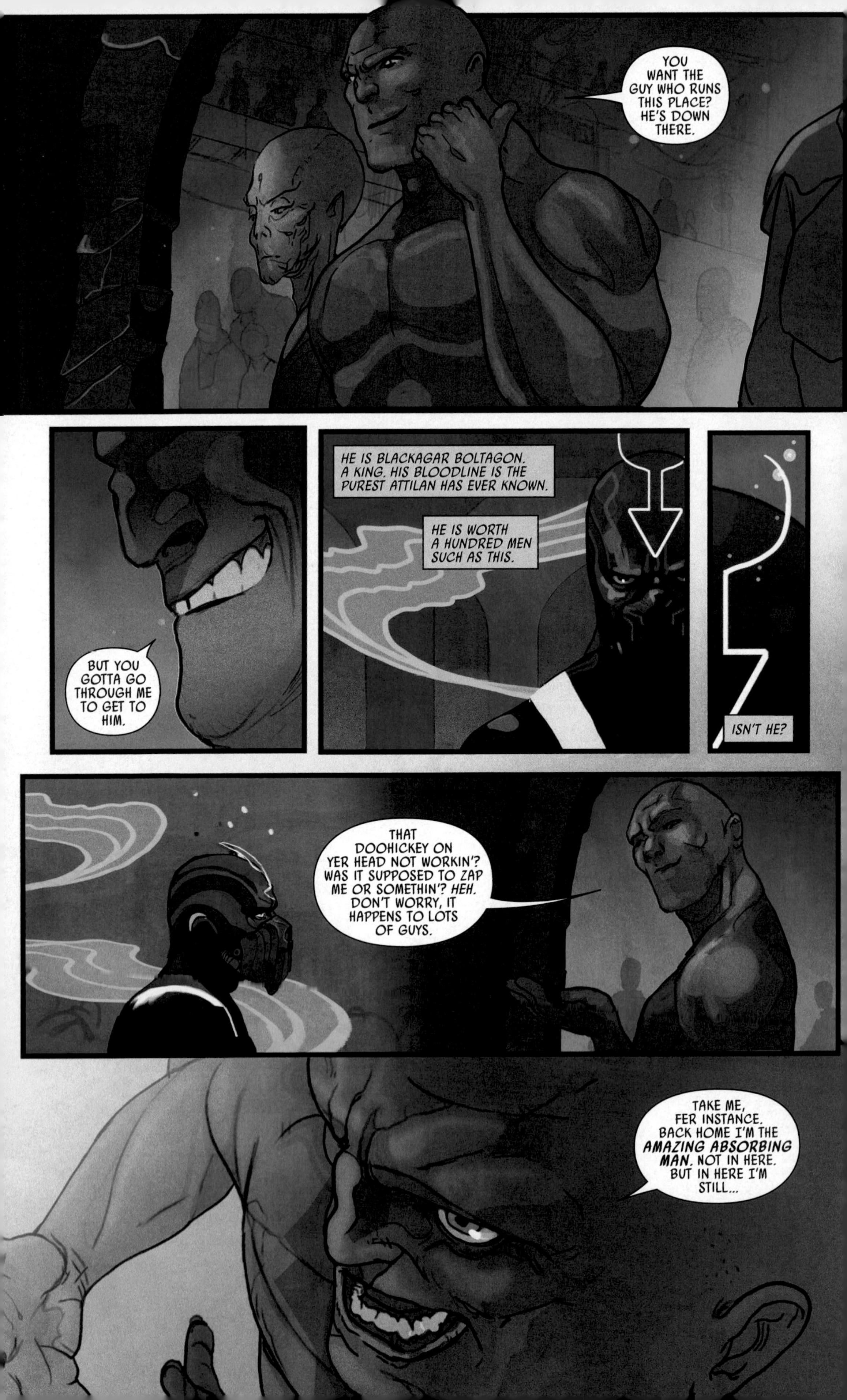
YOU WANT THE GUY WHO RUNS THIS PLACE? HE'S DOWN THERE.
BUT YOU GOTTA GO THROUGH ME TO GET TO HIM.
HE IS BLACKAGAR BOLTAGON. A KING. HIS BLOODLINE IS THE PUREST ATTILAN HAS EVER KNOWN.
HE IS WORTH A HUNDRED MEN SUCH AS THIS.
ISN'T HE?
THAT DOOHICKEY ON YER HEAD NOT WORKIN'? WAS IT SUPPOSED TO ZAP ME OR SOMETHIN'? HEH. DON'T WORRY, IT HAPPENS TO LOTS OF GUYS.
TAKE ME, FER INSTANCE. BACK HOME I'M THE AMAZING ABSORBING MAN. NOT IN HERE. BUT IN HERE I'M STILL...

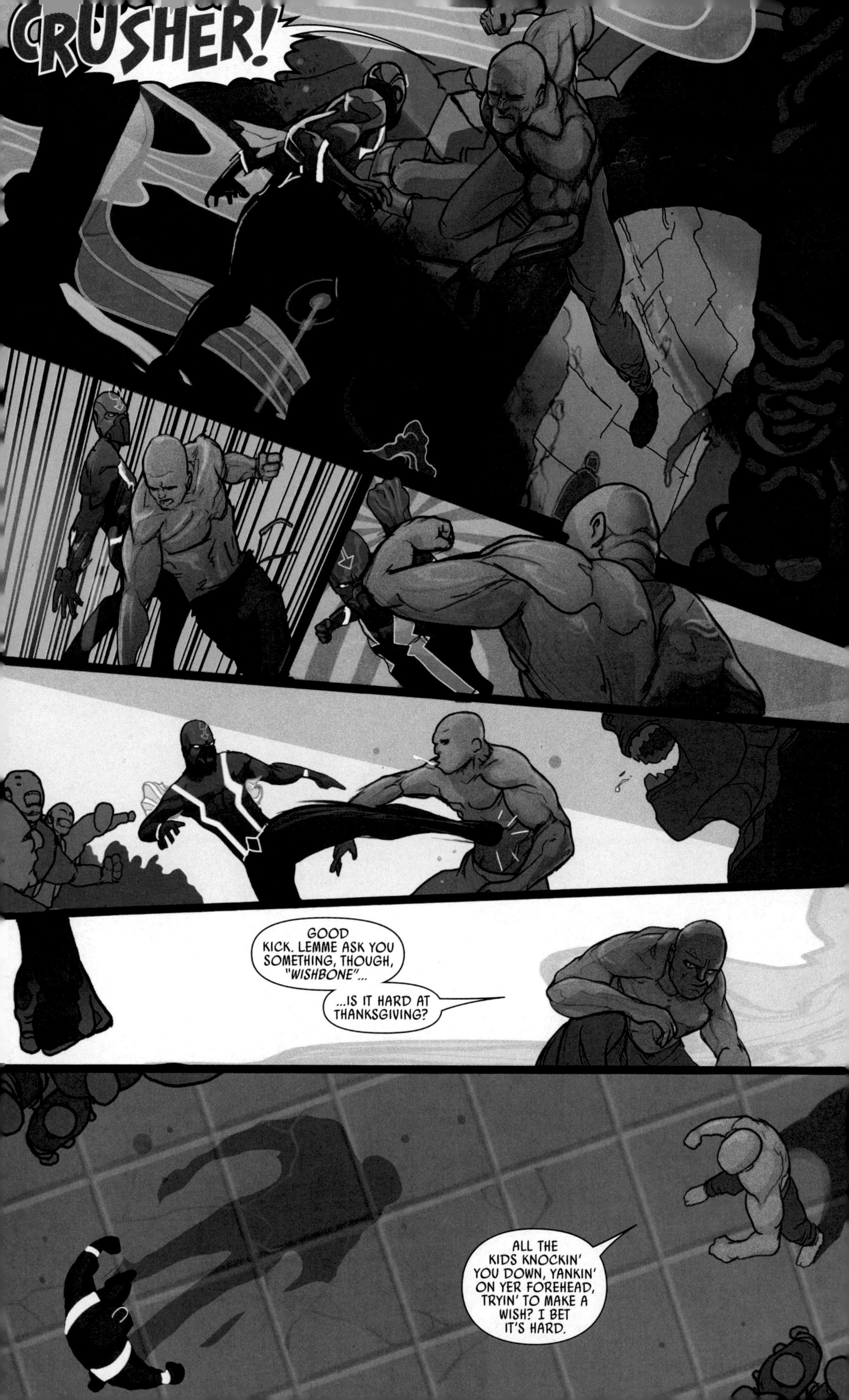
CRUSHER!
GOOD KICK. LEMME ASK YOU SOMETHING, THOUGH, "WISHBONE"...
...IS IT HARD AT THANKSGIVING?
ALL THE KIDS KNOCKIN' YOU DOWN, YANKIN' ON YER FOREHEAD, TRYIN' TO MAKE A WISH? I BET IT'S HARD.

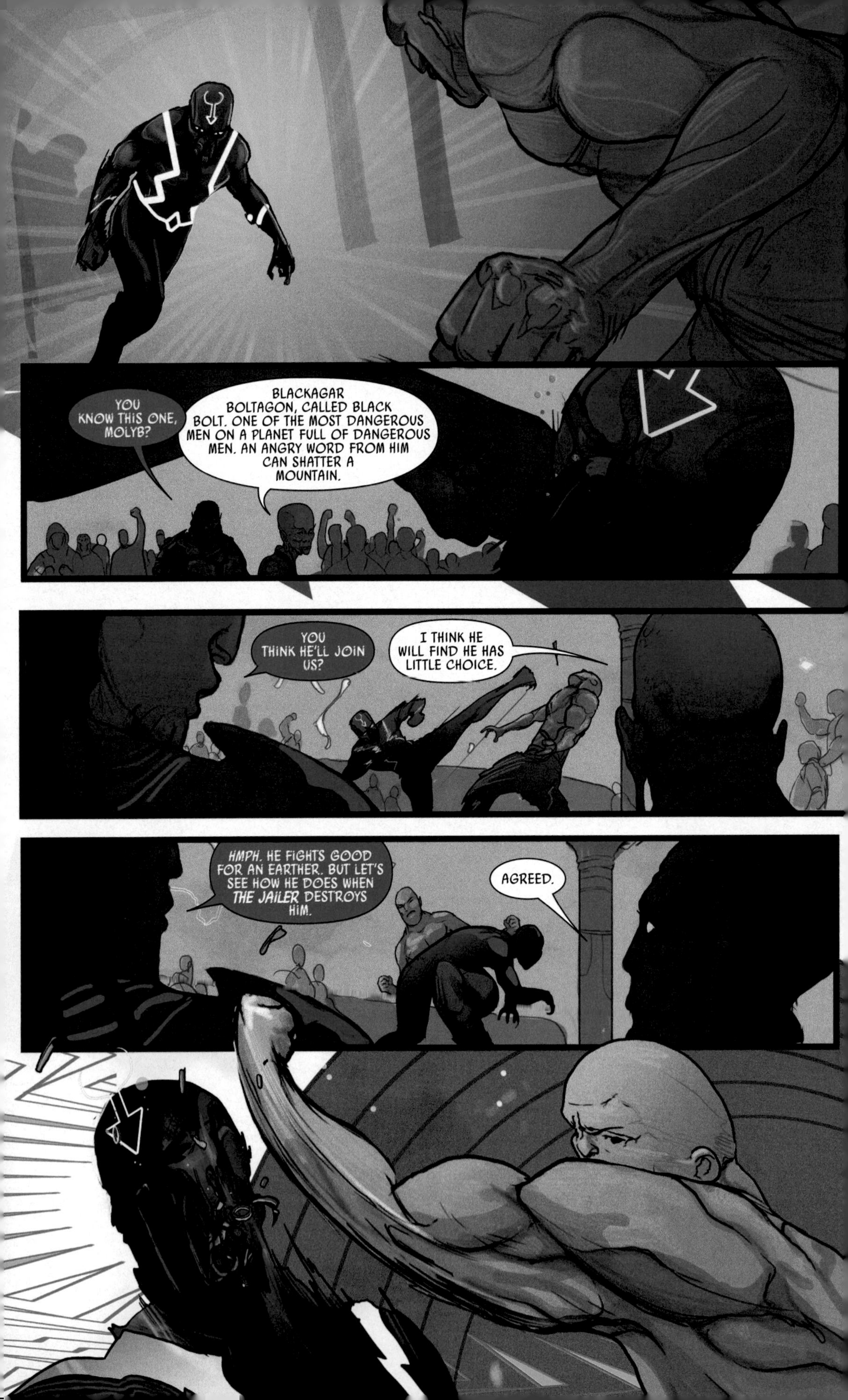
YOU KNOW THIS ONE, MOLYB?
BLACKAGAR BOLTAGON, CALLED BLACK BOLT. ONE OF THE MOST DANGEROUS MEN ON A PLANET FULL OF DANGEROUS MEN. AN ANGRY WORD FROM HIM CAN SHATTER A MOUNTAIN.
YOU THINK HE'LL JOIN US?
I THINK HE WILL FIND HE HAS LITTLE CHOICE.
HMPH. HE FIGHTS GOOD FOR AN EARTHER. BUT LET'S SEE HOW HE DOES WHEN THE JAILER DESTROYS HIM.
AGREED.

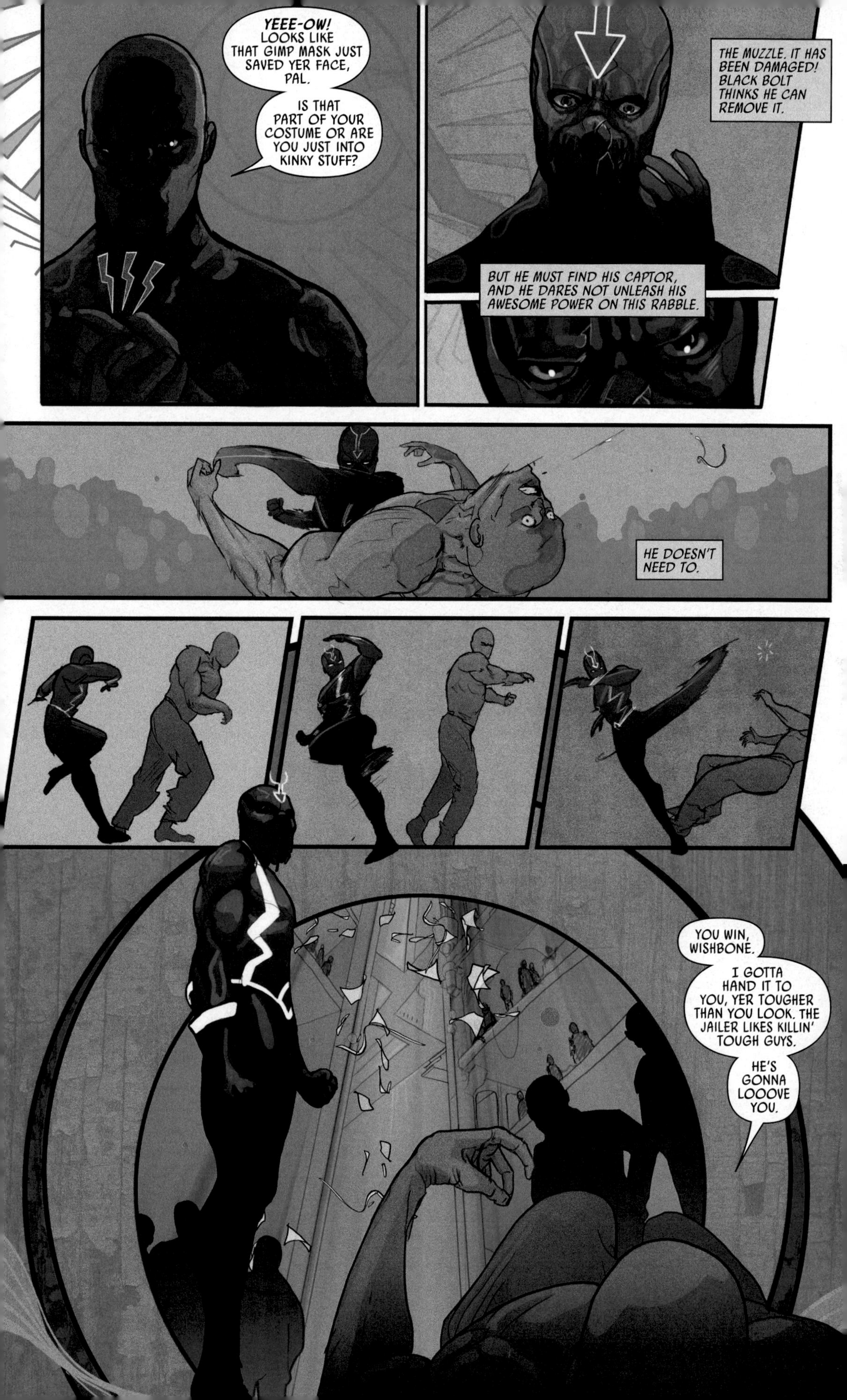
YEEE-OW! LOOKS LIKE THAT GIMP MASK JUST SAVED YER FACE, PAL.
IS THAT PART OF YOUR COSTUME OR ARE YOU JUST INTO KINKY STUFF?
THE MUZZLE. IT HAS BEEN DAMAGED! BLACK BOLT THINKS HE CAN REMOVE IT.
BUT HE MUST FIND HIS CAPTOR, AND HE DARES NOT UNLEASH HIS AWESOME POWER ON THIS RABBLE.
HE DOESN'T NEED TO.
YOU WIN, WISHBONE.
I GOTTA HAND IT TO YOU, YER TOUGHER THAN YOU LOOK. THE JAILER LIKES KILLIN' TOUGH GUYS.
HE'S GONNA LOOOVE YOU.

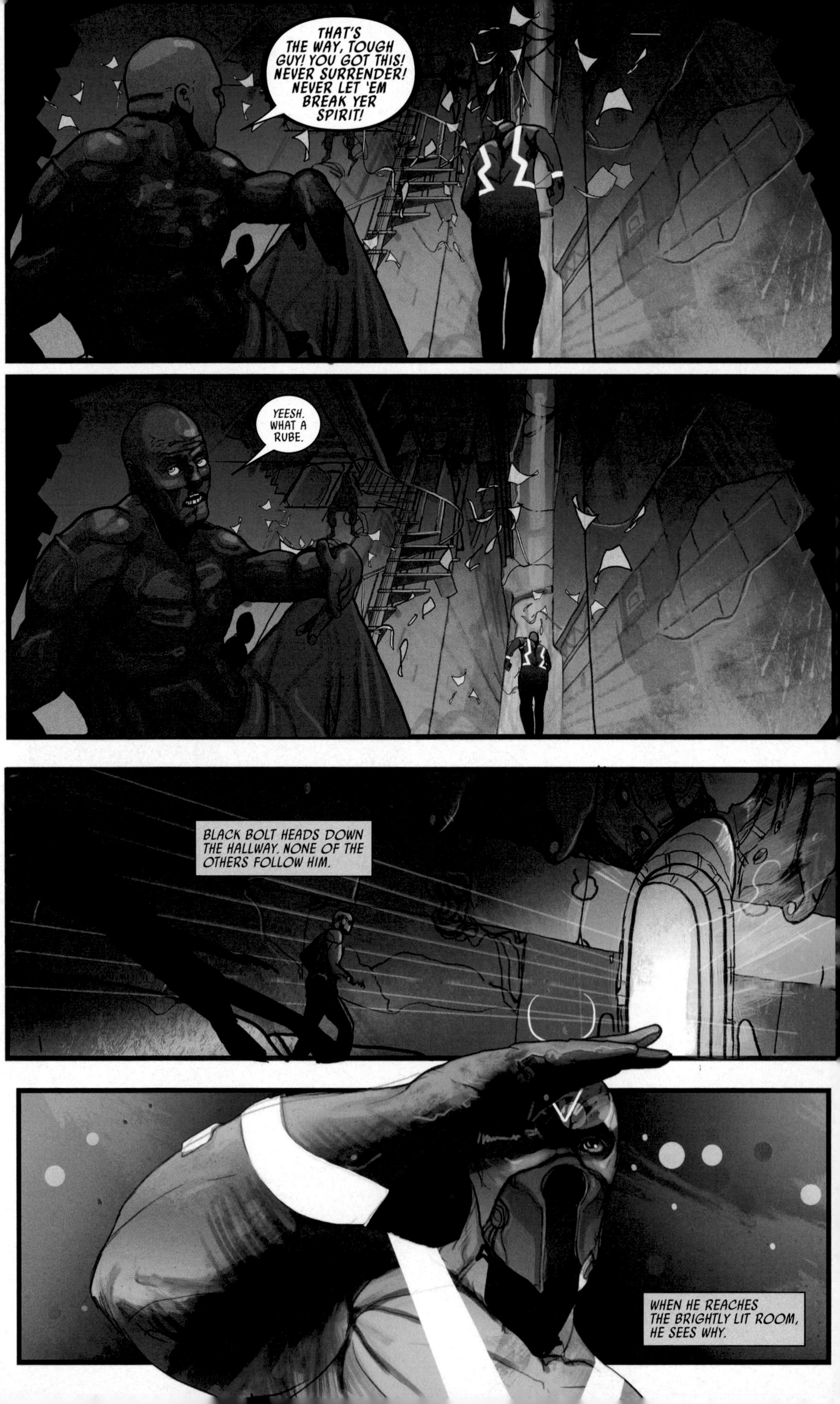
THAT'S THE WAY, TOUGH GUY! YOU GOT THIS! NEVER SURRENDER! NEVER LET 'EM BREAK YER SPIRIT!
YEESH. WHAT A RUBE.
BLACK BOLT HEADS DOWN THE HALLWAY. NONE OF THE OTHERS FOLLOW HIM.
WHEN HE REACHES THE BRIGHTLY LIT ROOM, HE SEES WHY.

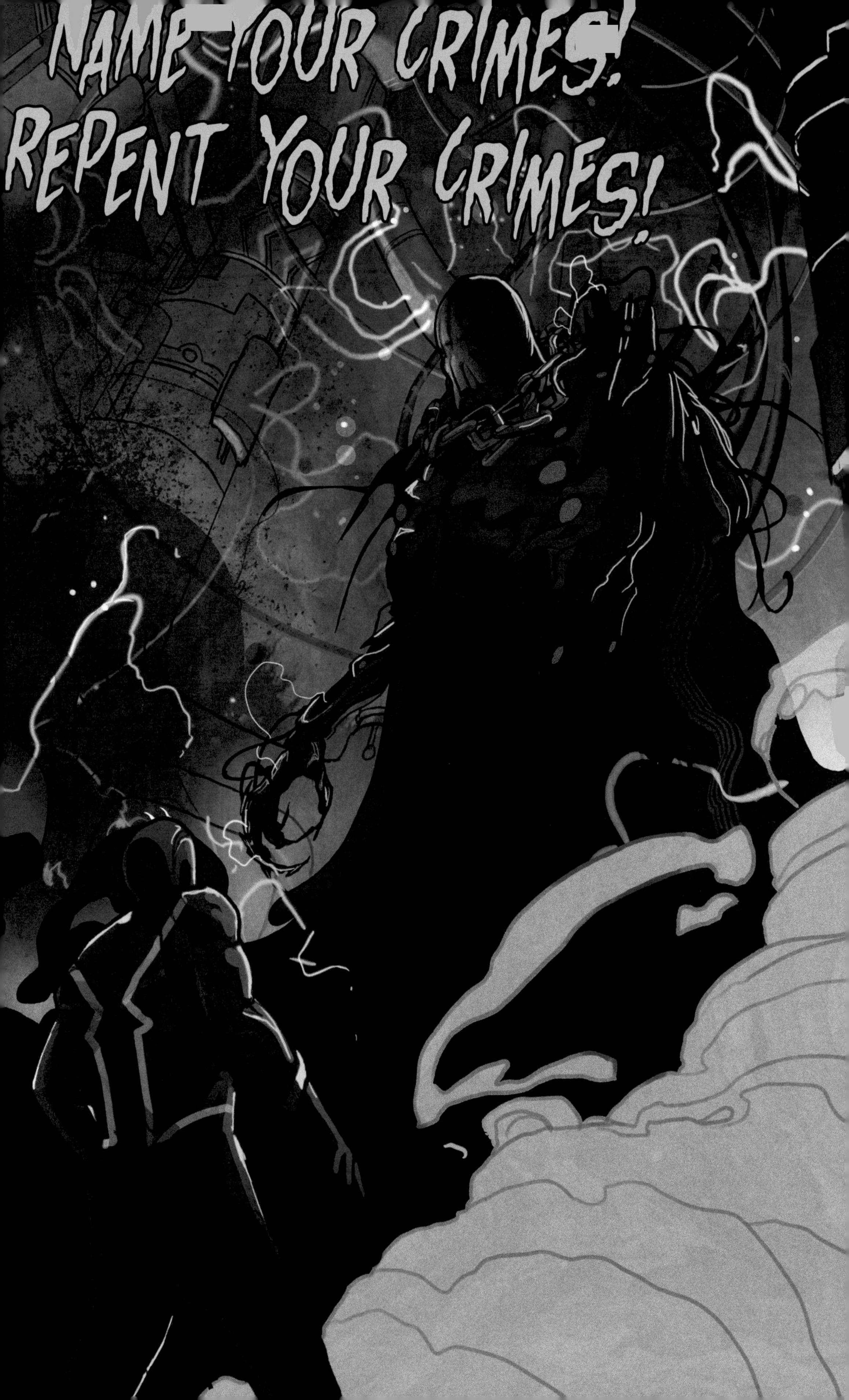
NAME YOUR CRIMES! REPENT YOUR CRIMES!

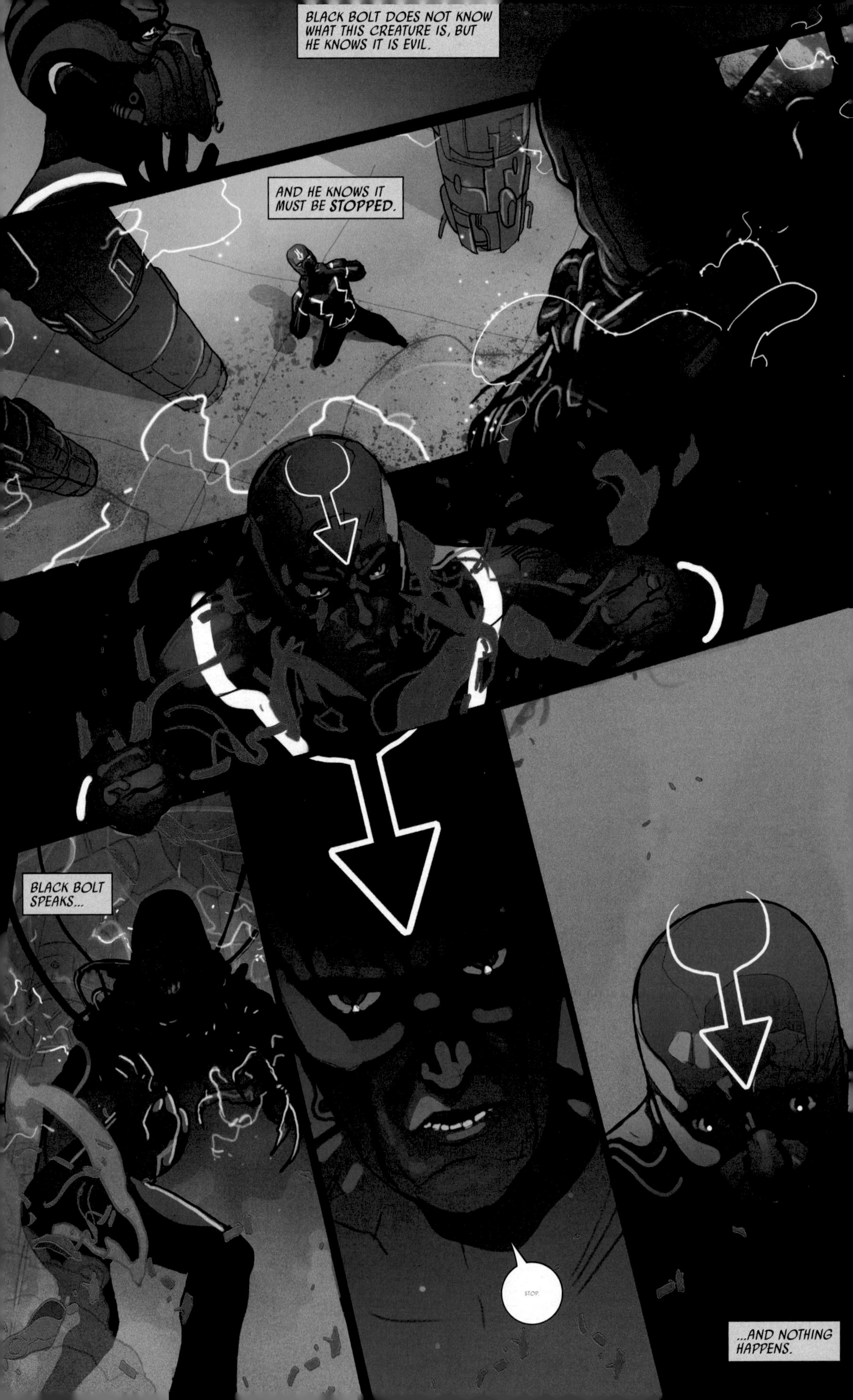
BLACK BOLT DOES NOT KNOW WHAT THIS CREATURE IS, BUT HE KNOWS IT IS EVIL.
AND HE KNOWS IT MUST BE STOPPED.
BLACK BOLT SPEAKS...
STOP.
...AND NOTHING HAPPENS.

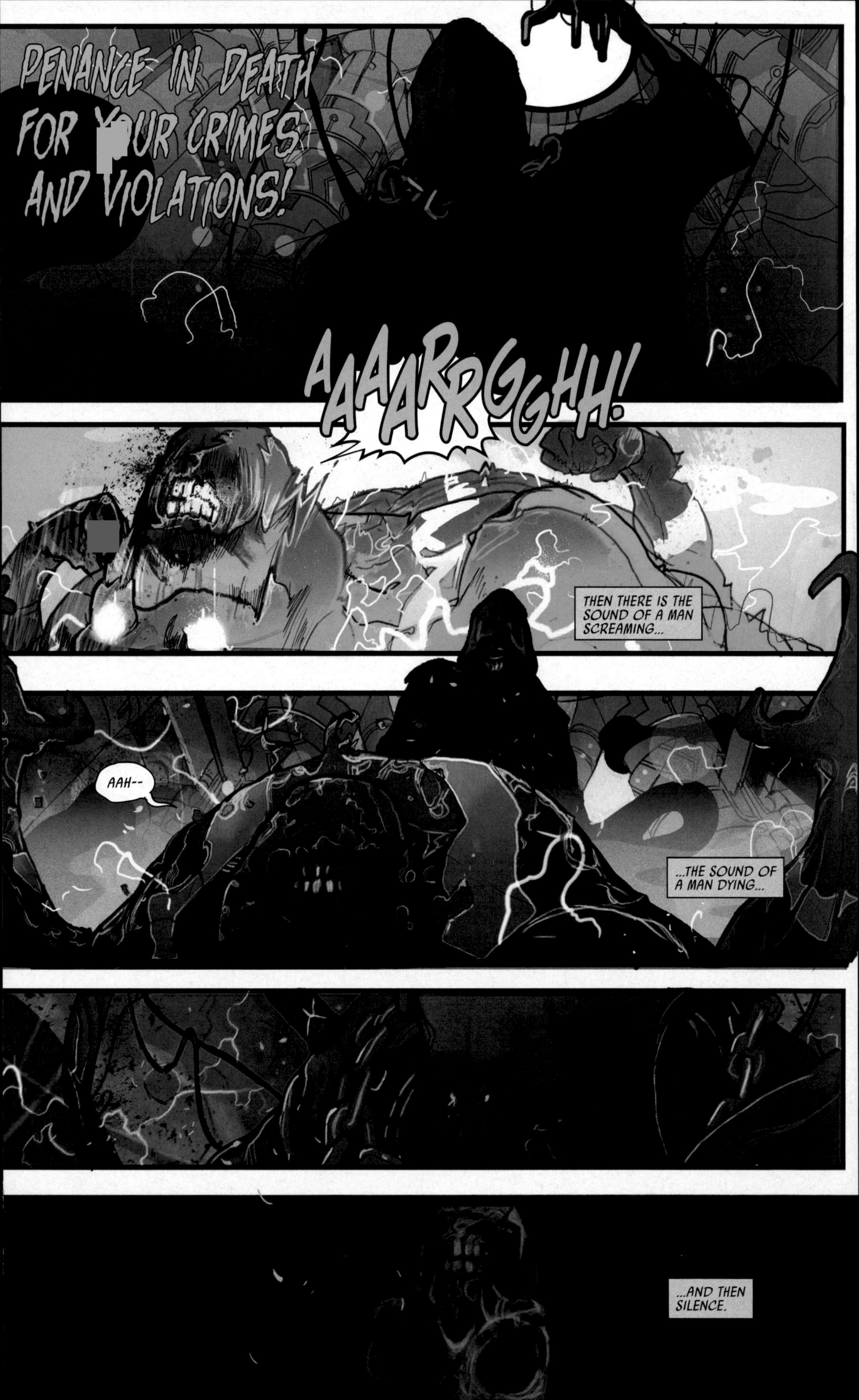
PENANCE IN DEATH FOR YOUR CRIMES AND VIOLATIONS!
AAARRGGHH!
THEN THERE IS THE SOUND OF A MAN SCREAMING...
AAH--
...THE SOUND OF A MAN DYING...
...AND THEN SILENCE.

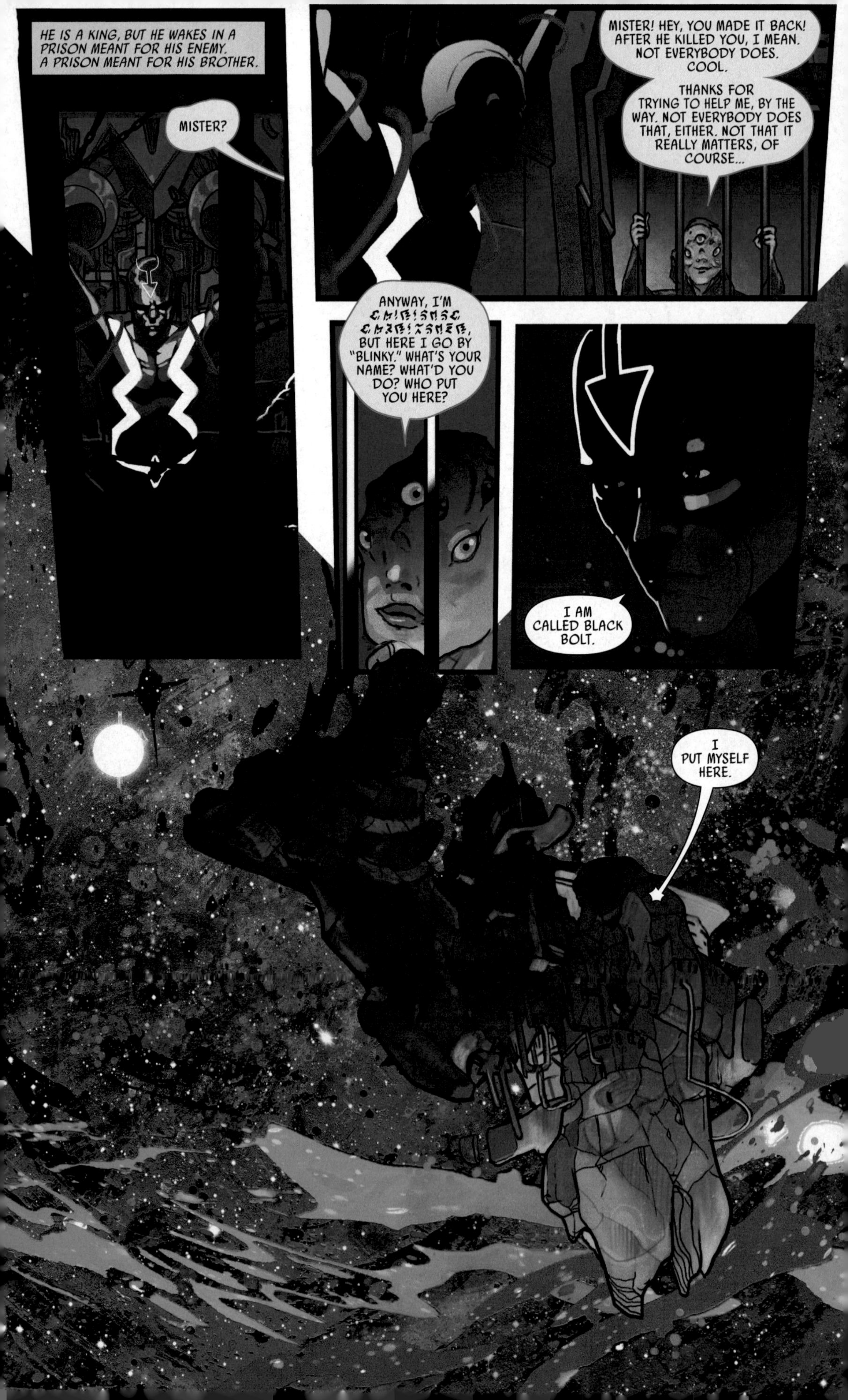
HE IS A KING, BUT HE WAKES IN A PRISON MEANT FOR HIS ENEMY. A PRISON MEANT FOR HIS BROTHER.
MISTER?
MISTER! HEY, YOU MADE IT BACK! AFTER HE KILLED YOU, I MEAN. NOT EVERYBODY DOES. COOL.
THANKS FOR TRYING TO HELP ME, BY THE WAY. NOT EVERYBODY DOES THAT, EITHER. NOT THAT IT REALLY MATTERS, OF COURSE...
ANYWAY, I'M
BUT HERE I GO BY "BLINKY." WHAT'S YOUR NAME? WHAT'D YOU DO? WHO PUT YOU HERE?
I AM CALLED BLACK BOLT.
I PUT MYSELF HERE.

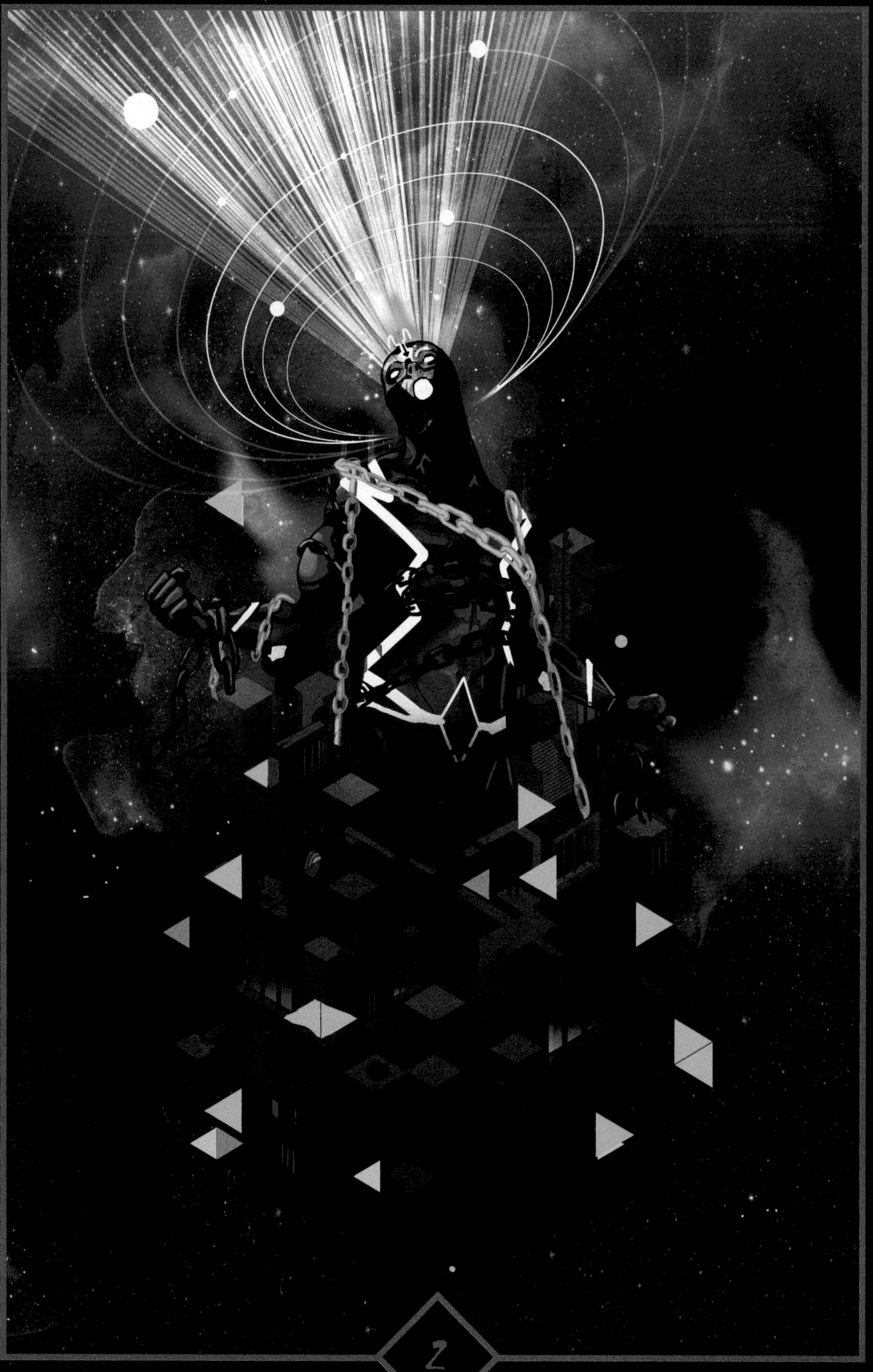

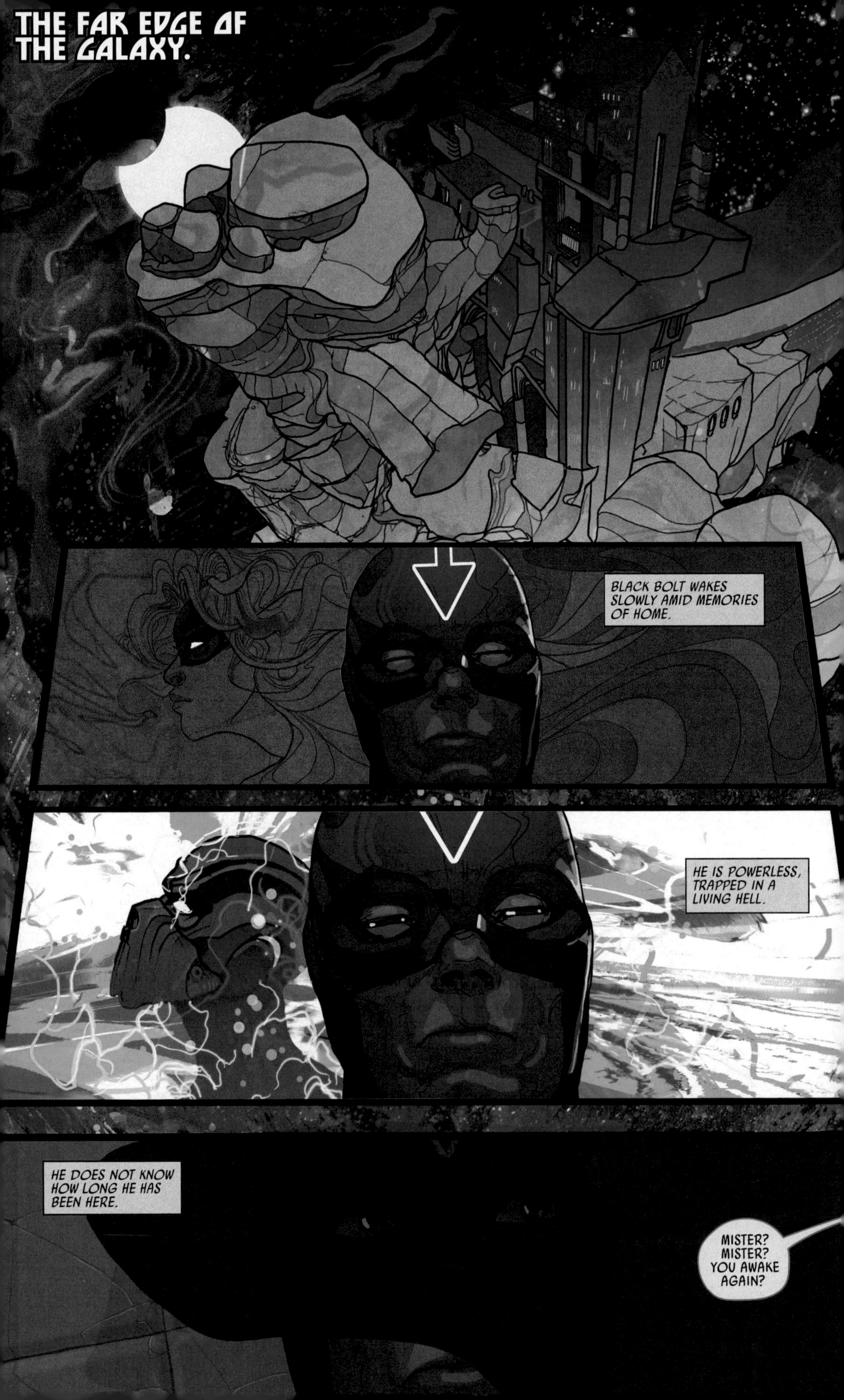

THE FAR EDGE OF THE GALAXY.
BLACK BOLT WAKES SLOWLY AMID MEMORIES OF HOME.
HE IS POWERLESS, TRAPPED IN A LIVING HELL.
HE DOES NOT KNOW HOW LONG HE HAS BEEN HERE.
MISTER? MISTER? YOU AWAKE AGAIN?

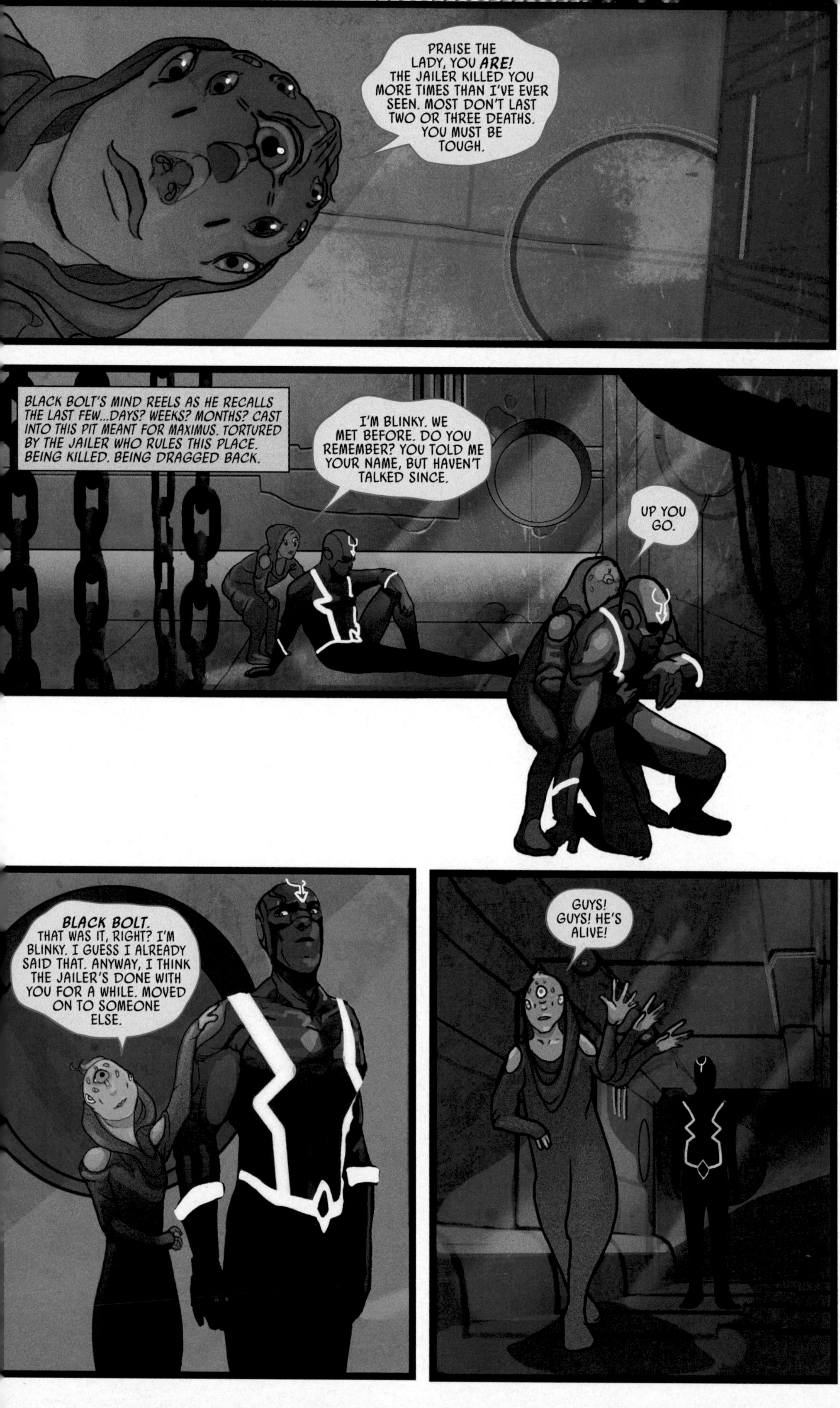
PRAISE THE LADY, YOU ARE! THE JAILER KILLED YOU MORE TIMES THAN I'VE EVER SEEN. MOST DON'T LAST TWO OR THREE DEATHS. YOU MUST BE TOUGH.
BLACK BOLT'S MIND REELS AS HE RECALLS THE LAST FEW...DAYS? WEEKS? MONTHS? CAST INTO THIS PIT MEANT FOR MAXIMUS. TORTURED BY THE JAILER WHO RULES THIS PLACE. BEING KILLED. BEING DRAGGED BACK.
I'M BLINKY. WE MET BEFORE. DO YOU REMEMBER? YOU TOLD ME YOUR NAME, BUT HAVEN'T TALKED SINCE.
UP YOU GO.
BLACK BOLT. THAT WAS IT, RIGHT? I'M BLINKY. I GUESS I ALREADY SAID THAT. ANYWAY, I THINK THE JAILER'S DONE WITH YOU FOR A WHILE. MOVED ON TO SOMEONE ELSE.
GUYS! GUYS! HE'S ALIVE!

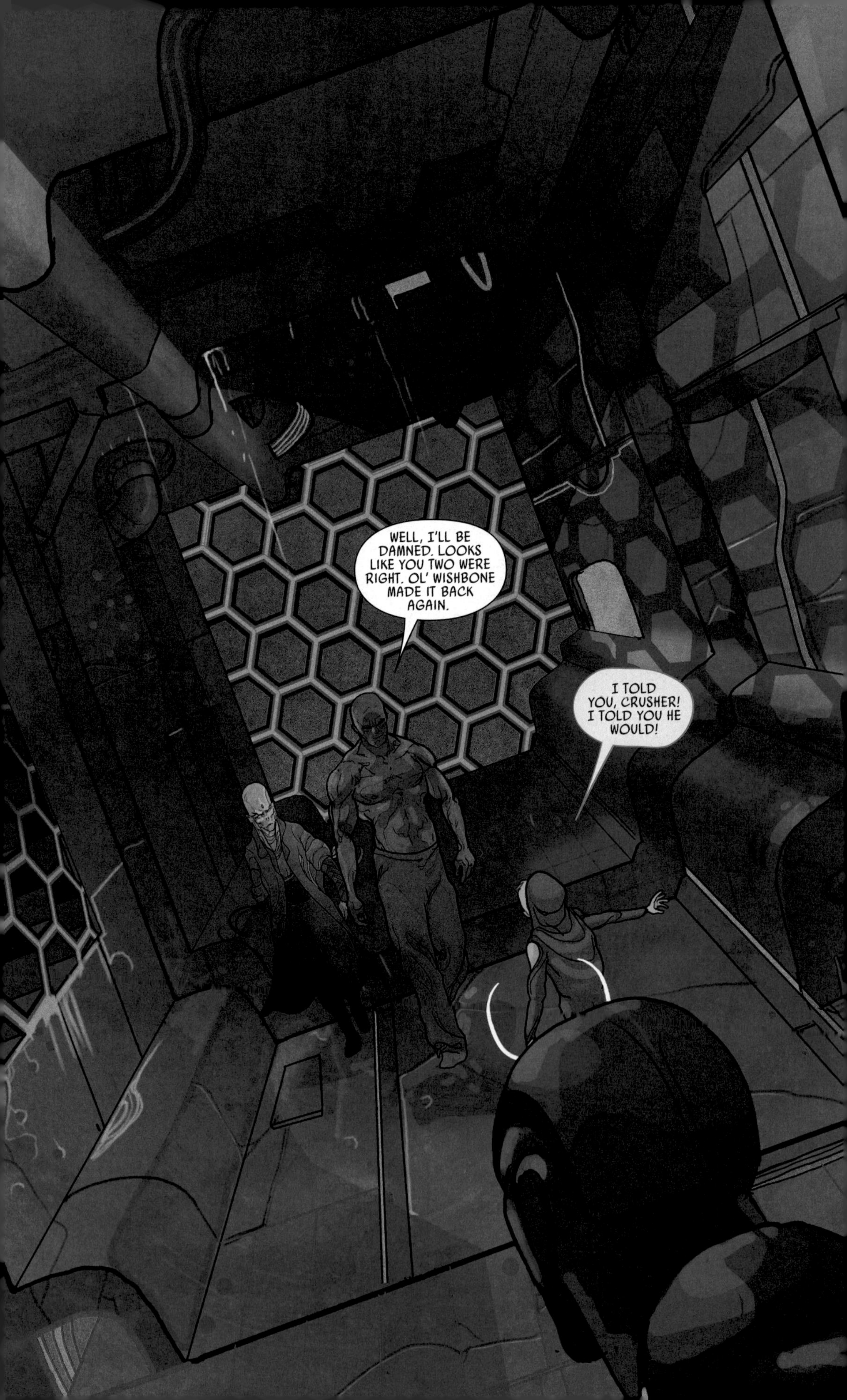
WELL, I'LL BE DAMNED. LOOKS LIKE YOU TWO WERE RIGHT. OL' WISHBONE MADE IT BACK AGAIN.
I TOLD YOU, CRUSHER! I TOLD YOU HE WOULD!

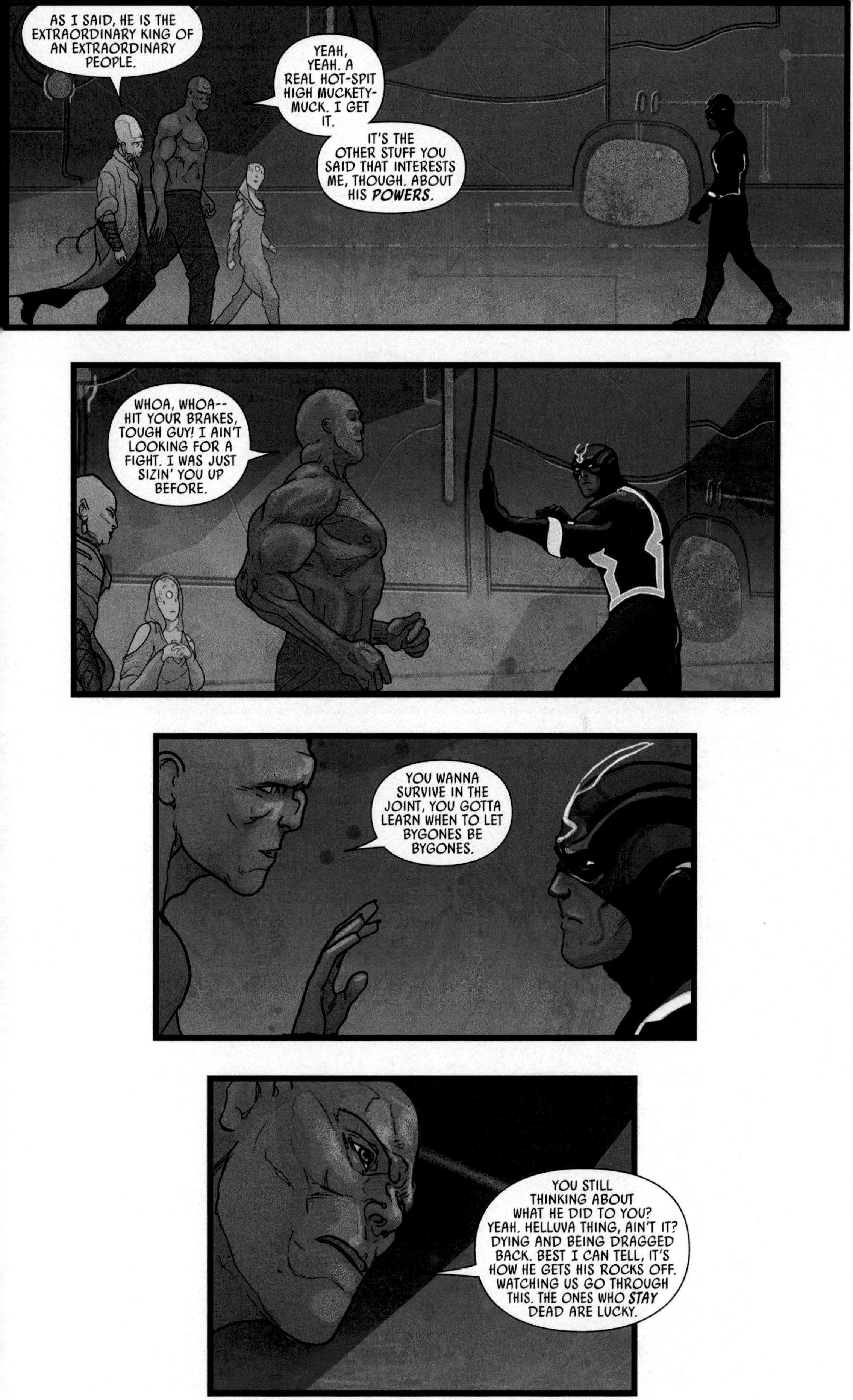
AS I SAID, HE IS THE EXTRAORDINARY KING OF AN EXTRAORDINARY PEOPLE.
YEAH, YEAH. A REAL HOT-SPIT HIGH MUCKETY-MUCK. I GET IT.
IT'S THE OTHER STUFF YOU SAID THAT INTERESTS ME, THOUGH. ABOUT HIS POWERS.
WHOA, WHOA--HIT YOUR BRAKES, TOUGH GUY! I AIN'T LOOKING FOR A FIGHT. I WAS JUST SIZIN' YOU UP BEFORE.
YOU WANNA SURVIVE IN THE JOINT, YOU GOTTA LEARN WHEN TO LET BYGONES BE BYGONES.
YOU STILL THINKING ABOUT WHAT HE DID TO YOU? YEAH. HELLUVA THING, AIN'T IT? DYING AND BEING DRAGGED BACK. BEST I CAN TELL, IT'S HOW HE GETS HIS ROCKS OFF. WATCHING US GO THROUGH THIS. THE ONES WHO STAY DEAD ARE LUCKY.

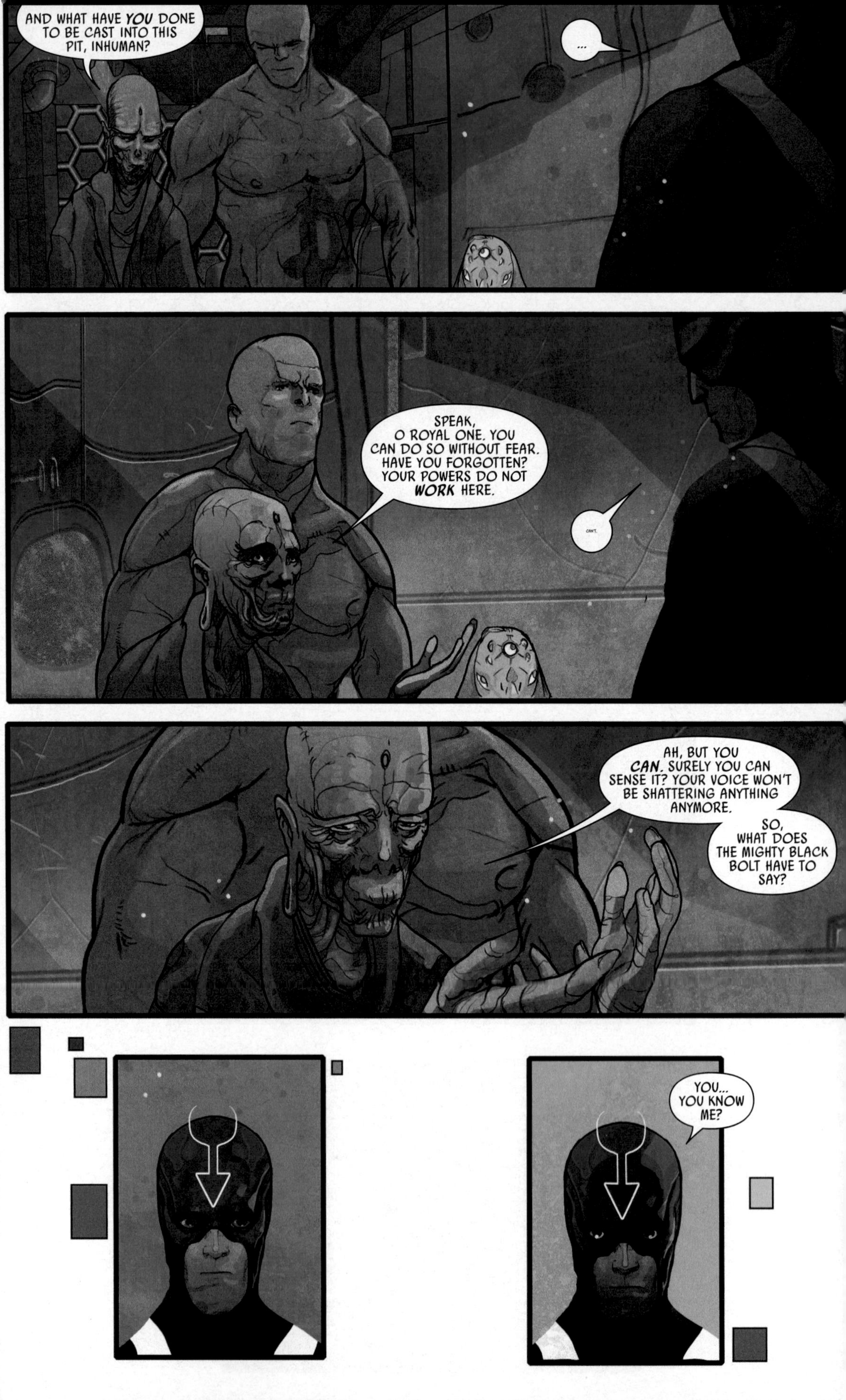
AND WHAT HAVE YOU DONE TO BE CAST INTO THIS PIT, INHUMAN?
...
SPEAK, O ROYAL ONE. YOU CAN DO SO WITHOUT FEAR. HAVE YOU FORGOTTEN? YOUR POWERS DO NOT WORK HERE.
CAN'T.
AH, BUT YOU CAN. SURELY YOU CAN SENSE IT? YOUR VOICE WON'T BE SHATTERING ANYTHING ANYMORE.
SO, WHAT DOES THE MIGHTY BLACK BOLT HAVE TO SAY?
YOU... YOU KNOW ME?

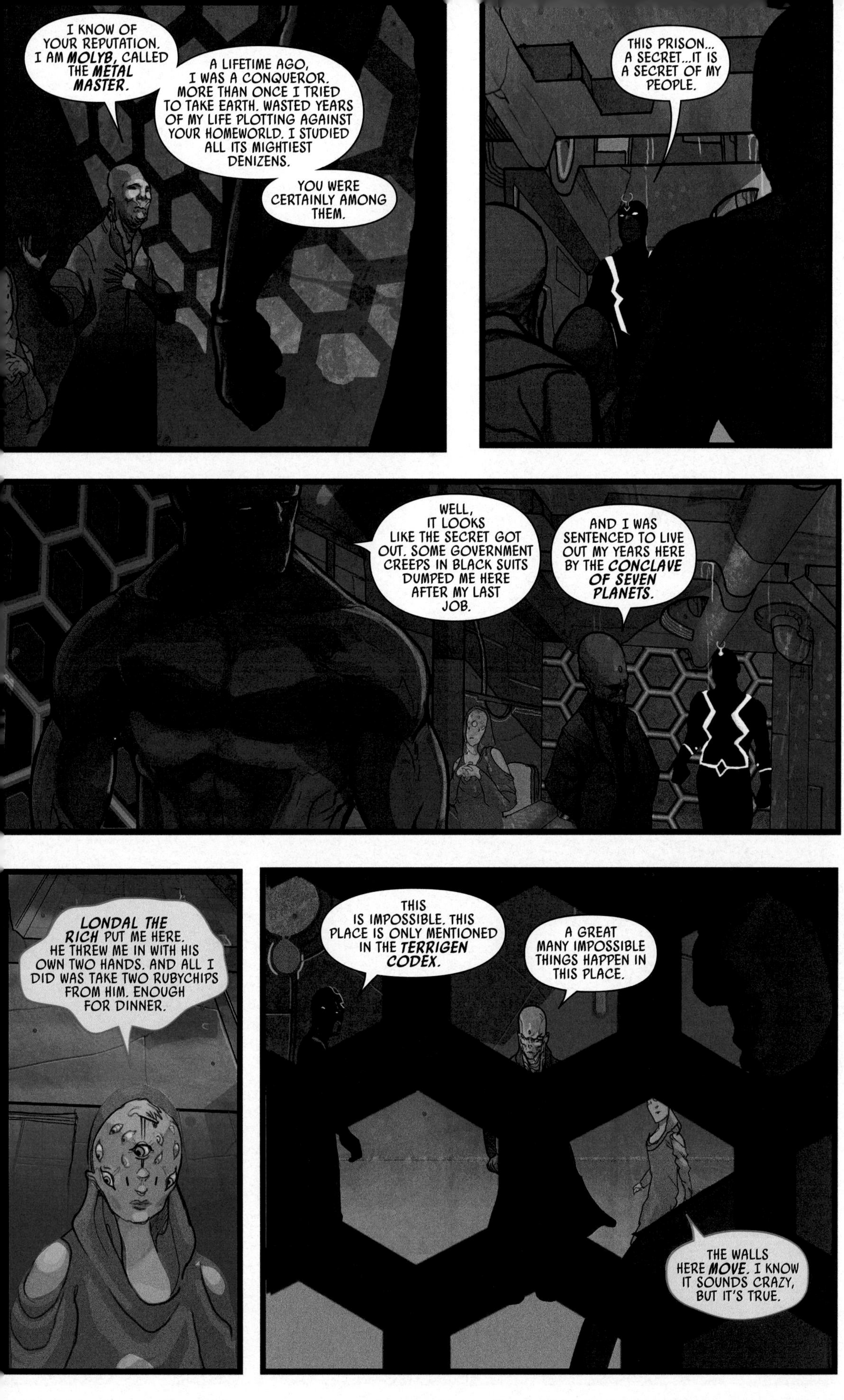
I KNOW OF YOUR REPUTATION. I AM MOLYB, CALLED THE METAL MASTER.
A LIFETIME AGO, I WAS A CONQUEROR. MORE THAN ONCE I TRIED TO TAKE EARTH. WASTED YEARS OF MY LIFE PLOTTING AGAINST YOUR HOMEWORLD. I STUDIED ALL ITS MIGHTIEST DENIZENS.
YOU WERE CERTAINLY AMONG THEM.
THIS PRISON... A SECRET...IT IS A SECRET OF MY PEOPLE.
WELL, IT LOOKS LIKE THE SECRET GOT OUT. SOME GOVERNMENT CREEPS IN BLACK SUITS DUMPED ME HERE AFTER MY LAST JOB.
AND I WAS SENTENCED TO LIVE OUT MY YEARS HERE BY THE CONCLAVE OF SEVEN PLANETS.
LONDAL THE RICH PUT ME HERE. HE THREW ME IN WITH HIS OWN TWO HANDS. AND ALL I DID WAS TAKE TWO RUBYCHIPS FROM HIM. ENOUGH FOR DINNER.
THIS IS IMPOSSIBLE. THIS PLACE IS ONLY MENTIONED IN THE TERRIGEN CODEX.
A GREAT MANY IMPOSSIBLE THINGS HAPPEN IN THIS PLACE.
THE WALLS HERE MOVE. I KNOW IT SOUNDS CRAZY, BUT IT'S TRUE.

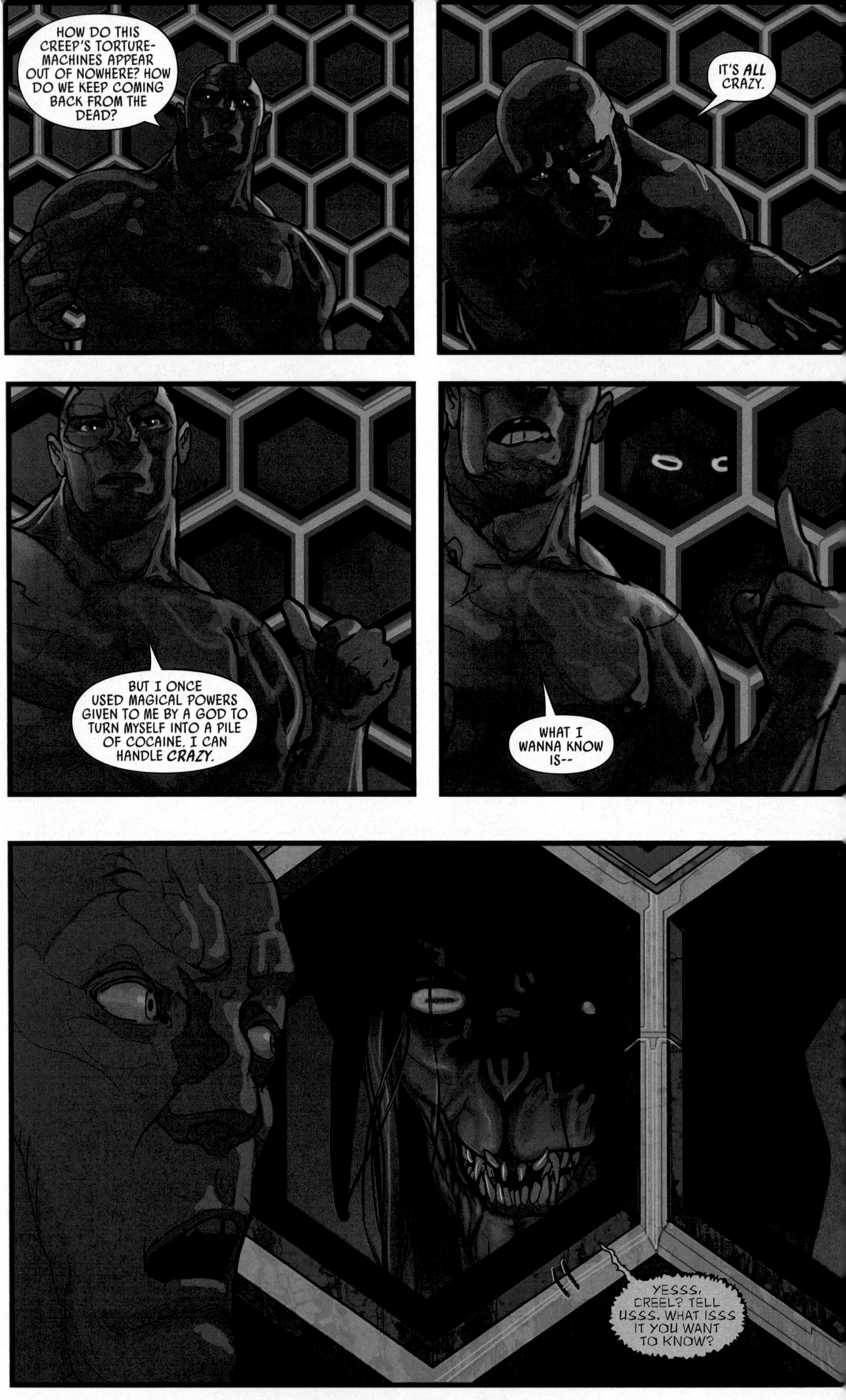
HOW DO THIS CREEP'S TORTURE-MACHINES APPEAR OUT OF NOWHERE? HOW DO WE KEEP COMING BACK FROM THE DEAD?
IT'S ALL CRAZY.
BUT I ONCE USED MAGICAL POWERS GIVEN TO ME BY A GOD TO TURN MYSELF INTO A PILE OF COCAINE. I CAN HANDLE CRAZY.
WHAT I WANNA KNOW IS--
YESSS, CREEL? TELL USSS. WHAT ISSS IT YOU WANT TO KNOW?

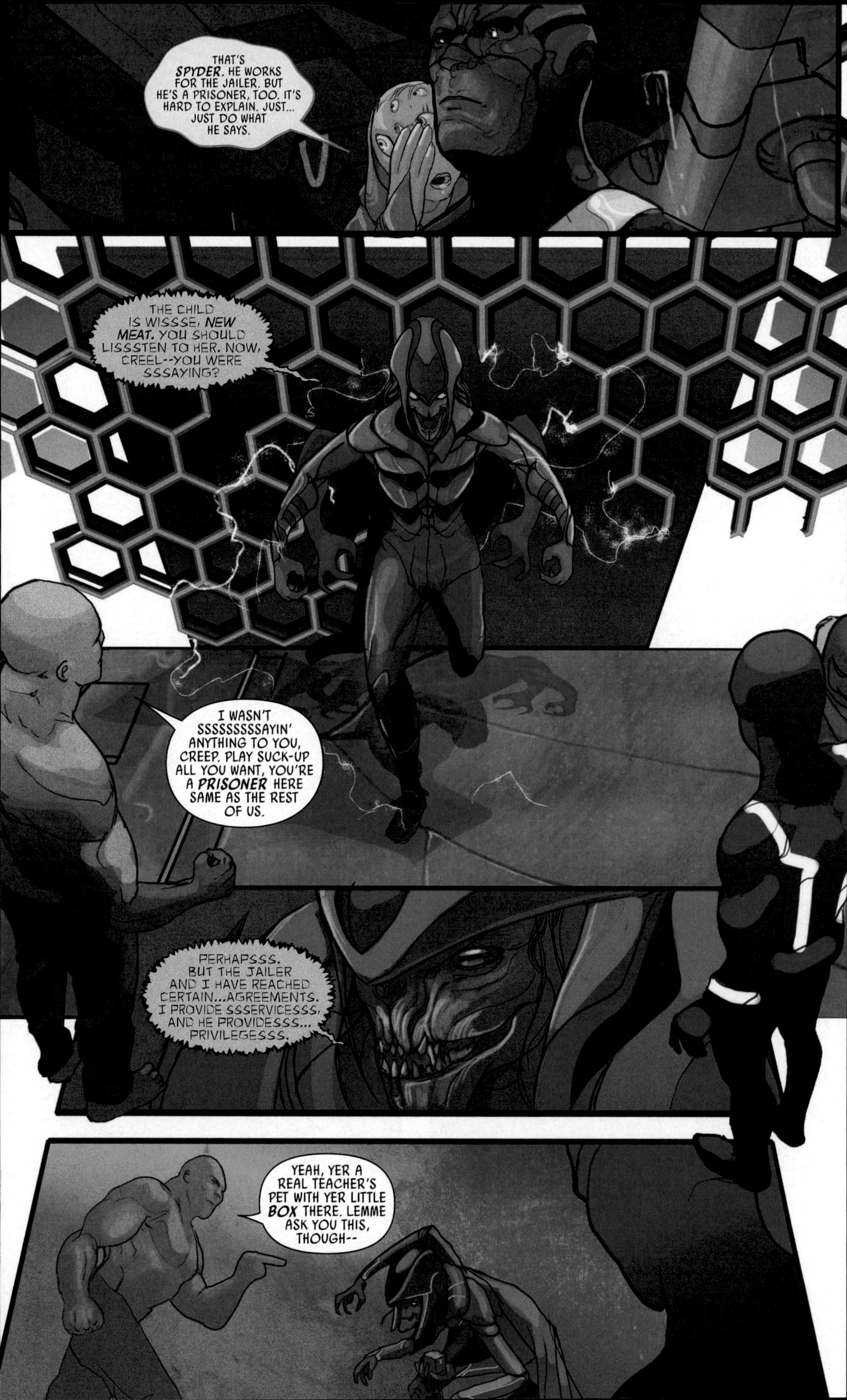
THAT'S SPYDER. HE WORKS FOR THE JAILER. BUT HE'S A PRISONER, TOO. IT'S HARD TO EXPLAIN. JUST... JUST DO WHAT HE SAYS.
THE CHILD IS WISSSE, NEW MEAT. YOU SHOULD LISSSTEN TO HER. NOW, CREEL--YOU WERE SSSAYING?
I WASN'T SSSSSSSSSAYIN' ANYTHING TO YOU, CREEP. PLAY SUCK-UP ALL YOU WANT, YOU'RE A PRISONER HERE SAME AS THE REST OF US.
PERHAPSSS. BUT THE JAILER AND I HAVE REACHED CERTAIN...AGREEMENTS. I PROVIDE SSSERVICESSS, AND HE PROVIDESSS... PRIVILEGESSS.
YEAH, YER A REAL TEACHER'S PET WITH YER LITTLE BOX THERE. LEMME ASK YOU THIS, THOUGH--

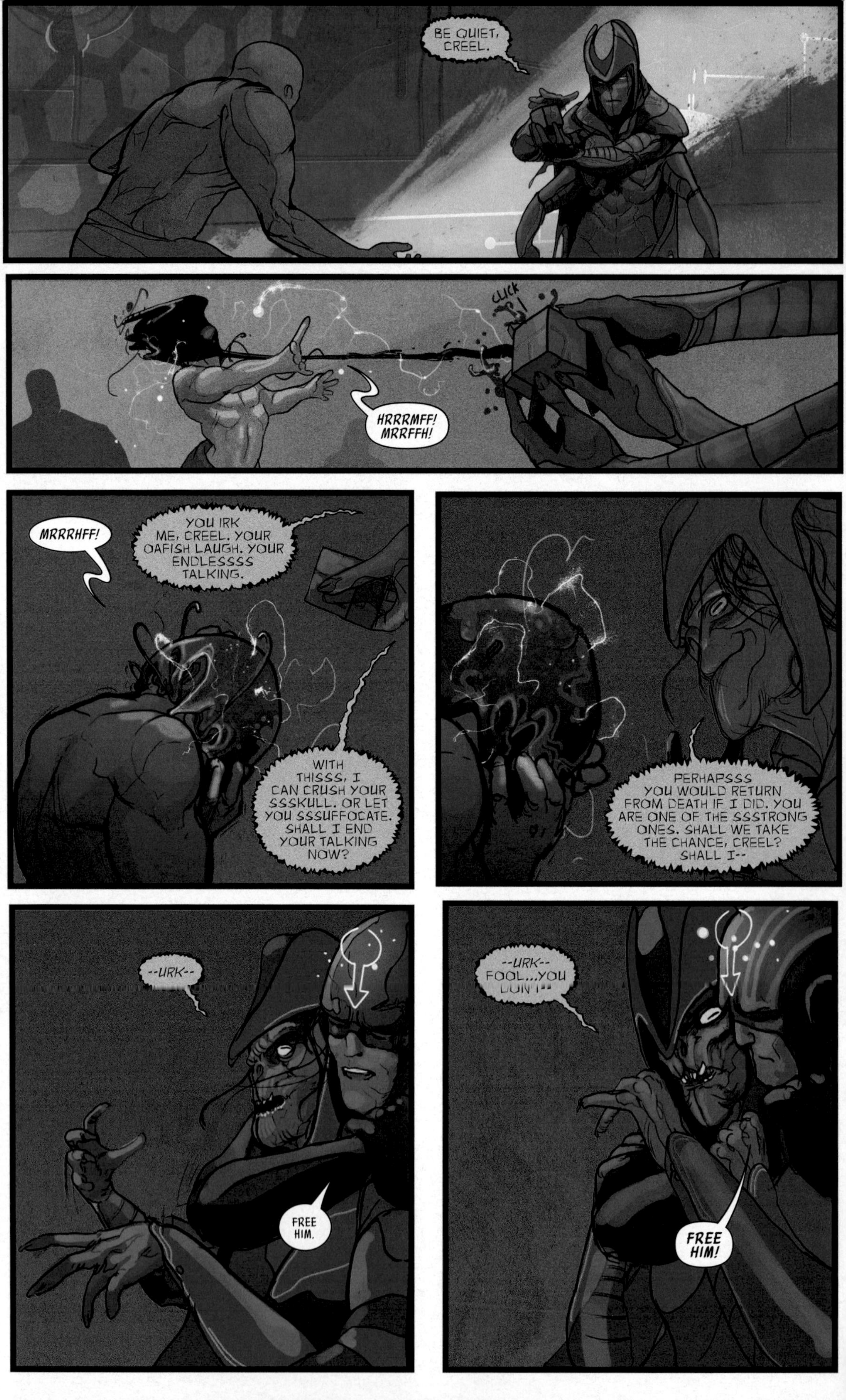
BE QUIET, CREEL.
CLICK
HRRRMFF! MRRFFH!
MRRRHFF!
YOU IRK ME, CREEL. YOUR OAFISH LAUGH. YOUR ENDLESSSS TALKING.
WITH THISSS, I CAN CRUSH YOUR SSSKULL. OR LET YOU SSSUFFOCATE. SHALL I END YOUR TALKING NOW?
PERHAPSSS YOU WOULD RETURN FROM DEATH IF I DID. YOU ARE ONE OF THE SSSTRONG ONES. SHALL WE TAKE THE CHANCE, CREEL? SHALL I--
--URK--
FREE HIM.
--URK-- FOOL...YOU
FREE HIM!

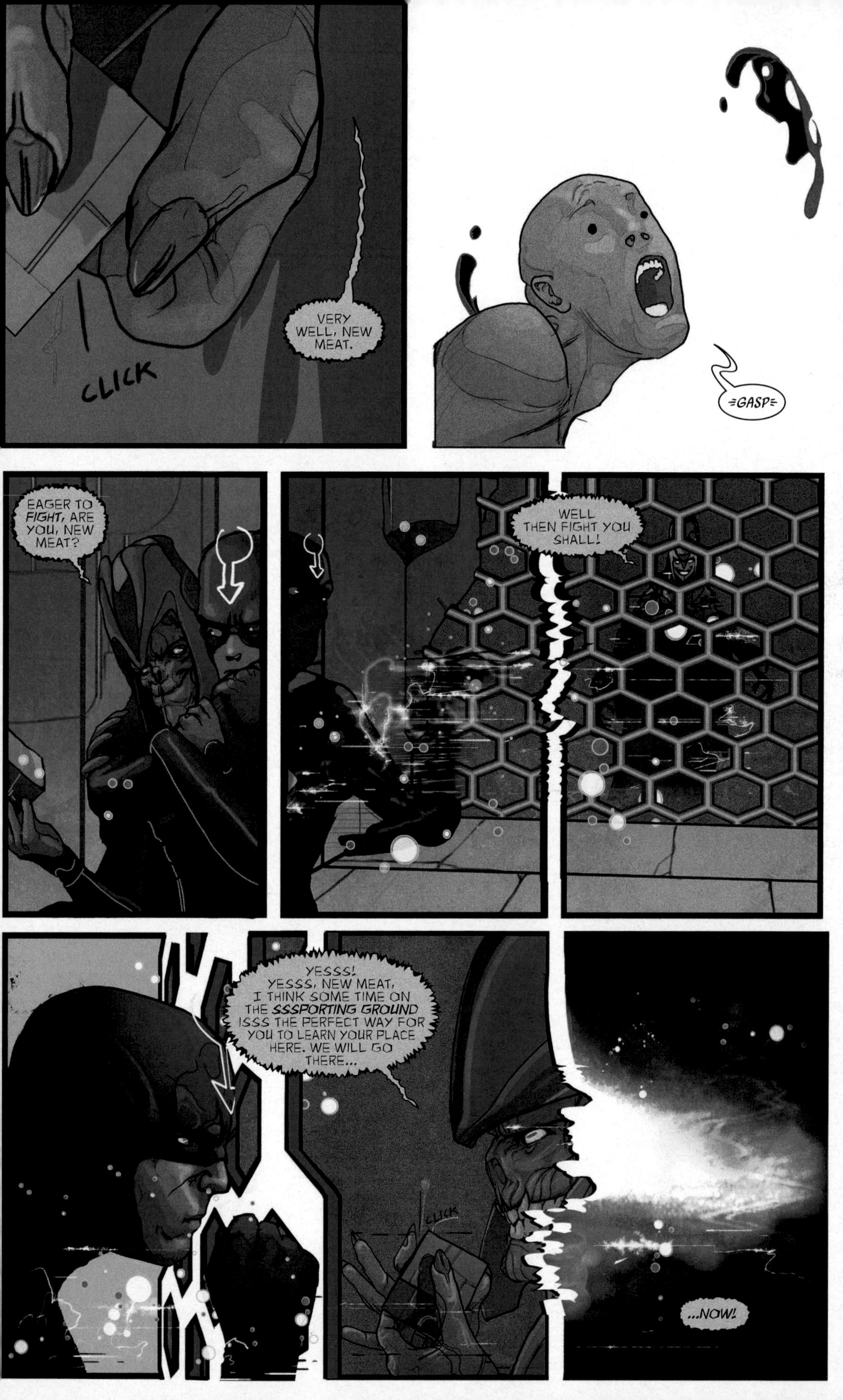
VERY WELL, NEW MEAT.
CLICK
GASP
EAGER TO FIGHT, ARE YOU, NEW MEAT?
WELL THEN FIGHT YOU SHALL!
YESSS! YESSS, NEW MEAT, I THINK SOME TIME ON THE SSSPORTING GROUND ISSS THE PERFECT WAY FOR YOU TO LEARN YOUR PLACE HERE. WE WILL GO THERE...
CLICK
...NOW!

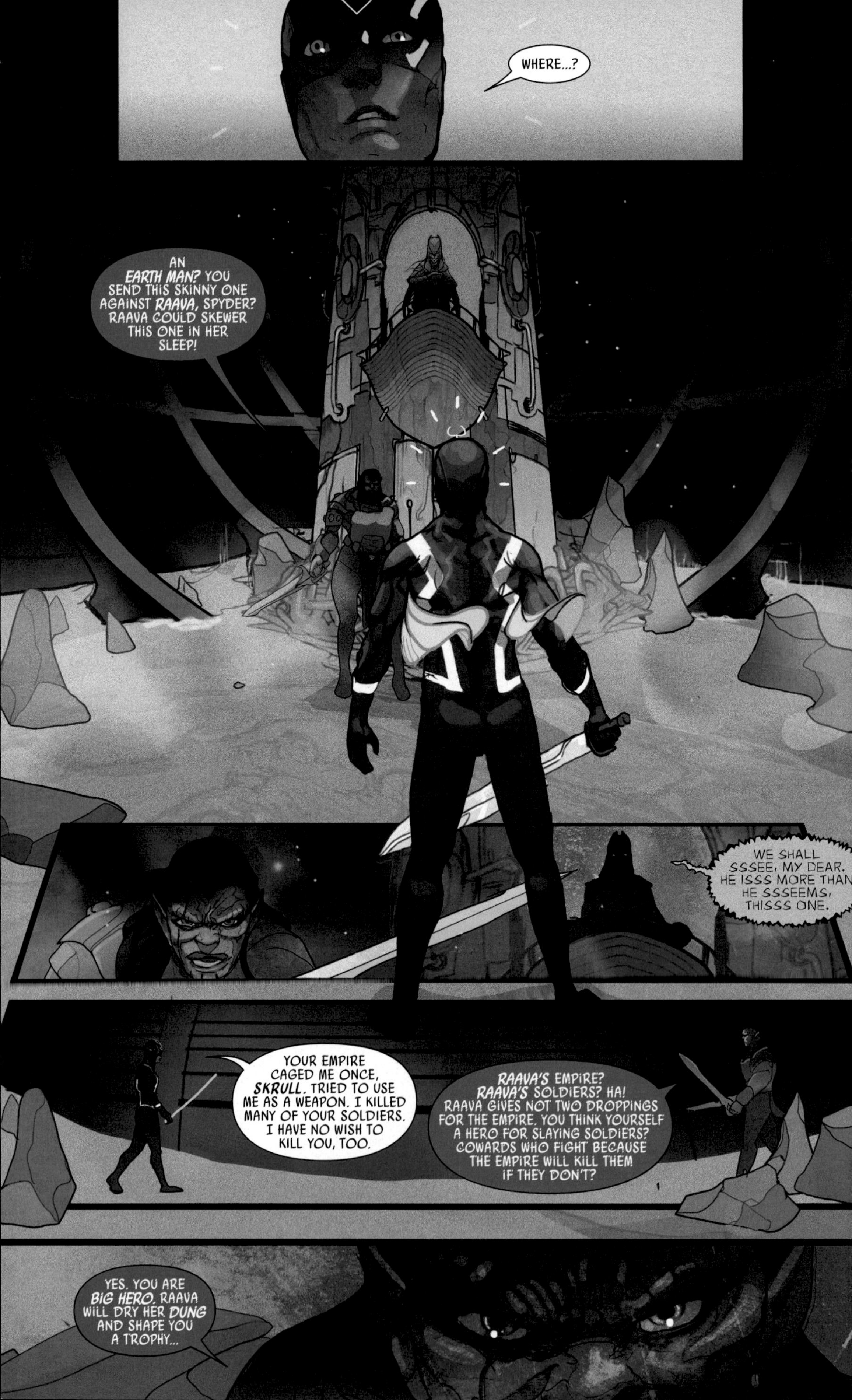
WHERE...?
AN EARTH MAN? YOU SEND THIS SKINNY ONE AGAINST RAAVA, SPYDER? RAAVA COULD SKEWER THIS ONE IN HER SLEEP!
WE SHALL SSSEE, MY DEAR. HE ISSS MORE THAN HE SSSEEMS, THISSS ONE.
YOUR EMPIRE CAGED ME ONCE, SKRULL. TRIED TO USE ME AS A WEAPON. I KILLED MANY OF YOUR SOLDIERS. I HAVE NO WISH TO KILL YOU, TOO.
RAAVA'S EMPIRE? RAAVA'S SOLDIERS? HA! RAAVA GIVES NOT TWO DROPPINGS FOR THE EMPIRE. YOU THINK YOURSELF A HERO FOR SLAYING SOLDIERS? COWARDS WHO FIGHT BECAUSE THE EMPIRE WILL KILL THEM IF THEY DON'T?
YES. YOU ARE BIG HERO. RAAVA WILL DRY HER DUNG AND SHAPE YOU A TROPHY...

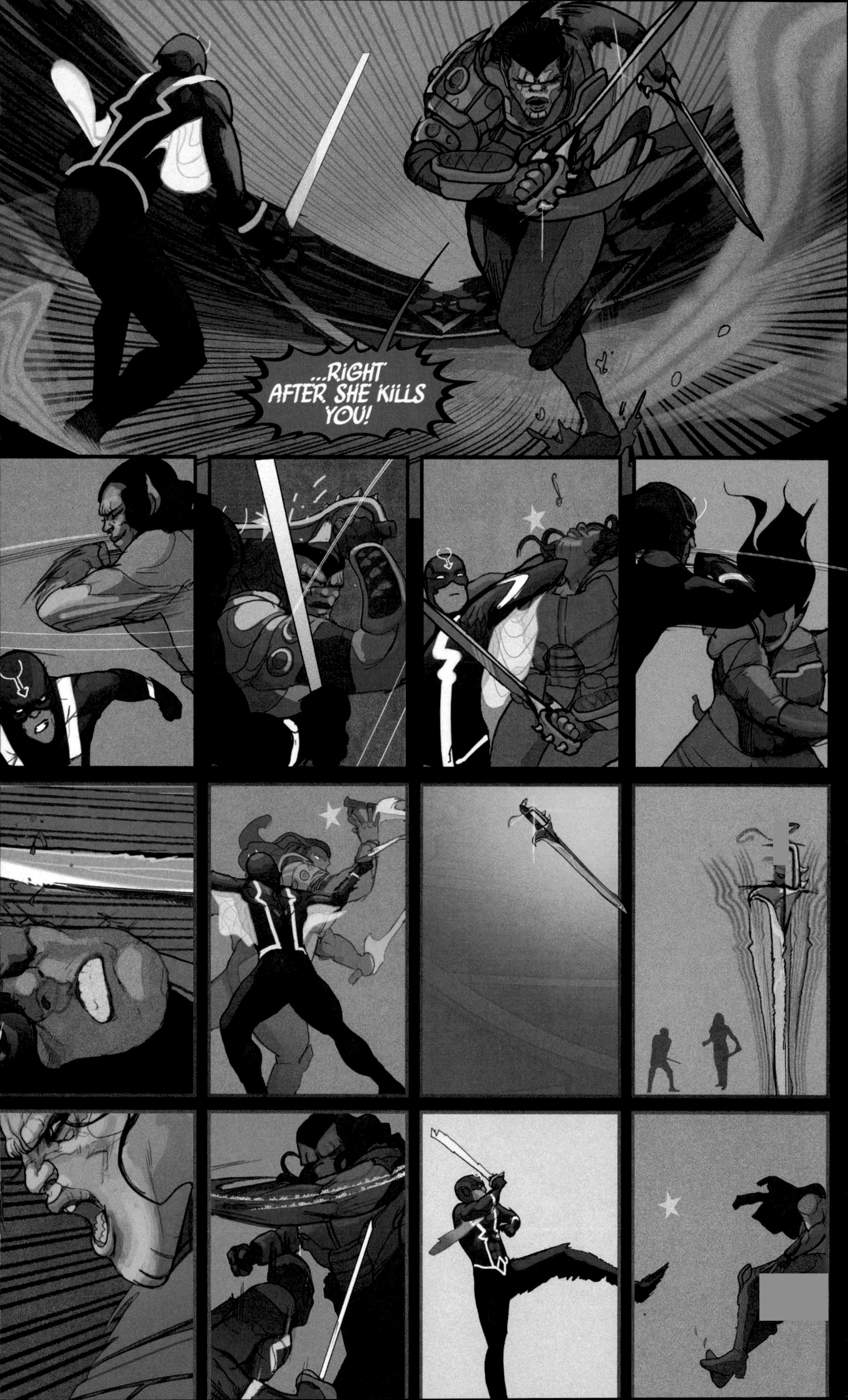
...RIGHT AFTER SHE KILLS YOU!

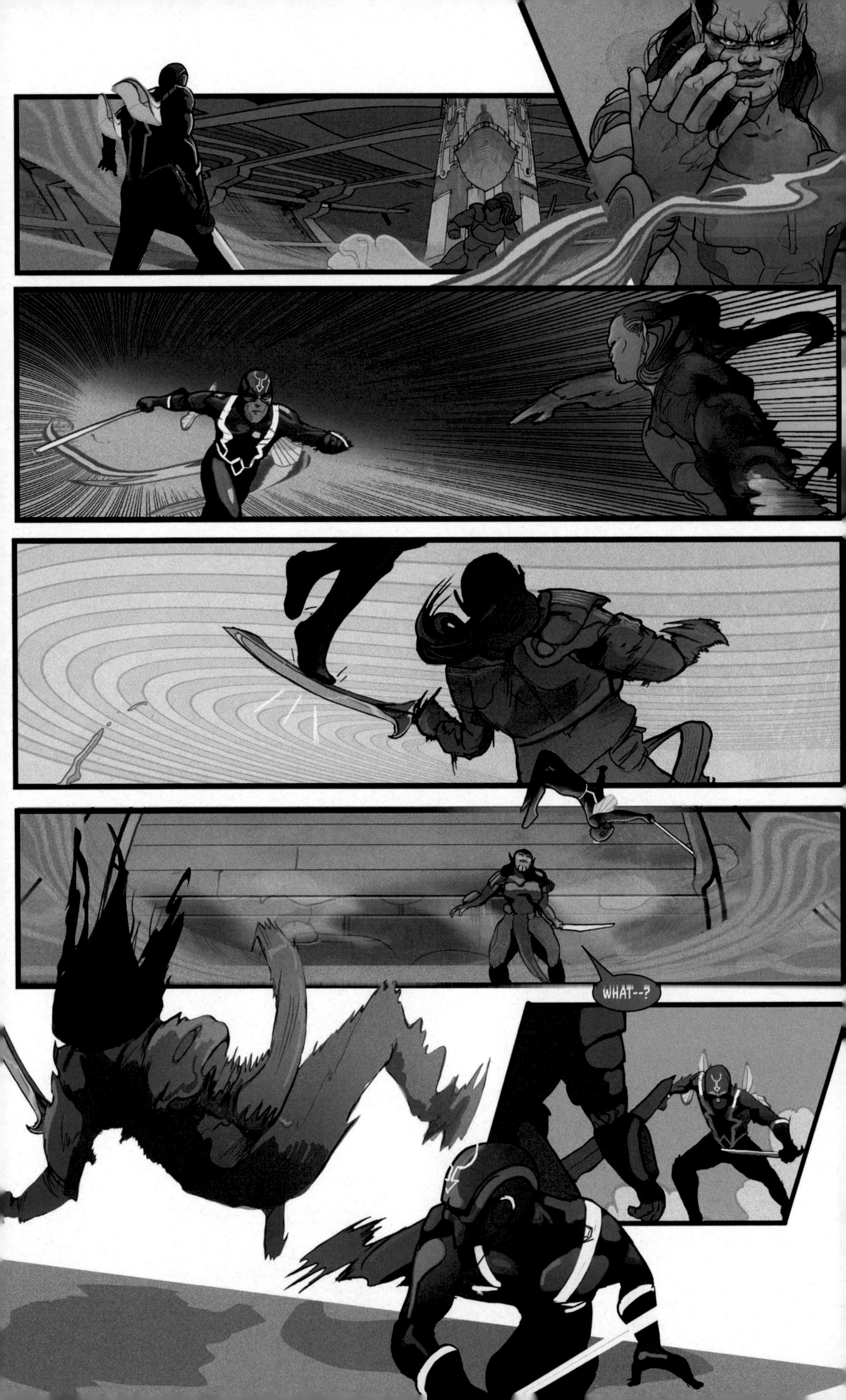
WHAT--?

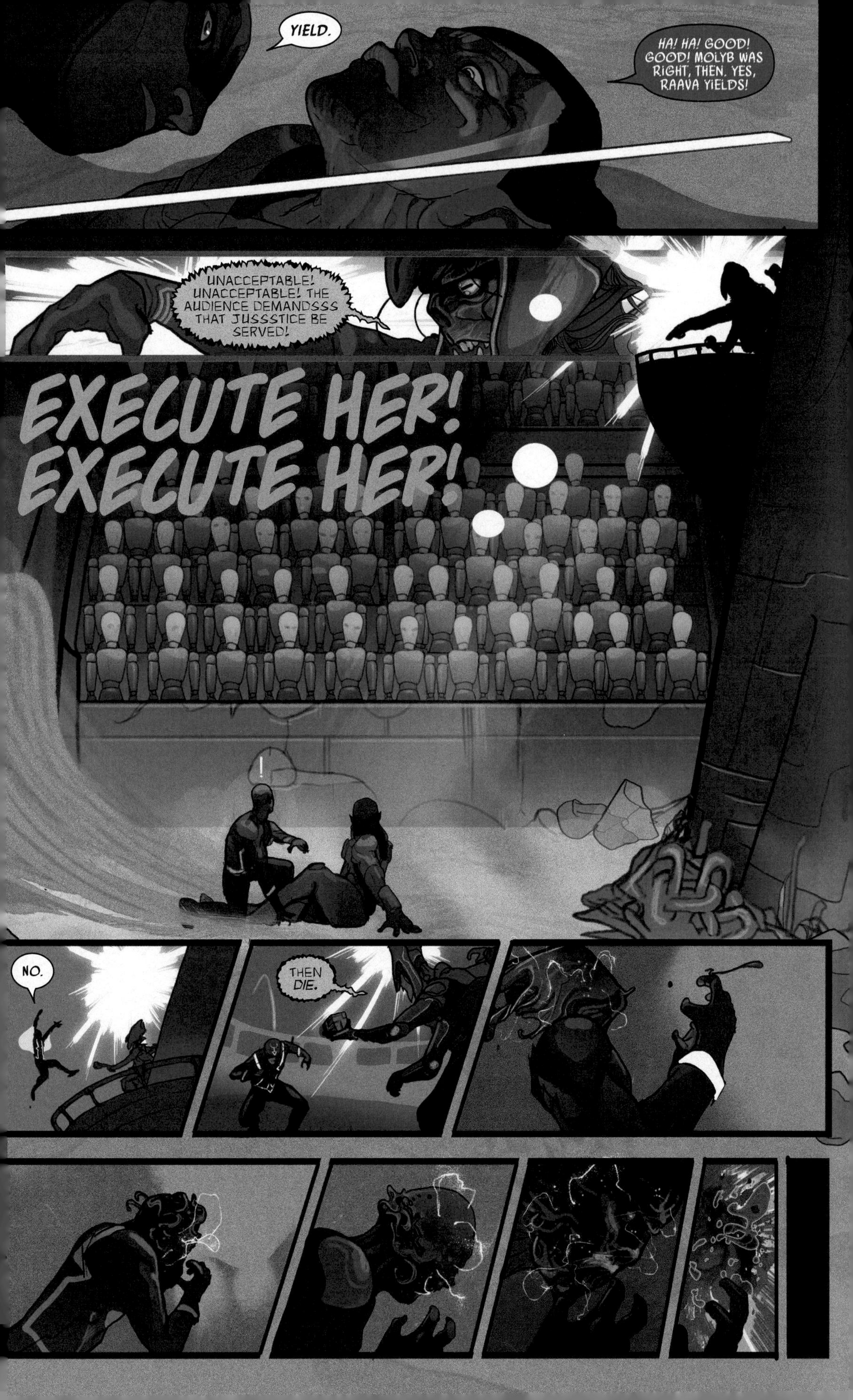
YIELD.
HA! HA! GOOD! GOOD! MOLYB WAS RIGHT, THEN. YES, RAAVA YIELDS!
UNACCEPTABLE! UNACCEPTABLE! THE AUDIENCE DEMANDSSS THAT JUSSSTICE BE SERVED!
EXECUTE HER! EXECUTE HER!
!
NO.
THEN DIE.

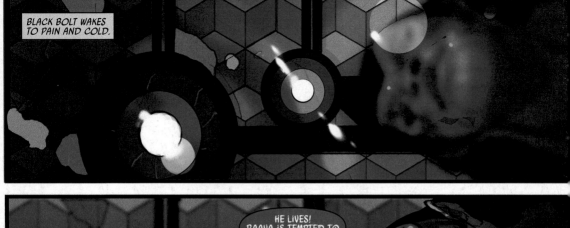

BLACK BOLT WAKES TO PAIN AND COLD.

HE LIVES! RAAVA IS TEMPTED TO FINISH HIM.

BEAT YOU ONCE...CAN BEAT YOU AGAIN...

YOU WHAT?

THIS SKINNY ONE THINKS HE *DEFEATED* RAAVA! THIS SKINNY ONE THINKS OUR BATTLE WAS IN *EARNEST!*

IT'S KINDA CUTE, AIN'T IT? I THINK HE THINKS HE BEAT ME WHEN WE TUSSLED, TOO. SO FULLA HIMSELF HE CAN'T EVEN SEE WHEN THE OTHER GUY THROWS THE FIGHT.

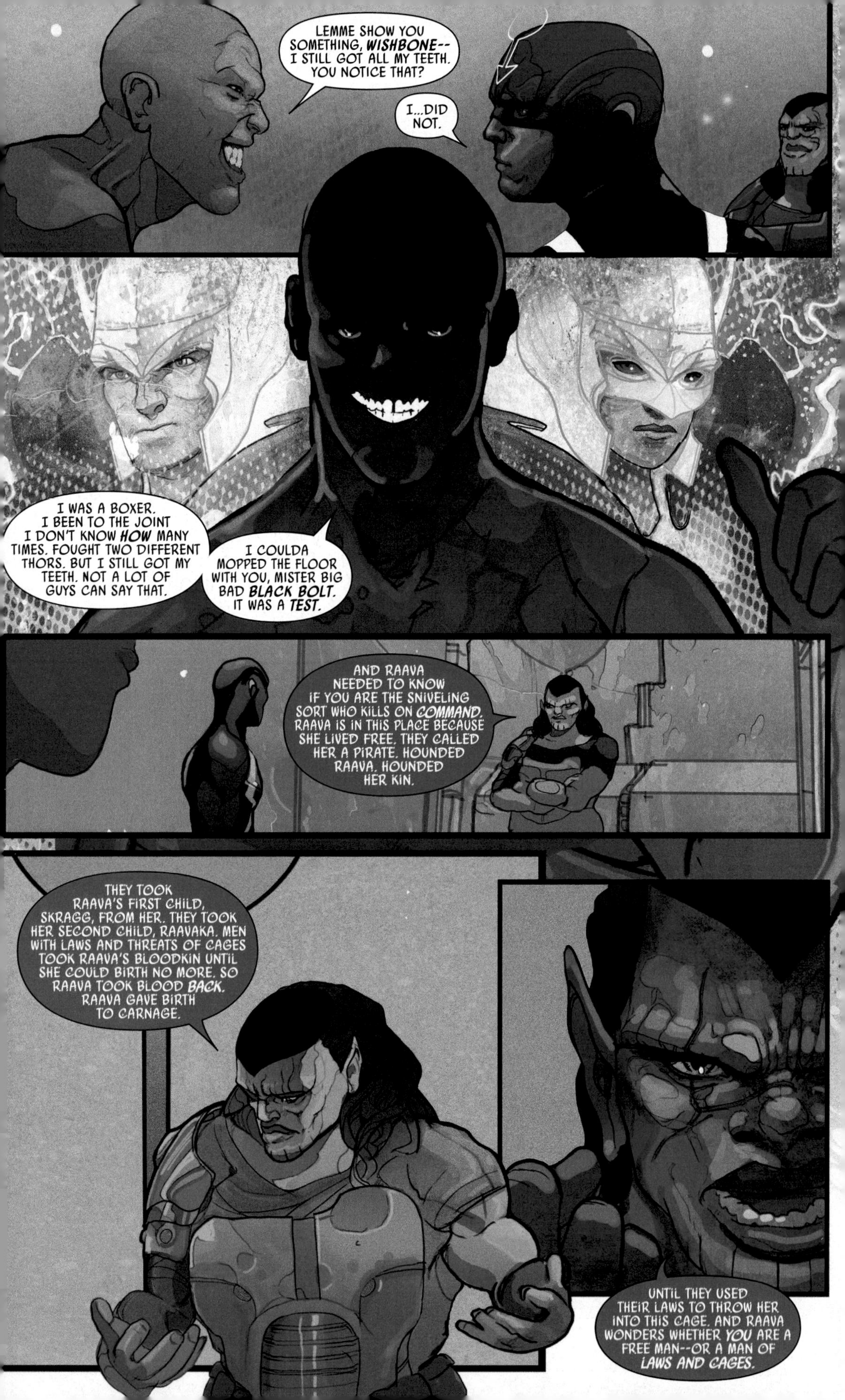

LEMME SHOW YOU SOMETHING, WISHBONE-- I STILL GOT ALL MY TEETH. YOU NOTICE THAT?
I...DID NOT.
I WAS A BOXER. I BEEN TO THE JOINT I DON'T KNOW HOW MANY TIMES. FOUGHT TWO DIFFERENT THORS. BUT I STILL GOT MY TEETH. NOT A LOT OF GUYS CAN SAY THAT.
I COULDA MOPPED THE FLOOR WITH YOU, MISTER BIG BAD BLACK BOLT. IT WAS A TEST.
AND RAAVA NEEDED TO KNOW IF YOU ARE THE SNIVELING SORT WHO KILLS ON COMMAND. RAAVA IS IN THIS PLACE BECAUSE SHE LIVED FREE. THEY CALLED HER A PIRATE. HOUNDED RAAVA. HOUNDED HER KIN.
THEY TOOK RAAVA'S FIRST CHILD, SKRAGG, FROM HER. THEY TOOK HER SECOND CHILD, RAAVAKA. MEN WITH LAWS AND THREATS OF CAGES TOOK RAAVA'S BLOODKIN UNTIL SHE COULD BIRTH NO MORE. SO RAAVA TOOK BLOOD BACK. RAAVA GAVE BIRTH TO CARNAGE.
UNTIL THEY USED THEIR LAWS TO THROW HER INTO THIS CAGE. AND RAAVA WONDERS WHETHER YOU ARE A FREE MAN--OR A MAN OF LAWS AND CAGES.

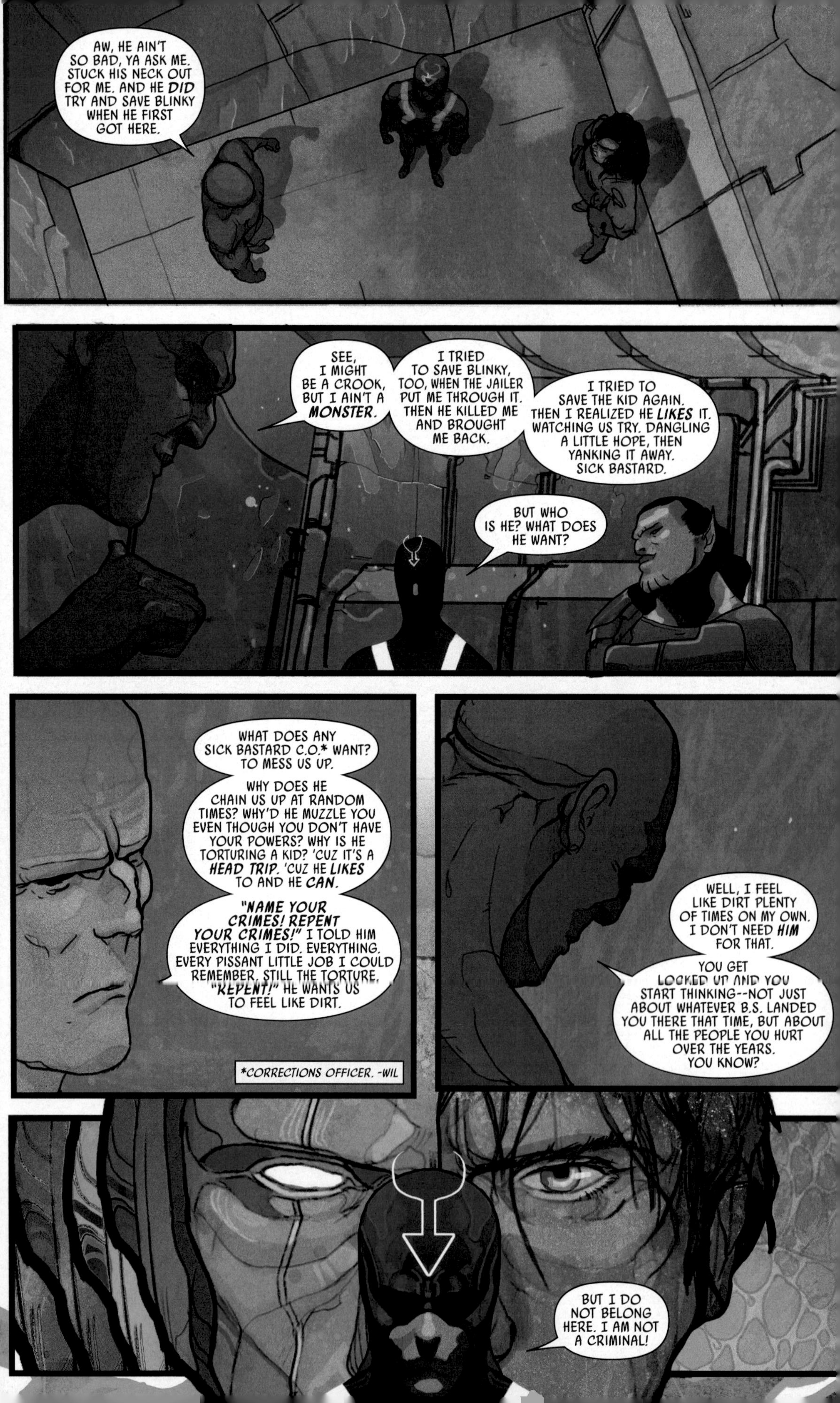
AW, HE AIN'T SO BAD, YA ASK ME. STUCK HIS NECK OUT FOR ME. AND HE DID TRY AND SAVE BLINKY WHEN HE FIRST GOT HERE.
SEE, I MIGHT BE A CROOK, BUT I AIN'T A MONSTER.
I TRIED TO SAVE BLINKY, TOO, WHEN THE JAILER PUT ME THROUGH IT. THEN HE KILLED ME AND BROUGHT ME BACK.
I TRIED TO SAVE THE KID AGAIN. THEN I REALIZED HE LIKES IT. WATCHING US TRY. DANGLING A LITTLE HOPE, THEN YANKING IT AWAY. SICK BASTARD.
BUT WHO IS HE? WHAT DOES HE WANT?
WHAT DOES ANY SICK BASTARD C.O.* WANT? TO MESS US UP.
WHY DOES HE CHAIN US UP AT RANDOM TIMES? WHY'D HE MUZZLE YOU EVEN THOUGH YOU DON'T HAVE YOUR POWERS? WHY IS HE TORTURING A KID? 'CUZ IT'S A HEAD TRIP. 'CUZ HE LIKES TO AND HE CAN.
"NAME YOUR CRIMES! REPENT YOUR CRIMES!" I TOLD HIM EVERYTHING I DID. EVERYTHING. EVERY PISSANT LITTLE JOB I COULD REMEMBER. STILL THE TORTURE. "REPENT!" HE WANTS US TO FEEL LIKE DIRT.
*CORRECTIONS OFFICER. -WIL
WELL, I FEEL LIKE DIRT PLENTY OF TIMES ON MY OWN. I DON'T NEED HIM FOR THAT.
YOU GET LOCKED UP AND YOU START THINKING--NOT JUST ABOUT WHATEVER B.S. LANDED YOU THERE THAT TIME, BUT ABOUT ALL THE PEOPLE YOU HURT OVER THE YEARS. YOU KNOW?
BUT I DO NOT BELONG HERE. I AM NOT A CRIMINAL!

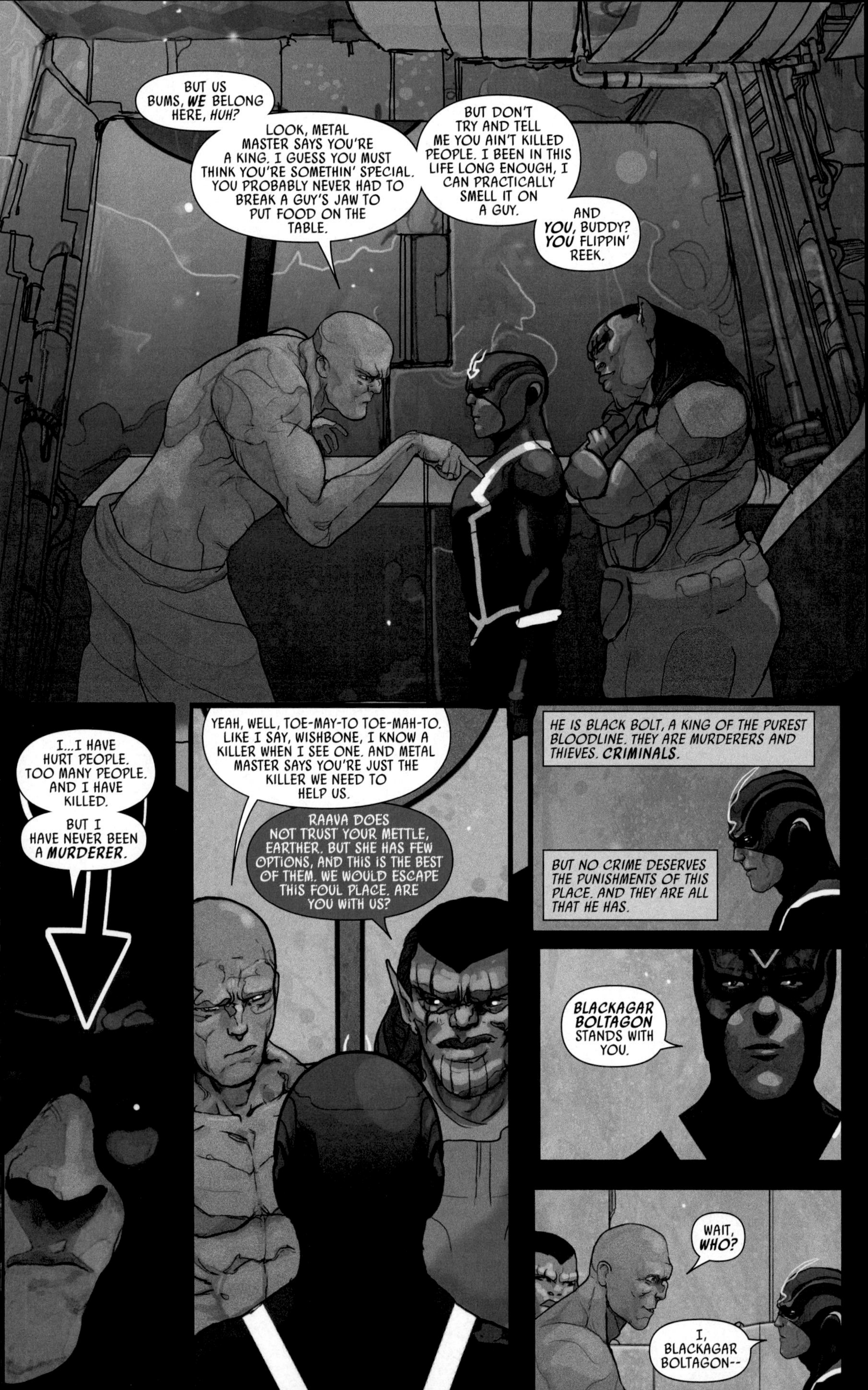
BUT US BUMS, WE BELONG HERE, HUH?
LOOK, METAL MASTER SAYS YOU'RE A KING. I GUESS YOU MUST THINK YOU'RE SOMETHIN' SPECIAL. YOU PROBABLY NEVER HAD TO BREAK A GUY'S JAW TO PUT FOOD ON THE TABLE.
BUT DON'T TRY AND TELL ME YOU AIN'T KILLED PEOPLE. I BEEN IN THIS LIFE LONG ENOUGH, I CAN PRACTICALLY SMELL IT ON A GUY.
AND YOU, BUDDY? YOU FLIPPIN' REEK.
I...I HAVE HURT PEOPLE. TOO MANY PEOPLE. AND I HAVE KILLED.
BUT I HAVE NEVER BEEN A MURDERER.
YEAH, WELL, TOE-MAY-TO TOE-MAH-TO. LIKE I SAY, WISHBONE, I KNOW A KILLER WHEN I SEE ONE. AND METAL MASTER SAYS YOU'RE JUST THE KILLER WE NEED TO HELP US.
RAAVA DOES NOT TRUST YOUR METTLE, EARTHER. BUT SHE HAS FEW OPTIONS, AND THIS IS THE BEST OF THEM. WE WOULD ESCAPE THIS FOUL PLACE. ARE YOU WITH US?
HE IS BLACK BOLT, A KING OF THE PUREST BLOODLINE. THEY ARE MURDERERS AND THIEVES. CRIMINALS.
BUT NO CRIME DESERVES THE PUNISHMENTS OF THIS PLACE. AND THEY ARE ALL THAT HE HAS.
BLACKAGAR BOLTAGON STANDS WITH YOU.
WAIT, WHO?
I, BLACKAGAR BOLTAGON--

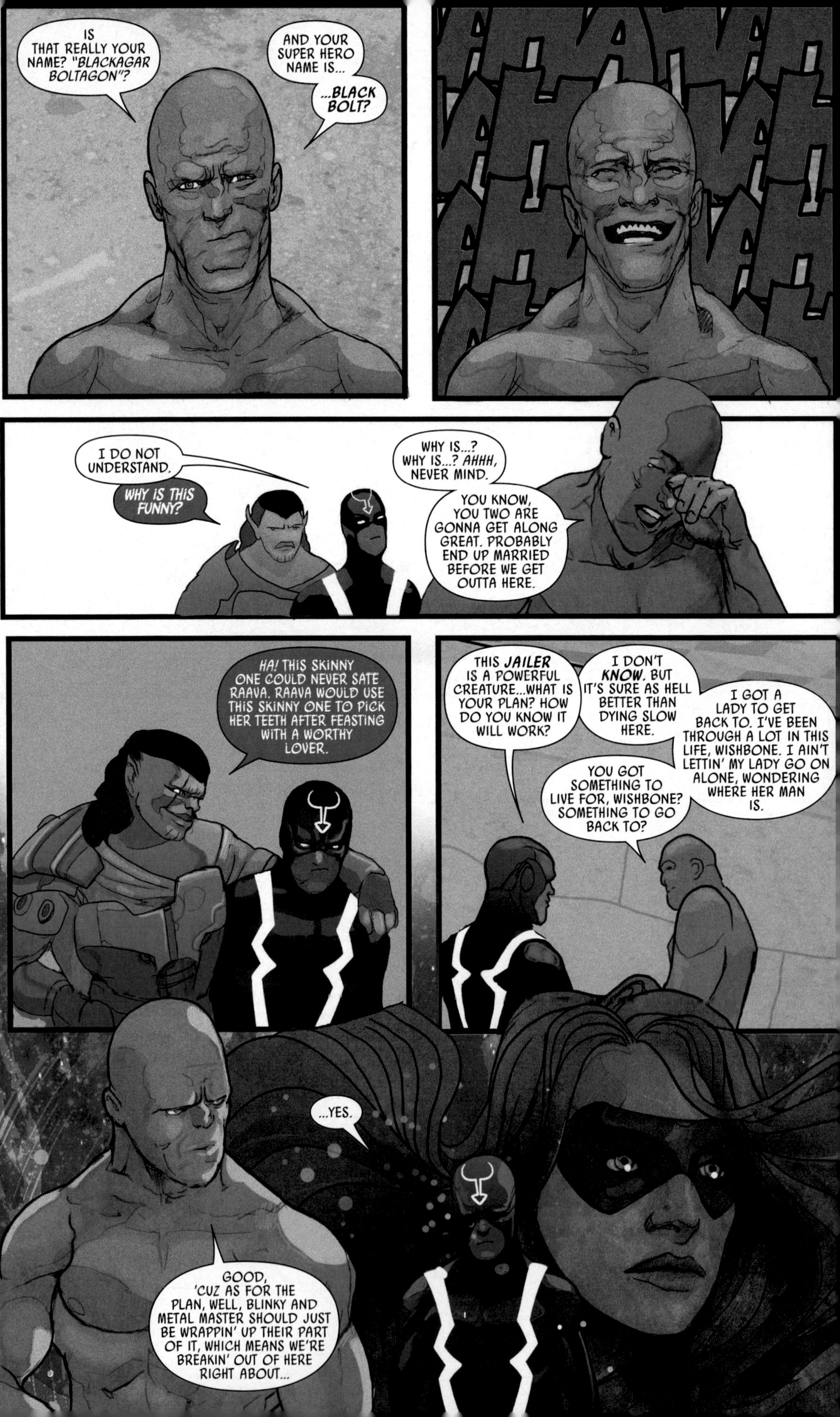
IS THAT REALLY YOUR NAME? "BLACKAGAR BOLTAGON"?
AND YOUR SUPER HERO NAME IS...
...BLACK BOLT?
I DO NOT UNDERSTAND.
WHY IS THIS FUNNY?
WHY IS...? WHY IS...? AHHH, NEVER MIND.
YOU KNOW, YOU TWO ARE GONNA GET ALONG GREAT. PROBABLY END UP MARRIED BEFORE WE GET OUTTA HERE.
HA! THIS SKINNY ONE COULD NEVER SATE RAAVA. RAAVA WOULD USE THIS SKINNY ONE TO PICK HER TEETH AFTER FEASTING WITH A WORTHY LOVER.
THIS JAILER IS A POWERFUL CREATURE...WHAT IS YOUR PLAN? HOW DO YOU KNOW IT WILL WORK?
I DON'T KNOW. BUT IT'S SURE AS HELL BETTER THAN DYING SLOW HERE.
I GOT A LADY TO GET BACK TO. I'VE BEEN THROUGH A LOT IN THIS LIFE, WISHBONE. I AIN'T LETTIN' MY LADY GO ON ALONE, WONDERING WHERE HER MAN IS.
YOU GOT SOMETHING TO LIVE FOR, WISHBONE? SOMETHING TO GO BACK TO?
...YES.
GOOD, 'CUZ AS FOR THE PLAN, WELL, BLINKY AND METAL MASTER SHOULD JUST BE WRAPPIN' UP THEIR PART OF IT, WHICH MEANS WE'RE BREAKIN' OUT OF HERE RIGHT ABOUT...

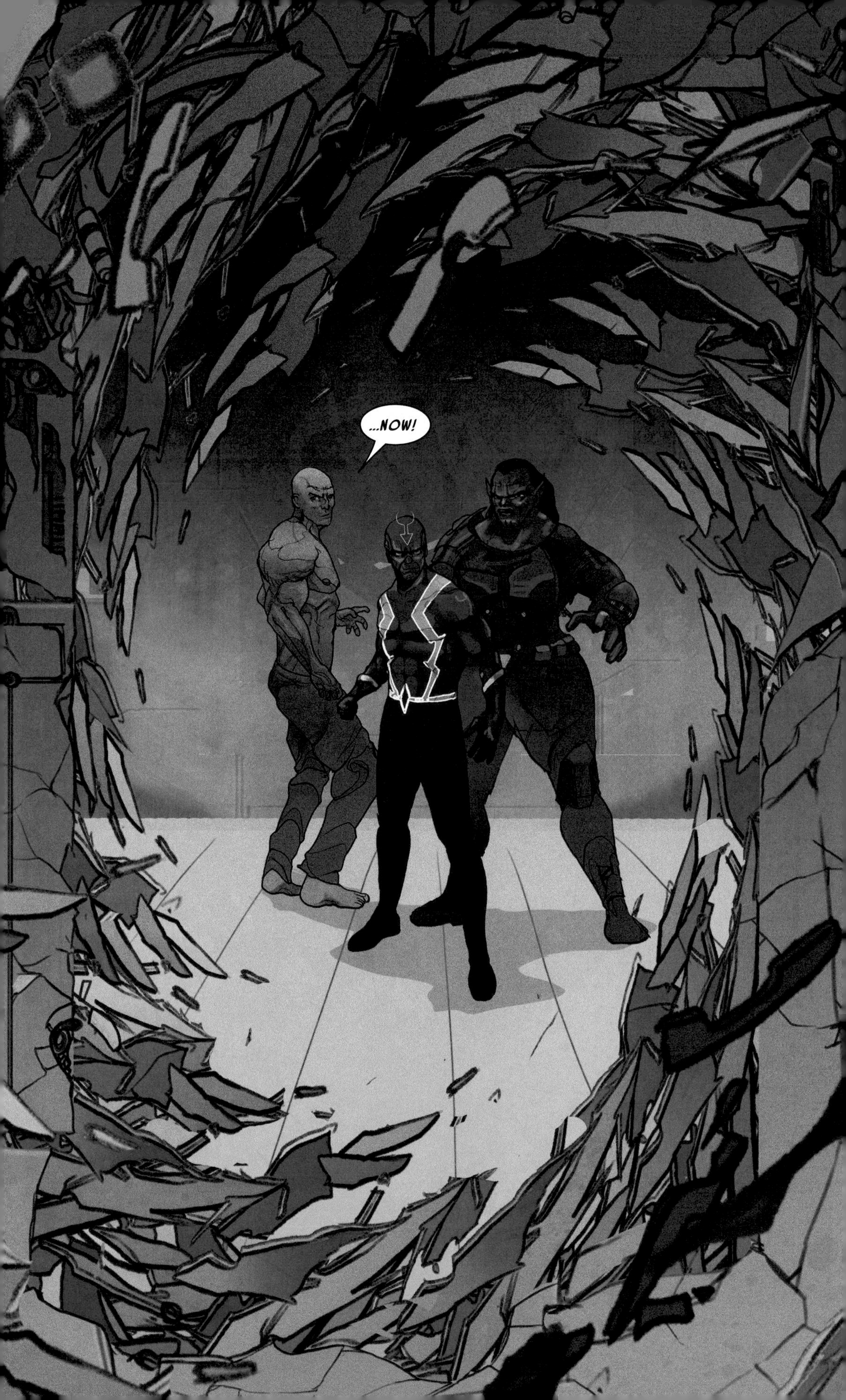
...NOW!

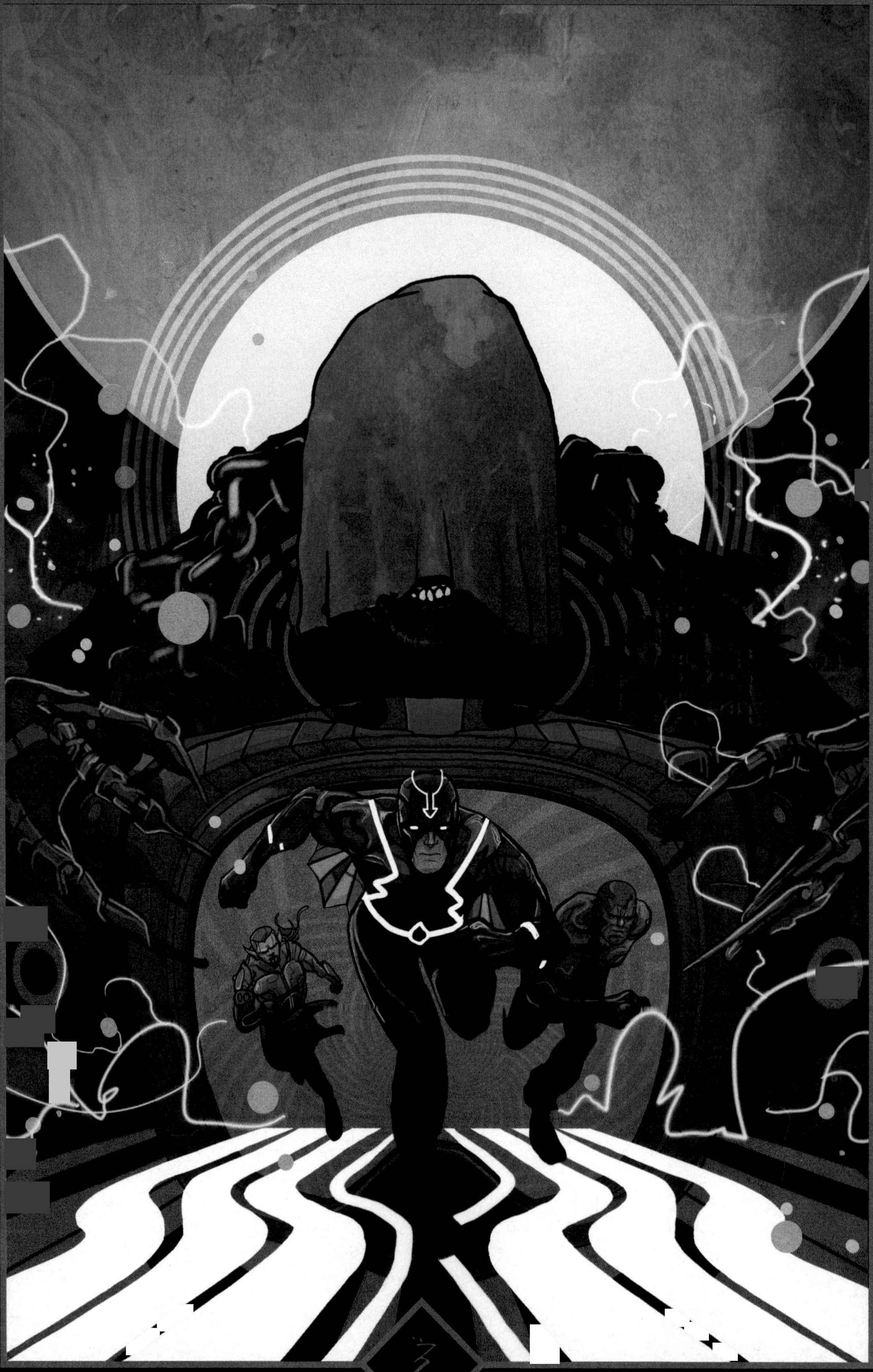

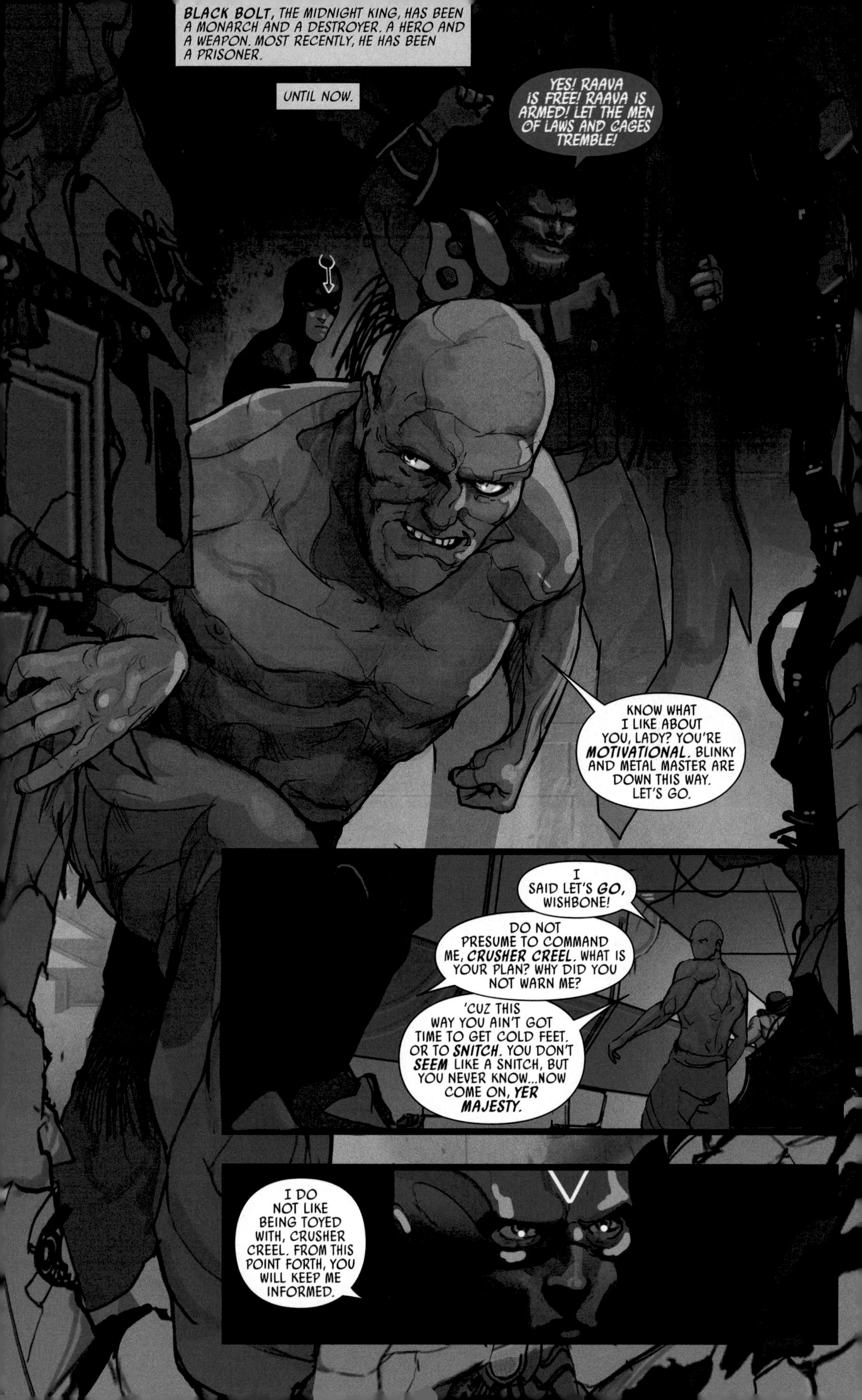
BLACK BOLT, THE MIDNIGHT KING, HAS BEEN A MONARCH AND A DESTROYER. A HERO AND A WEAPON. MOST RECENTLY, HE HAS BEEN A PRISONER.
UNTIL NOW.
YES! RAAVA IS FREE! RAAVA IS ARMED! LET THE MEN OF LAWS AND CAGES TREMBLE!
KNOW WHAT I LIKE ABOUT YOU, LADY? YOU'RE MOTIVATIONAL. BLINKY AND METAL MASTER ARE DOWN THIS WAY. LET'S GO.
I SAID LET'S GO, WISHBONE!
DO NOT PRESUME TO COMMAND ME, CRUSHER CREEL. WHAT IS YOUR PLAN? WHY DID YOU NOT WARN ME?
'CUZ THIS WAY YOU AIN'T GOT TIME TO GET COLD FEET. OR TO SNITCH. YOU DON'T SEEM LIKE A SNITCH, BUT YOU NEVER KNOW...NOW COME ON, YER MAJESTY.
I DO NOT LIKE BEING TOYED WITH, CRUSHER CREEL. FROM THIS POINT FORTH, YOU WILL KEEP ME INFORMED.

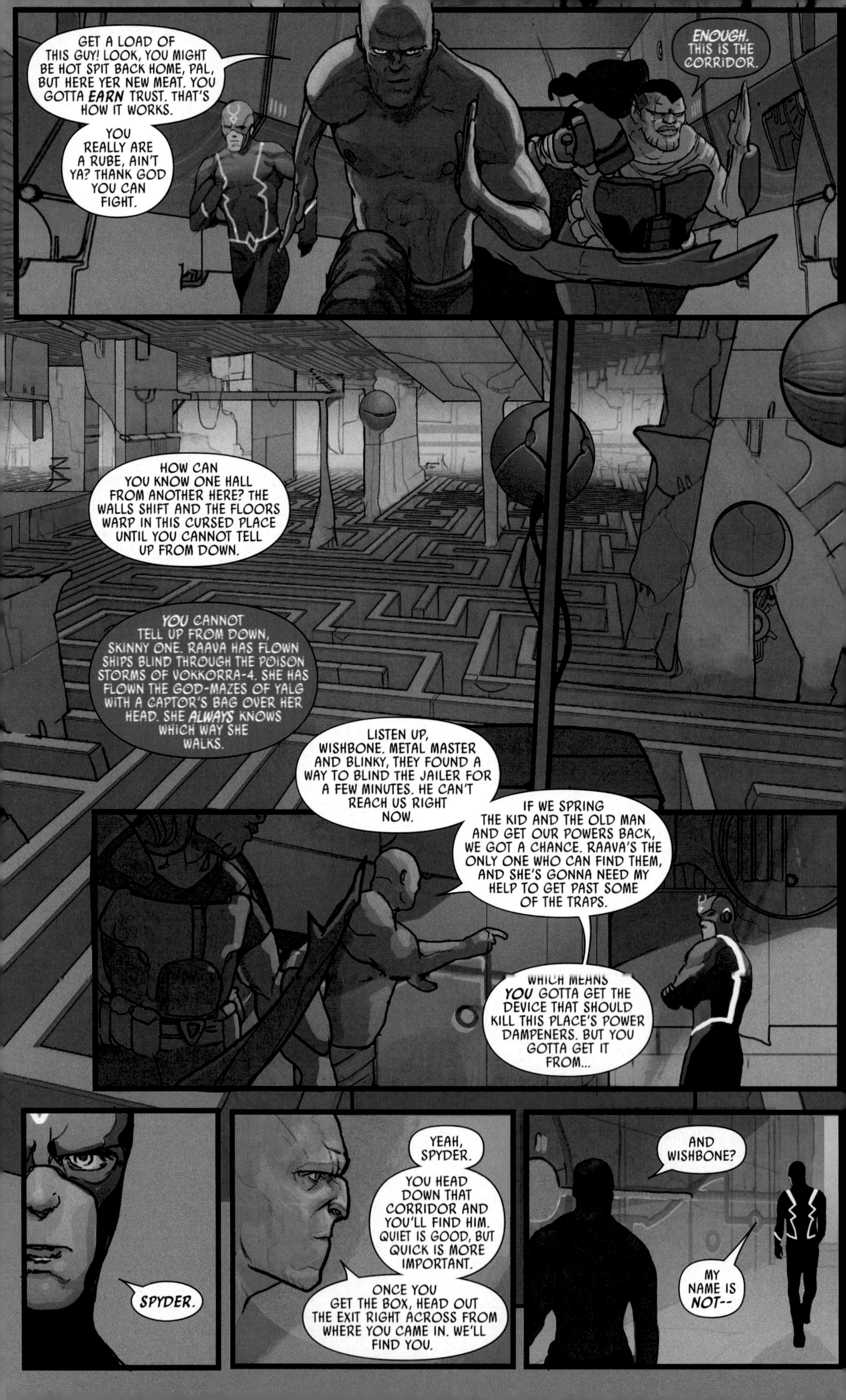

GET A LOAD OF THIS GUY! LOOK, YOU MIGHT BE HOT SPIT BACK HOME, PAL, BUT HERE YER NEW MEAT. YOU GOTTA EARN TRUST. THAT'S HOW IT WORKS.
YOU REALLY ARE A RUBE, AIN'T YA? THANK GOD YOU CAN FIGHT.
ENOUGH. THIS IS THE CORRIDOR.
HOW CAN YOU KNOW ONE HALL FROM ANOTHER HERE? THE WALLS SHIFT AND THE FLOORS WARP IN THIS CURSED PLACE UNTIL YOU CANNOT TELL UP FROM DOWN.
YOU CANNOT TELL UP FROM DOWN, SKINNY ONE. RAAVA HAS FLOWN SHIPS BLIND THROUGH THE POISON STORMS OF VOKKORRA-4. SHE HAS FLOWN THE GOD-MAZES OF YALG WITH A CAPTOR'S BAG OVER HER HEAD. SHE ALWAYS KNOWS WHICH WAY SHE WALKS.
LISTEN UP, WISHBONE. METAL MASTER AND BLINKY, THEY FOUND A WAY TO BLIND THE JAILER FOR A FEW MINUTES. HE CAN'T REACH US RIGHT NOW.
IF WE SPRING THE KID AND THE OLD MAN AND GET OUR POWERS BACK, WE GOT A CHANCE. RAAVA'S THE ONLY ONE WHO CAN FIND THEM, AND SHE'S GONNA NEED MY HELP TO GET PAST SOME OF THE TRAPS.
WHICH MEANS YOU GOTTA GET THE DEVICE THAT SHOULD KILL THIS PLACE'S POWER DAMPENERS. BUT YOU GOTTA GET IT FROM...
SPYDER.
YEAH, SPYDER.
YOU HEAD DOWN THAT CORRIDOR AND YOU'LL FIND HIM. QUIET IS GOOD, BUT QUICK IS MORE IMPORTANT.
ONCE YOU GET THE BOX, HEAD OUT THE EXIT RIGHT ACROSS FROM WHERE YOU CAME IN. WE'LL FIND YOU.
AND WISHBONE?
MY NAME IS NOT--

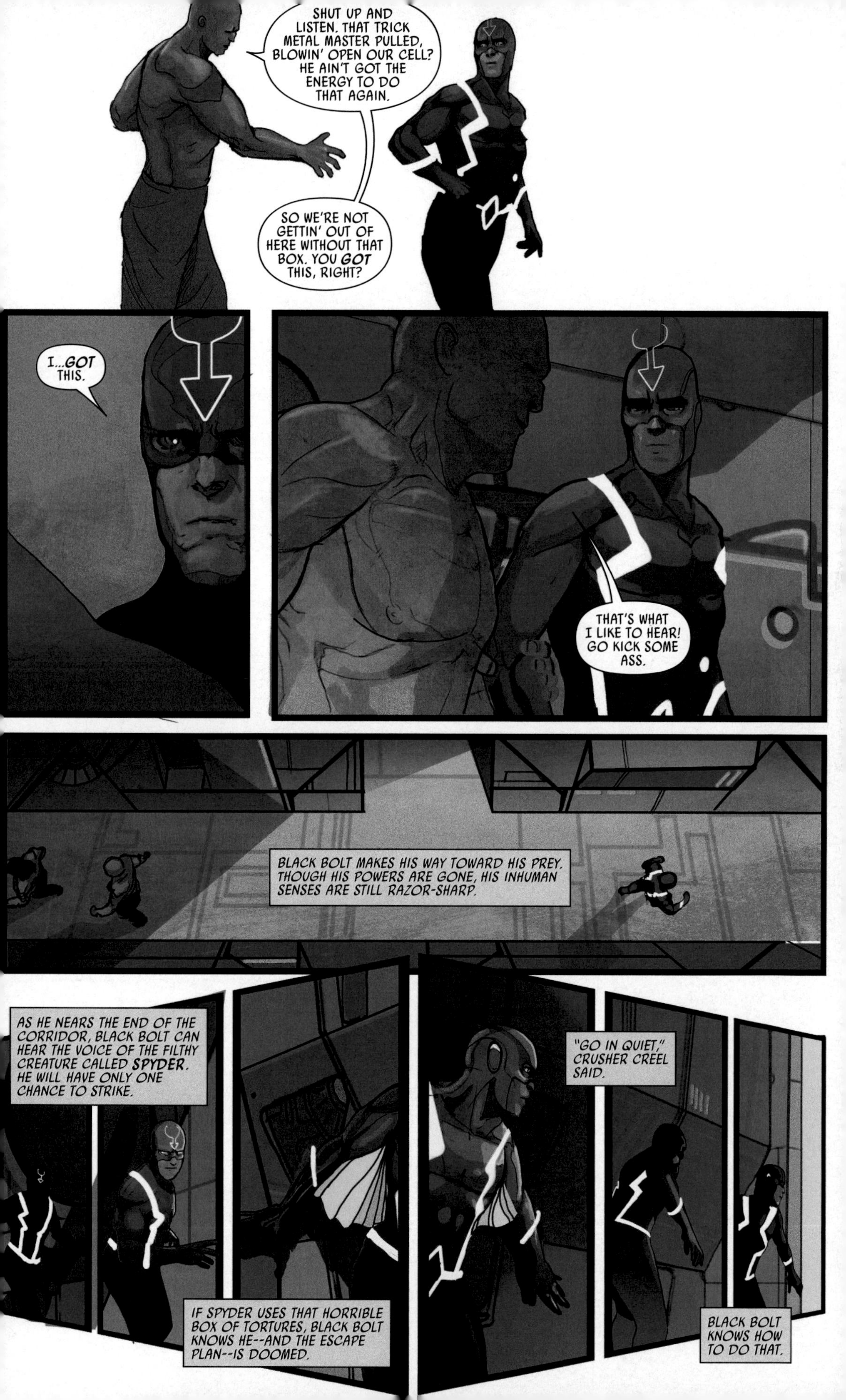
SHUT UP AND LISTEN. THAT TRICK METAL MASTER PULLED, BLOWIN' OPEN OUR CELL? HE AIN'T GOT THE ENERGY TO DO THAT AGAIN.
SO WE'RE NOT GETTIN' OUT OF HERE WITHOUT THAT BOX. YOU **GOT** THIS, RIGHT?
I...**GOT** THIS.
THAT'S WHAT I LIKE TO HEAR! GO KICK SOME ASS.
BLACK BOLT MAKES HIS WAY TOWARD HIS PREY. THOUGH HIS POWERS ARE GONE, HIS INHUMAN SENSES ARE STILL RAZOR-SHARP.
AS HE NEARS THE END OF THE CORRIDOR, BLACK BOLT CAN HEAR THE VOICE OF THE FILTHY CREATURE CALLED **SPYDER**. HE WILL HAVE ONLY ONE CHANCE TO STRIKE.
IF SPYDER USES THAT HORRIBLE BOX OF TORTURES, BLACK BOLT KNOWS HE--AND THE ESCAPE PLAN--IS DOOMED.
"GO IN QUIET," CRUSHER CREEL SAID.
BLACK BOLT KNOWS HOW TO DO THAT.

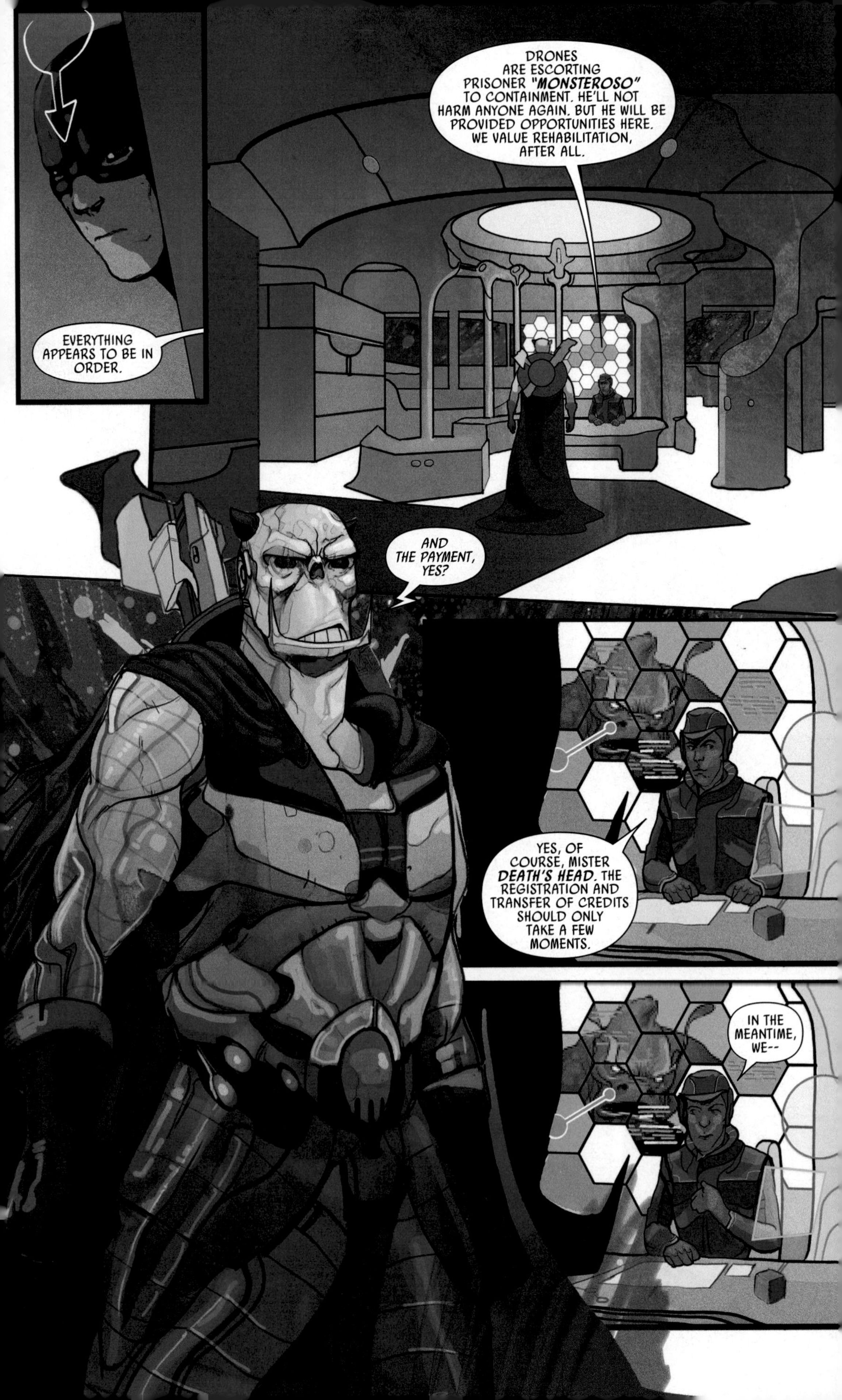

EVERYTHING APPEARS TO BE IN ORDER.
DRONES ARE ESCORTING PRISONER "MONSTEROSO" TO CONTAINMENT. HE'LL NOT HARM ANYONE AGAIN. BUT HE WILL BE PROVIDED OPPORTUNITIES HERE. WE VALUE REHABILITATION, AFTER ALL.
AND THE PAYMENT, YES?
YES, OF COURSE, MISTER DEATH'S HEAD. THE REGISTRATION AND TRANSFER OF CREDITS SHOULD ONLY TAKE A FEW MOMENTS.
IN THE MEANTIME, WE--

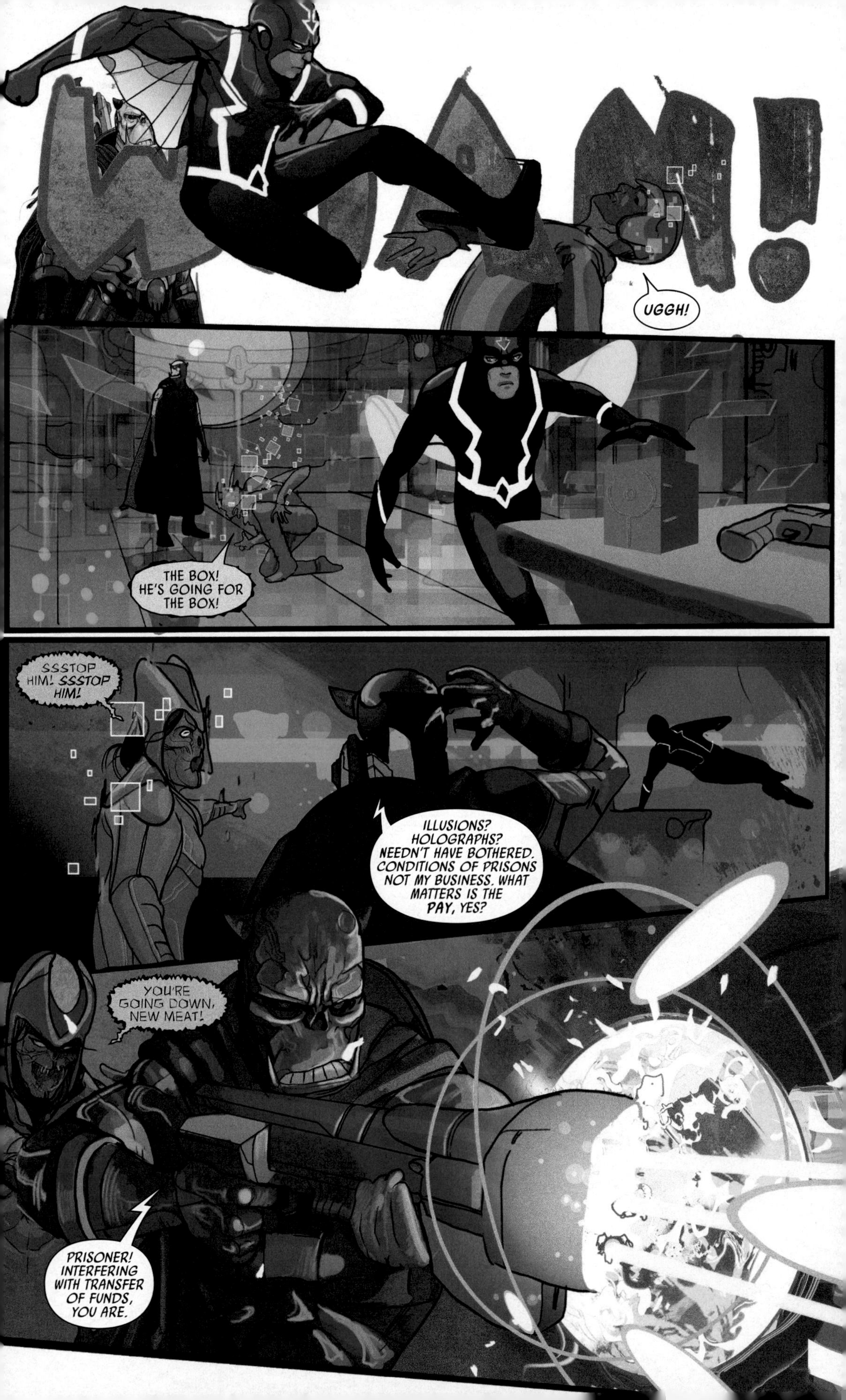
WHAM!
UGGH!
THE BOX! HE'S GOING FOR THE BOX!
SSSTOP HIM! SSSTOP HIM!
ILLUSIONS? HOLOGRAPHS? NEEDN'T HAVE BOTHERED. CONDITIONS OF PRISONS NOT MY BUSINESS. WHAT MATTERS IS THE PAY, YES?
YOU'RE GOING DOWN, NEW MEAT!
PRISONER! INTERFERING WITH TRANSFER OF FUNDS, YOU ARE.

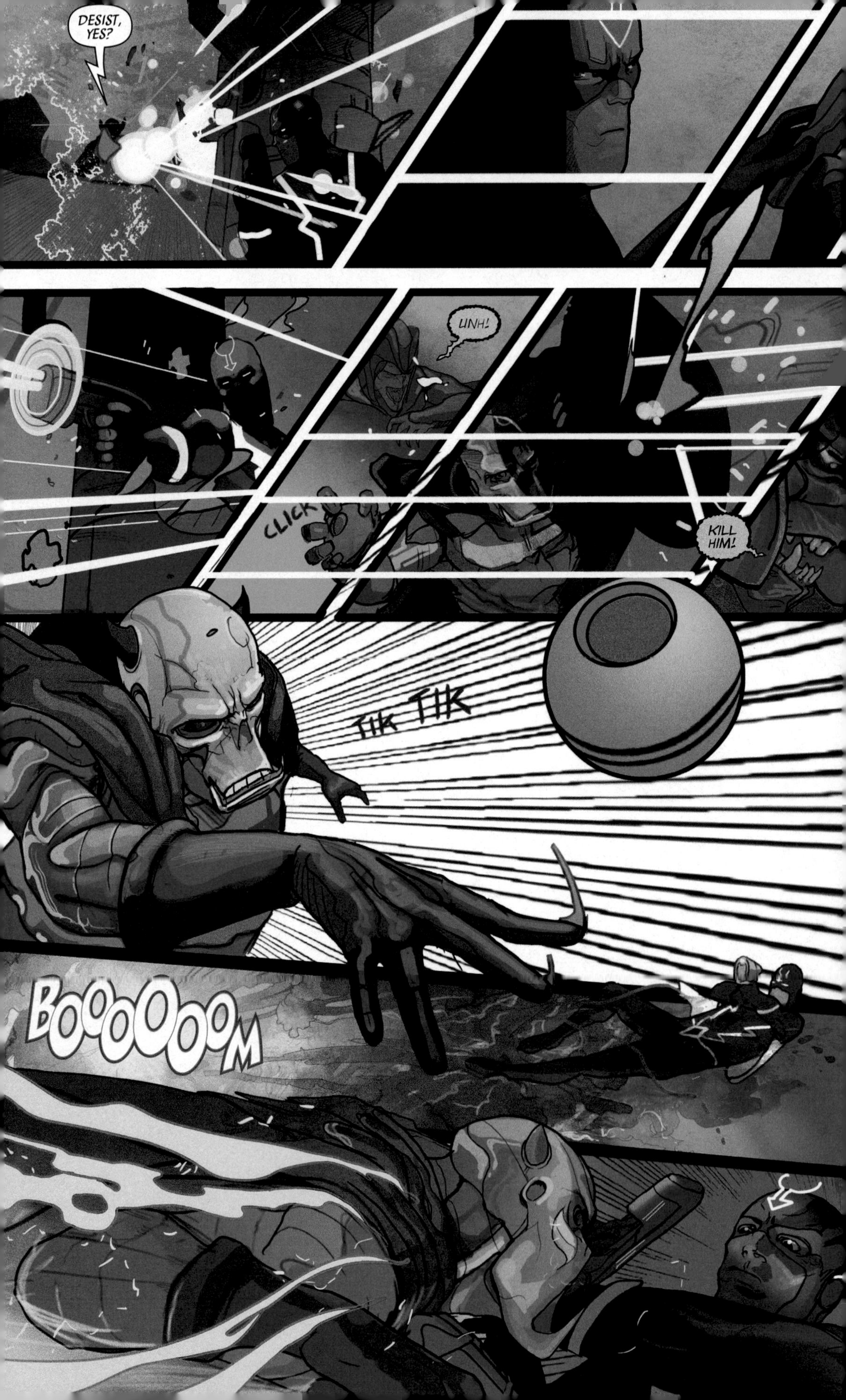
DESIST, YES?
UNH!
CLICK
KILL HIM!
TIK TIK
BOOOOOOM

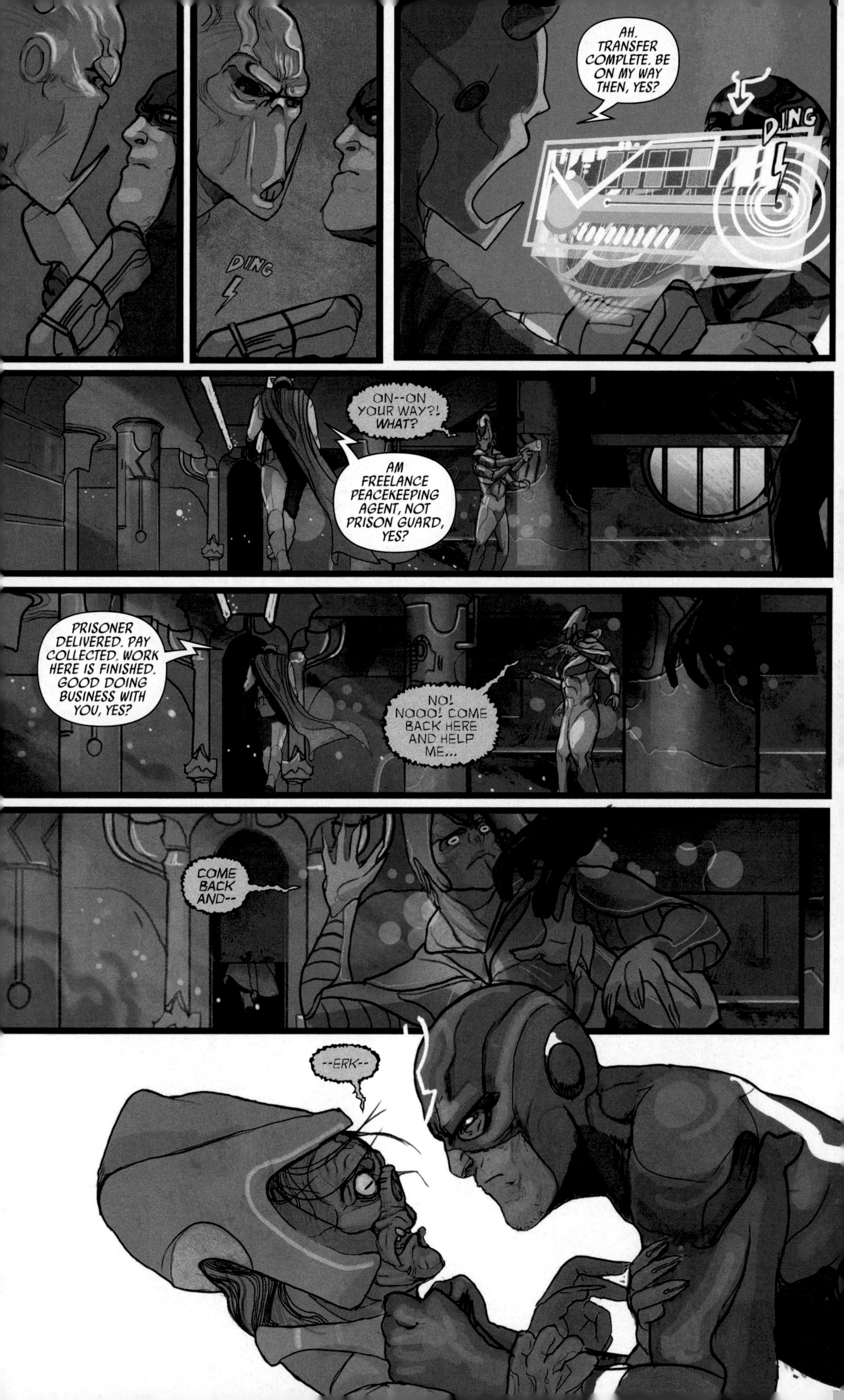
DING
AH. TRANSFER COMPLETE. BE ON MY WAY THEN, YES?
DING
ON--ON YOUR WAY?! WHAT?
AM FREELANCE PEACEKEEPING AGENT, NOT PRISON GUARD, YES?
PRISONER DELIVERED. PAY COLLECTED. WORK HERE IS FINISHED. GOOD DOING BUSINESS WITH YOU, YES?
NO! NOOO! COME BACK HERE AND HELP ME...
COME BACK AND--
--ERK--

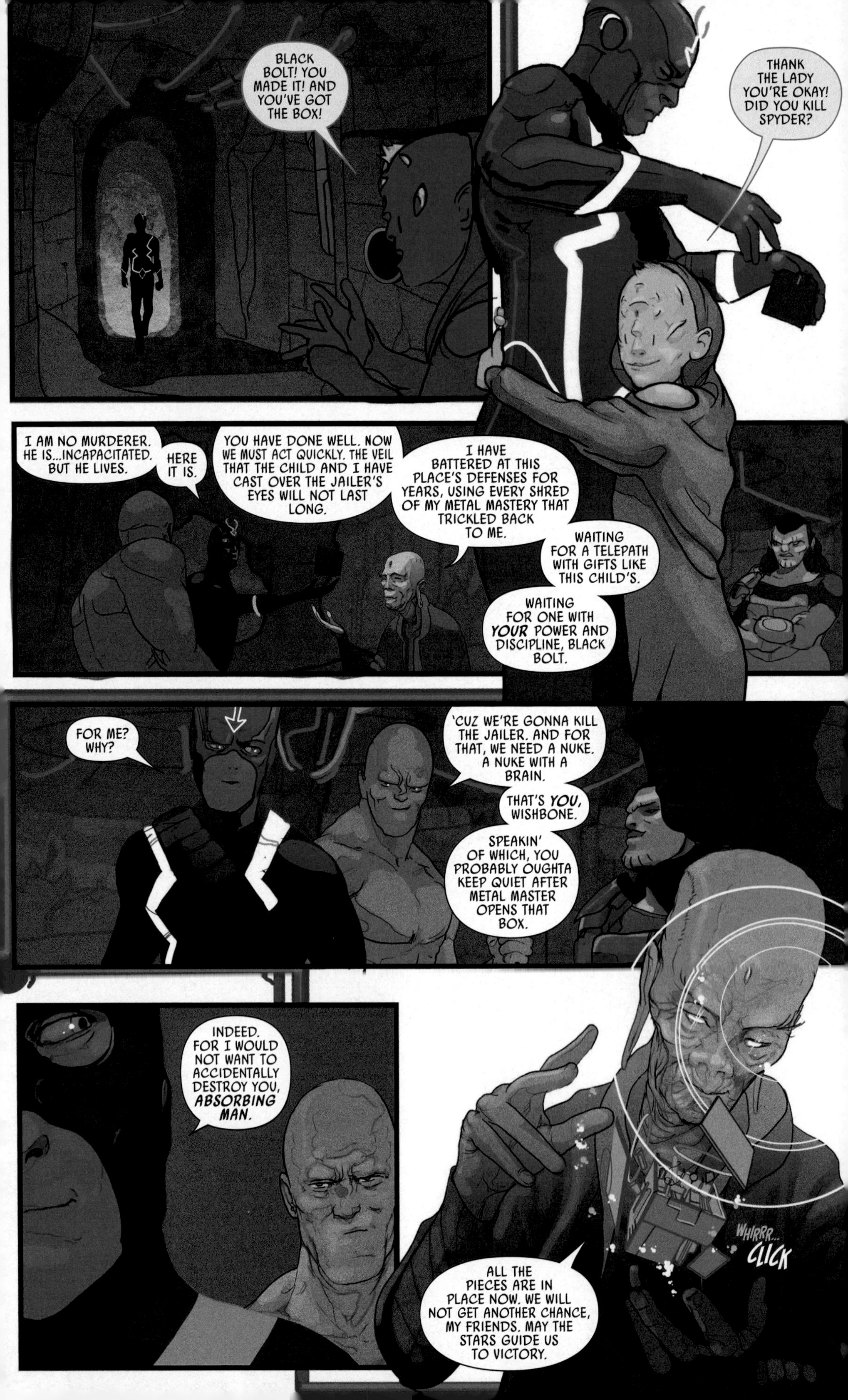
BLACK BOLT! YOU MADE IT! AND YOU'VE GOT THE BOX!
THANK THE LADY YOU'RE OKAY! DID YOU KILL SPYDER?
I AM NO MURDERER. HE IS...INCAPACITATED. BUT HE LIVES.
HERE IT IS.
YOU HAVE DONE WELL. NOW WE MUST ACT QUICKLY. THE VEIL THAT THE CHILD AND I HAVE CAST OVER THE JAILER'S EYES WILL NOT LAST LONG.
I HAVE BATTERED AT THIS PLACE'S DEFENSES FOR YEARS, USING EVERY SHRED OF MY METAL MASTERY THAT TRICKLED BACK TO ME.
WAITING FOR A TELEPATH WITH GIFTS LIKE THIS CHILD'S.
WAITING FOR ONE WITH *YOUR* POWER AND DISCIPLINE, BLACK BOLT.
FOR ME? WHY?
'CUZ WE'RE GONNA KILL THE JAILER. AND FOR THAT, WE NEED A NUKE. A NUKE WITH A BRAIN.
THAT'S *YOU*, WISHBONE.
SPEAKIN' OF WHICH, YOU PROBABLY OUGHTA KEEP QUIET AFTER METAL MASTER OPENS THAT BOX.
INDEED. FOR I WOULD NOT WANT TO ACCIDENTALLY DESTROY YOU, *ABSORBING MAN*.
WHIRRR...
CLICK
ALL THE PIECES ARE IN PLACE NOW. WE WILL NOT GET ANOTHER CHANCE, MY FRIENDS. MAY THE STARS GUIDE US TO VICTORY.

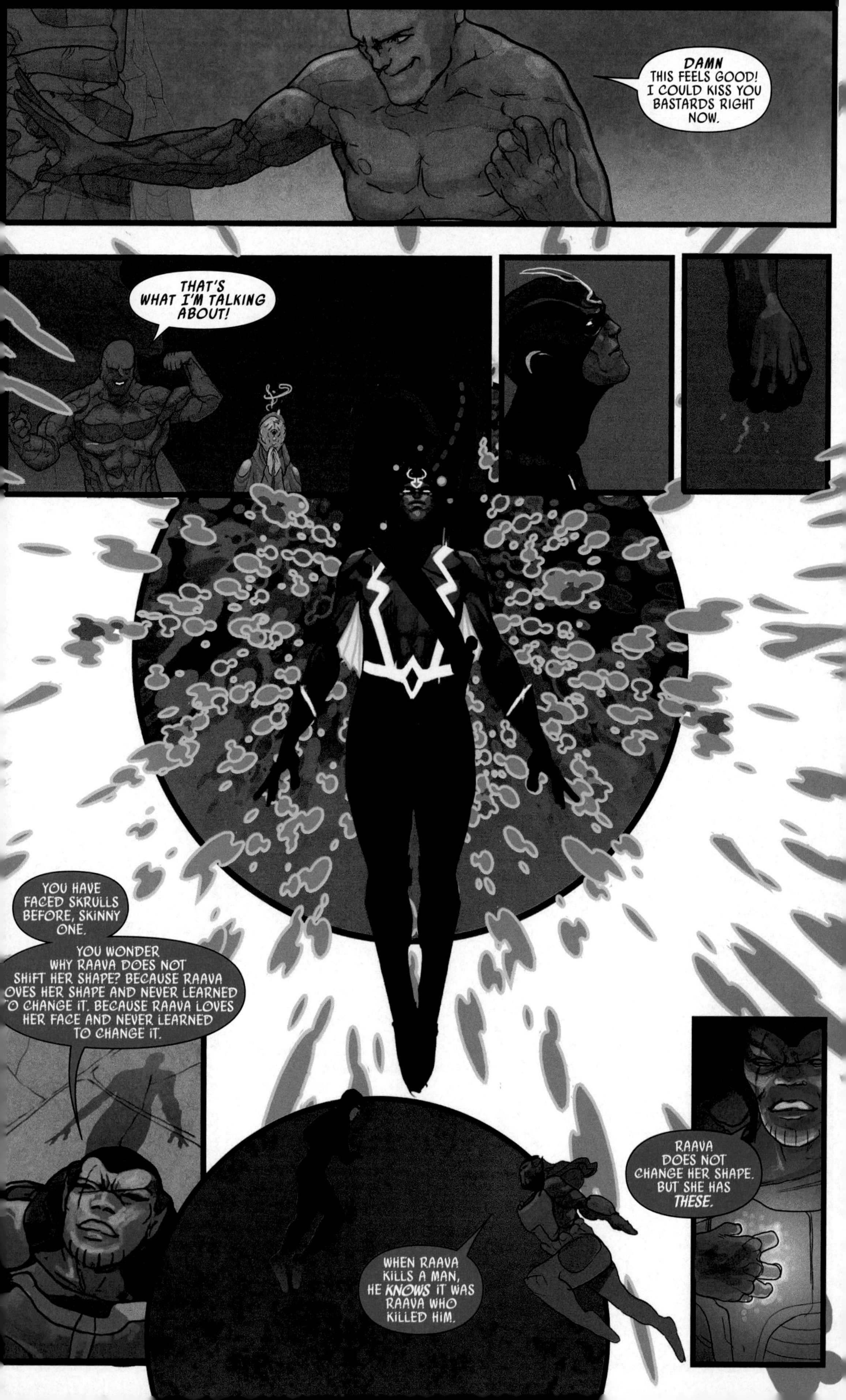
DAMN
THIS FEELS GOOD! I COULD KISS YOU BASTARDS RIGHT NOW.
THAT'S WHAT I'M TALKING ABOUT!
YOU HAVE FACED SKRULLS BEFORE, SKINNY ONE.
YOU WONDER WHY RAAVA DOES NOT SHIFT HER SHAPE? BECAUSE RAAVA LOVES HER SHAPE AND NEVER LEARNED TO CHANGE IT. BECAUSE RAAVA LOVES HER FACE AND NEVER LEARNED TO CHANGE IT.
WHEN RAAVA KILLS A MAN, HE KNOWS IT WAS RAAVA WHO KILLED HIM.
RAAVA DOES NOT CHANGE HER SHAPE. BUT SHE HAS THESE.

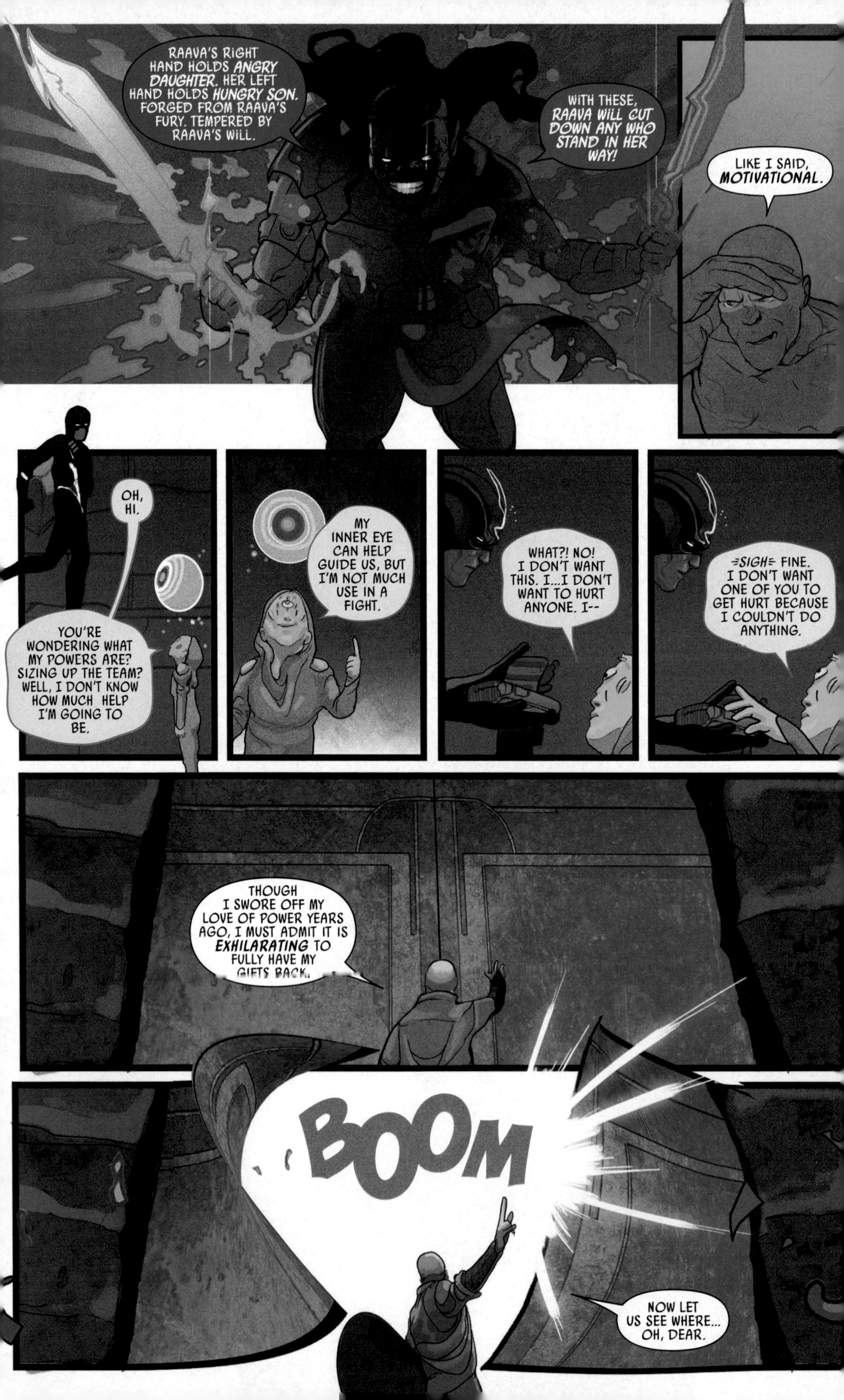
RAAVA'S RIGHT HAND HOLDS ANGRY DAUGHTER. HER LEFT HAND HOLDS HUNGRY SON. FORGED FROM RAAVA'S FURY. TEMPERED BY RAAVA'S WILL.
WITH THESE, RAAVA WILL CUT DOWN ANY WHO STAND IN HER WAY!
LIKE I SAID, MOTIVATIONAL.
OH, HI.
YOU'RE WONDERING WHAT MY POWERS ARE? SIZING UP THE TEAM? WELL, I DON'T KNOW HOW MUCH HELP I'M GOING TO BE.
MY INNER EYE CAN HELP GUIDE US, BUT I'M NOT MUCH USE IN A FIGHT.
WHAT?! NO! I DON'T WANT THIS. I...I DON'T WANT TO HURT ANYONE. I--
=SIGH= FINE. I DON'T WANT ONE OF YOU TO GET HURT BECAUSE I COULDN'T DO ANYTHING.
THOUGH I SWORE OFF MY LOVE OF POWER YEARS AGO, I MUST ADMIT IT IS EXHILARATING TO FULLY HAVE MY GIFTS BACK.
BOOM
NOW LET US SEE WHERE... OH, DEAR.

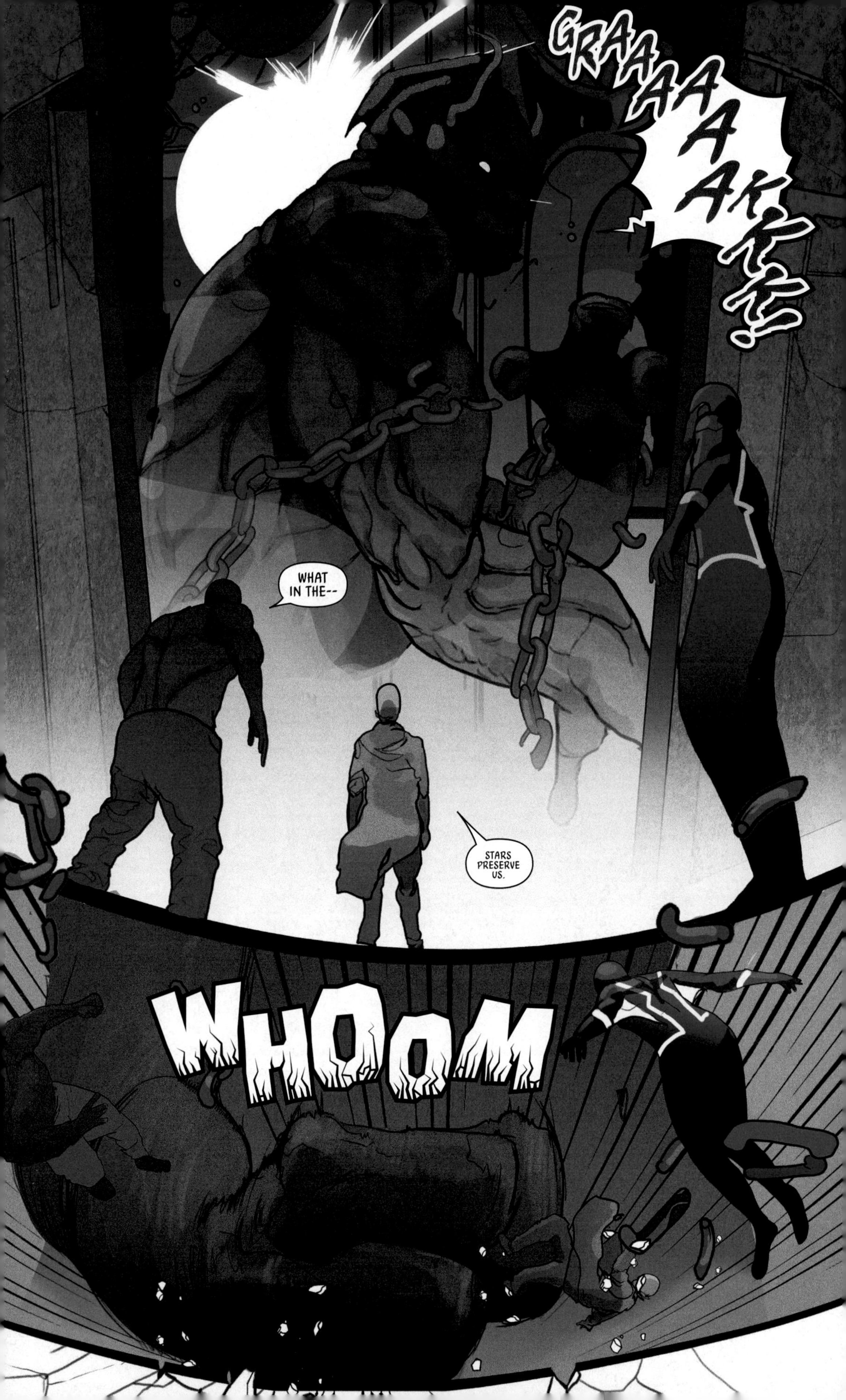
GRAAAAAKKK!
WHAT IN THE--
STARS PRESERVE US.
WHOOM

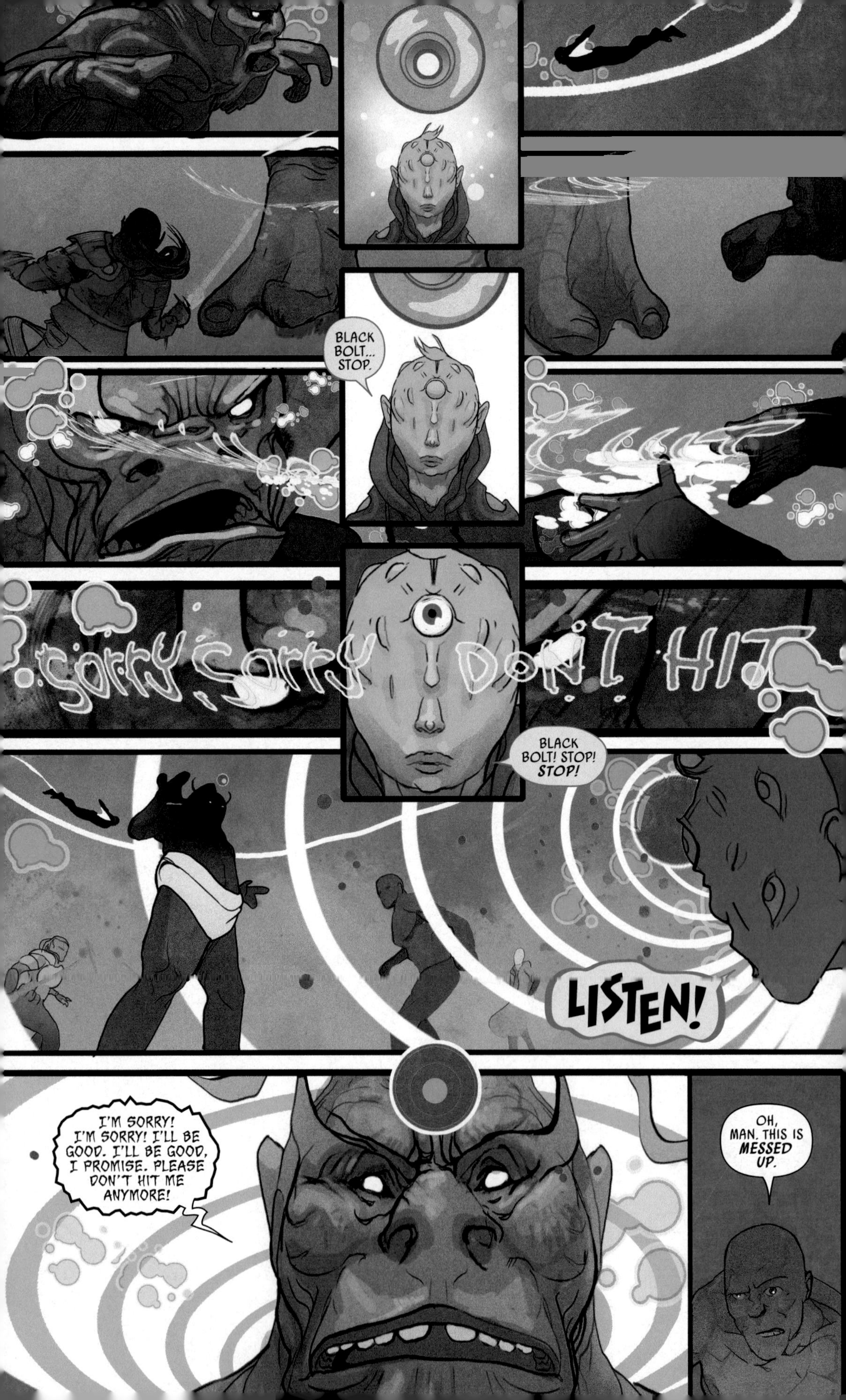
BLACK BOLT... STOP.
SORRY SORRY DON'T HIT
BLACK BOLT! STOP! STOP!
LISTEN!
I'M SORRY! I'M SORRY! I'LL BE GOOD. I'LL BE GOOD, I PROMISE. PLEASE DON'T HIT ME ANYMORE!
OH, MAN. THIS IS MESSED UP.

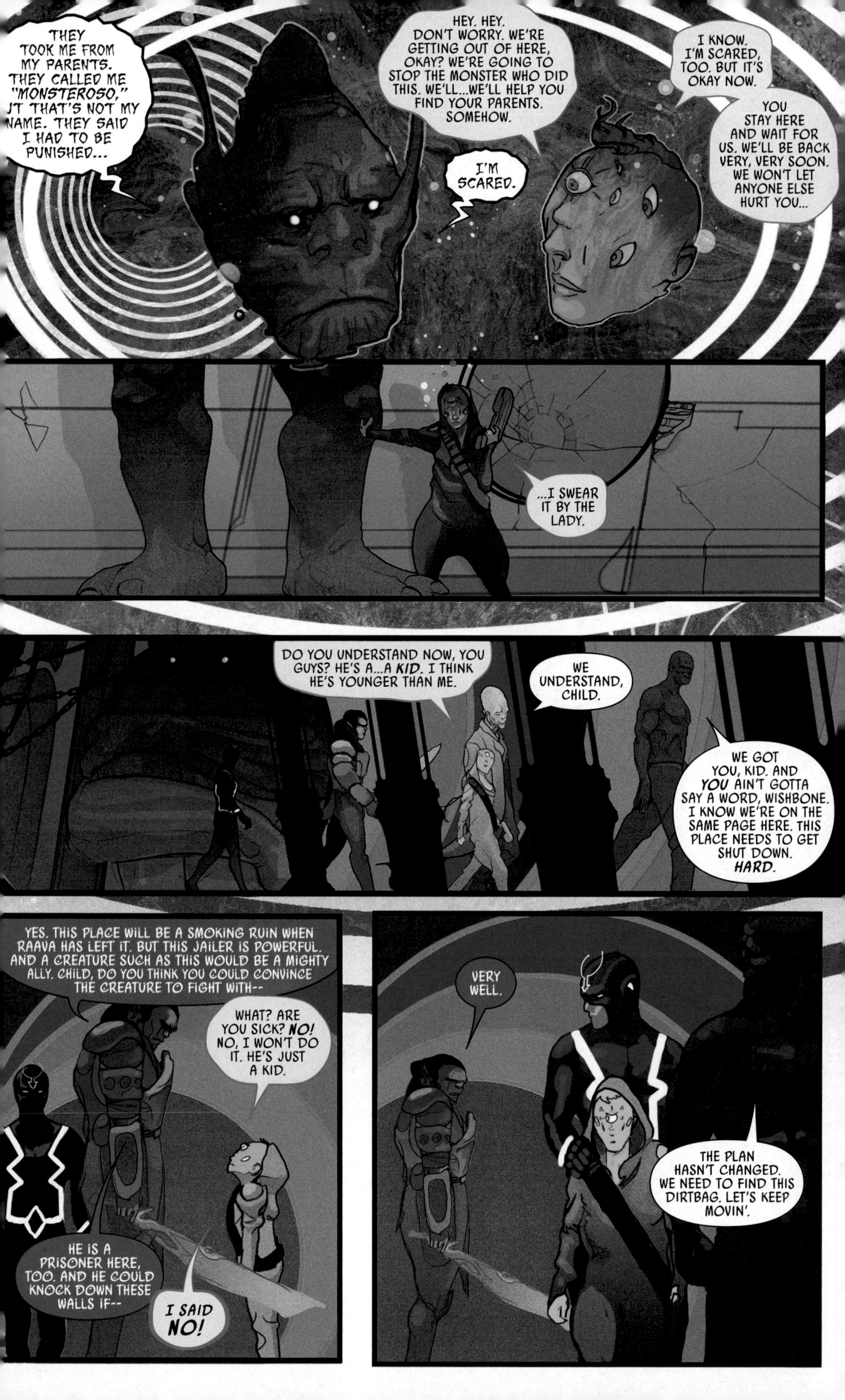

THEY TOOK ME FROM MY PARENTS. THEY CALLED ME "MONSTEROSO," JT THAT'S NOT MY NAME. THEY SAID I HAD TO BE PUNISHED...
HEY. HEY. DON'T WORRY. WE'RE GETTING OUT OF HERE, OKAY? WE'RE GOING TO STOP THE MONSTER WHO DID THIS. WE'LL...WE'LL HELP YOU FIND YOUR PARENTS. SOMEHOW.
I'M SCARED.
I KNOW. I'M SCARED, TOO. BUT IT'S OKAY NOW.
YOU STAY HERE AND WAIT FOR US. WE'LL BE BACK VERY, VERY SOON. WE WON'T LET ANYONE ELSE HURT YOU...
...I SWEAR IT BY THE LADY.
DO YOU UNDERSTAND NOW, YOU GUYS? HE'S A...A KID. I THINK HE'S YOUNGER THAN ME.
WE UNDERSTAND, CHILD.
WE GOT YOU, KID. AND YOU AIN'T GOTTA SAY A WORD, WISHBONE. I KNOW WE'RE ON THE SAME PAGE HERE. THIS PLACE NEEDS TO GET SHUT DOWN. HARD.
YES. THIS PLACE WILL BE A SMOKING RUIN WHEN RAAVA HAS LEFT IT. BUT THIS JAILER IS POWERFUL. AND A CREATURE SUCH AS THIS WOULD BE A MIGHTY ALLY. CHILD, DO YOU THINK YOU COULD CONVINCE THE CREATURE TO FIGHT WITH--
WHAT? ARE YOU SICK? NO! NO, I WON'T DO IT. HE'S JUST A KID.
HE IS A PRISONER HERE, TOO. AND HE COULD KNOCK DOWN THESE WALLS IF--
I SAID NO!
VERY WELL.
THE PLAN HASN'T CHANGED. WE NEED TO FIND THIS DIRTBAG. LET'S KEEP MOVIN'.

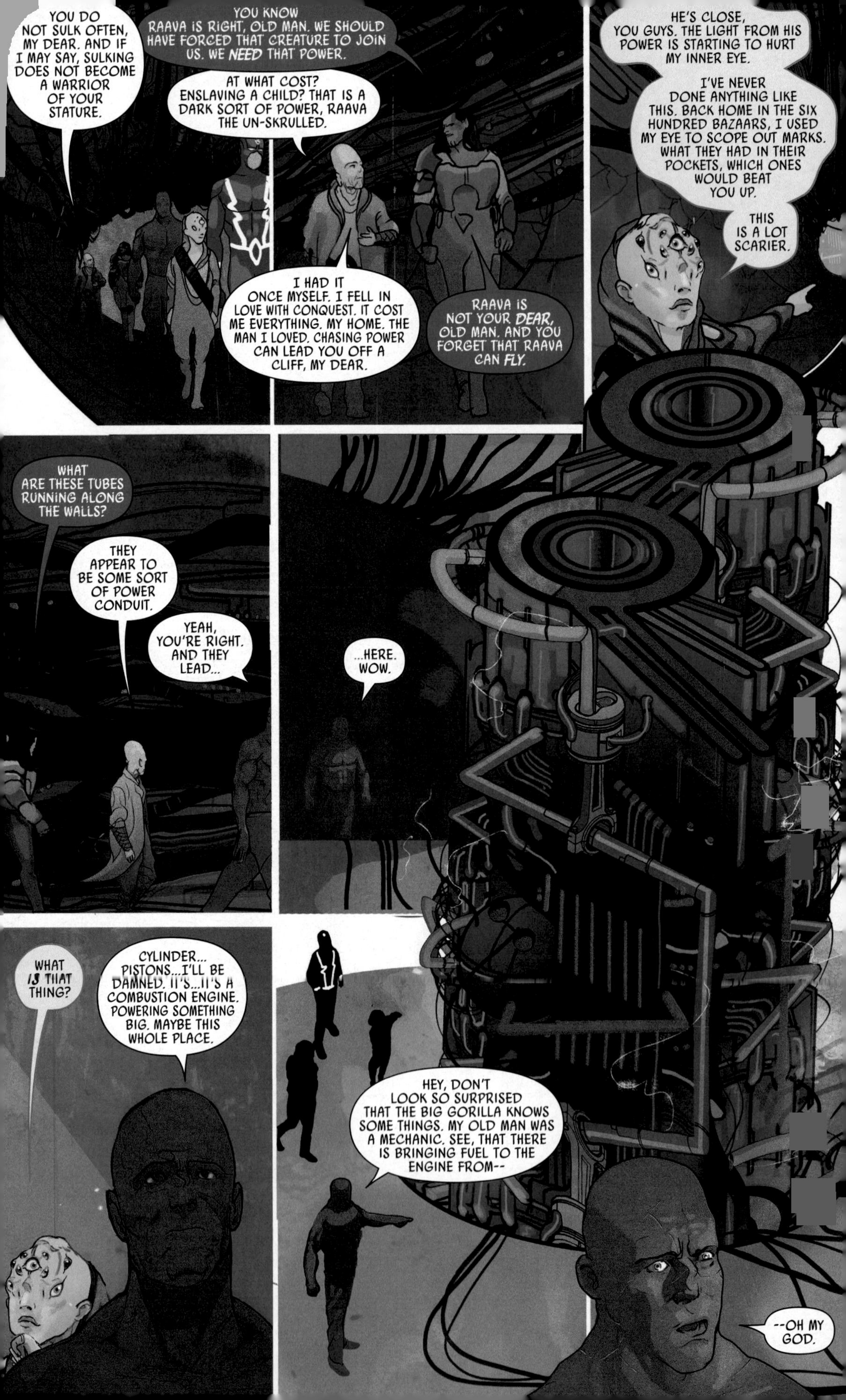
YOU DO NOT SULK OFTEN, MY DEAR. AND IF I MAY SAY, SULKING DOES NOT BECOME A WARRIOR OF YOUR STATURE.
YOU KNOW RAAVA IS RIGHT, OLD MAN. WE SHOULD HAVE FORCED THAT CREATURE TO JOIN US. WE *NEED* THAT POWER.
AT WHAT COST? ENSLAVING A CHILD? THAT IS A DARK SORT OF POWER, RAAVA THE UN-SKRULLED.
I HAD IT ONCE MYSELF. I FELL IN LOVE WITH CONQUEST. IT COST ME EVERYTHING. MY HOME. THE MAN I LOVED. CHASING POWER CAN LEAD YOU OFF A CLIFF, MY DEAR.
RAAVA IS NOT YOUR *DEAR*, OLD MAN. AND YOU FORGET THAT RAAVA CAN *FLY*.
HE'S CLOSE, YOU GUYS. THE LIGHT FROM HIS POWER IS STARTING TO HURT MY INNER EYE.
I'VE NEVER DONE ANYTHING LIKE THIS. BACK HOME IN THE SIX HUNDRED BAZAARS, I USED MY EYE TO SCOPE OUT MARKS. WHAT THEY HAD IN THEIR POCKETS, WHICH ONES WOULD BEAT YOU UP.
THIS IS A LOT SCARIER.
WHAT ARE THESE TUBES RUNNING ALONG THE WALLS?
THEY APPEAR TO BE SOME SORT OF POWER CONDUIT.
YEAH, YOU'RE RIGHT. AND THEY LEAD...
...HERE. WOW.
WHAT *IS* THAT THING?
CYLINDER... PISTONS...I'LL BE DAMNED. IT'S...IT'S A COMBUSTION ENGINE. POWERING SOMETHING BIG. MAYBE THIS WHOLE PLACE.
HEY, DON'T LOOK SO SURPRISED THAT THE BIG GORILLA KNOWS SOME THINGS. MY OLD MAN WAS A MECHANIC. SEE, THAT THERE IS BRINGING FUEL TO THE ENGINE FROM--
--OH MY GOD.

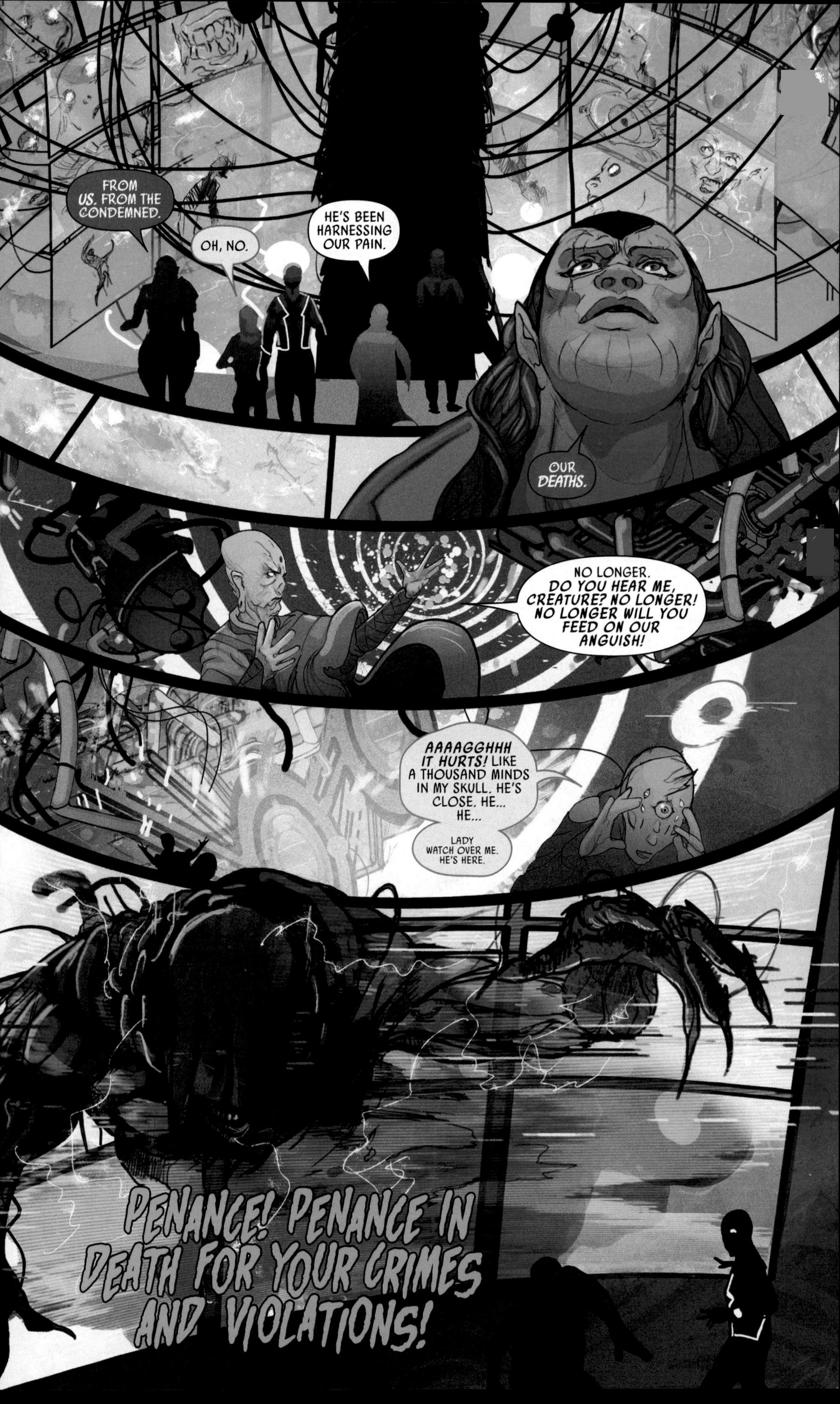
FROM US. FROM THE CONDEMNED.
OH, NO.
HE'S BEEN HARNESSING OUR PAIN.
OUR DEATHS.
NO LONGER. DO YOU HEAR ME, CREATURE? NO LONGER! NO LONGER WILL YOU FEED ON OUR ANGUISH!
AAAAGGHHH IT HURTS! LIKE A THOUSAND MINDS IN MY SKULL. HE'S CLOSE. HE... HE...
LADY WATCH OVER ME. HE'S HERE.
PENANCE! PENANCE IN DEATH FOR YOUR CRIMES AND VIOLATIONS!

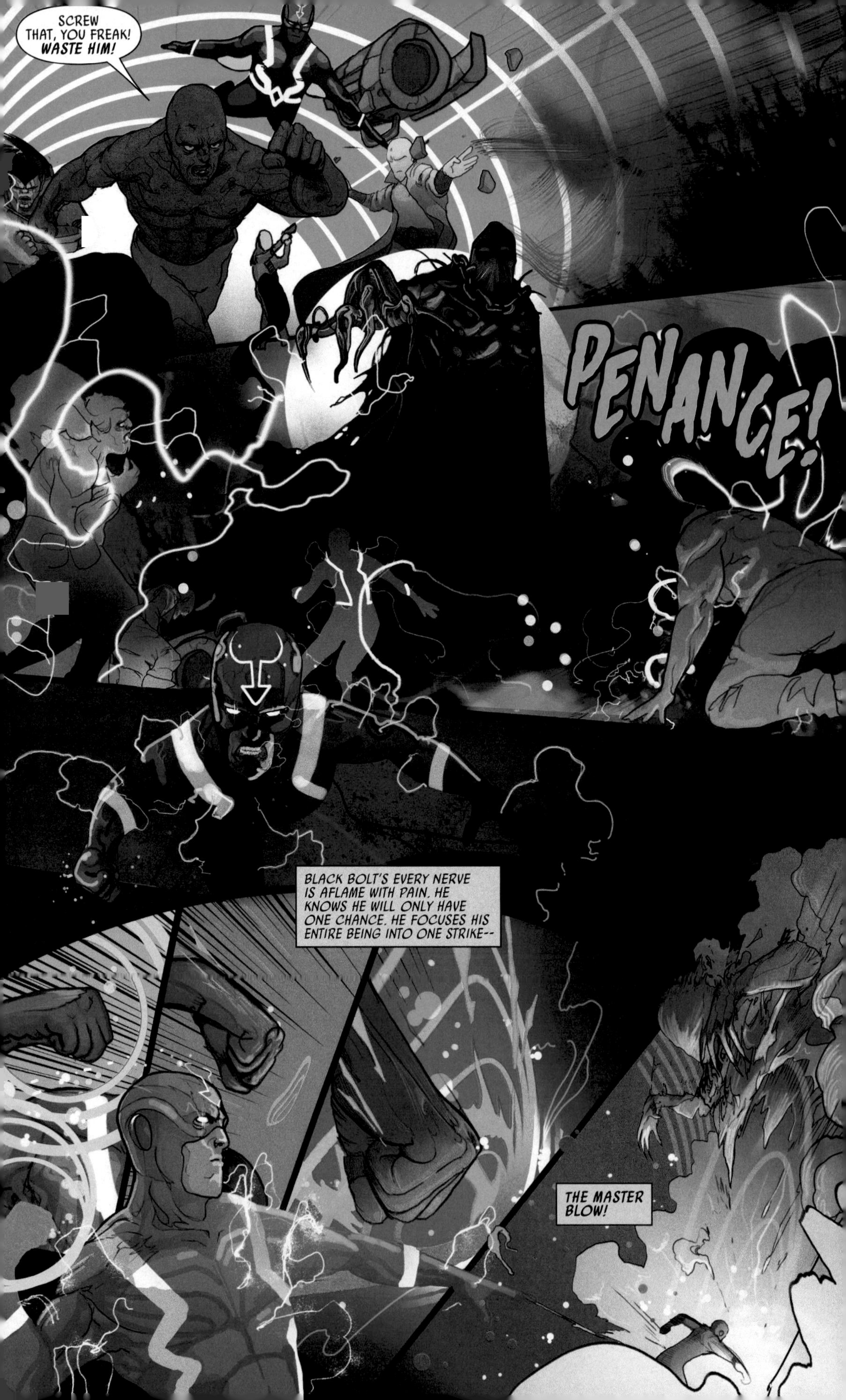
SCREW THAT, YOU FREAK! WASTE HIM!
PENANCE!
BLACK BOLT'S EVERY NERVE IS AFLAME WITH PAIN. HE KNOWS HE WILL ONLY HAVE ONE CHANCE. HE FOCUSES HIS ENTIRE BEING INTO ONE STRIKE--
THE MASTER BLOW!

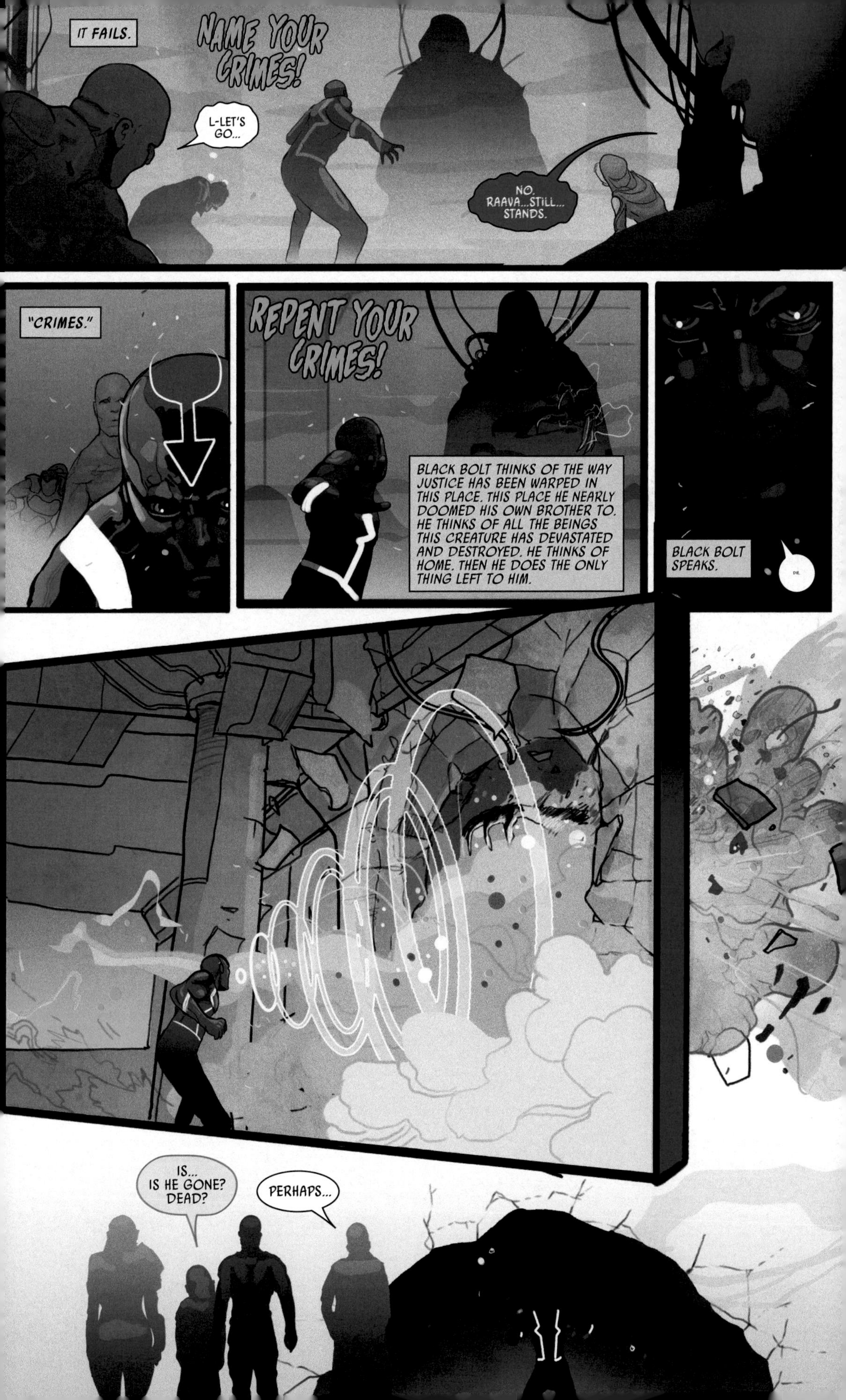
IT FAILS.
NAME YOUR CRIMES!
L-LET'S GO...
NO. RAAVA...STILL... STANDS.
"CRIMES."
REPENT YOUR CRIMES!
BLACK BOLT THINKS OF THE WAY JUSTICE HAS BEEN WARPED IN THIS PLACE. THIS PLACE HE NEARLY DOOMED HIS OWN BROTHER TO. HE THINKS OF ALL THE BEINGS THIS CREATURE HAS DEVASTATED AND DESTROYED. HE THINKS OF HOME. THEN HE DOES THE ONLY THING LEFT TO HIM.
BLACK BOLT SPEAKS.
DIE.
IS... IS HE GONE? DEAD?
PERHAPS...

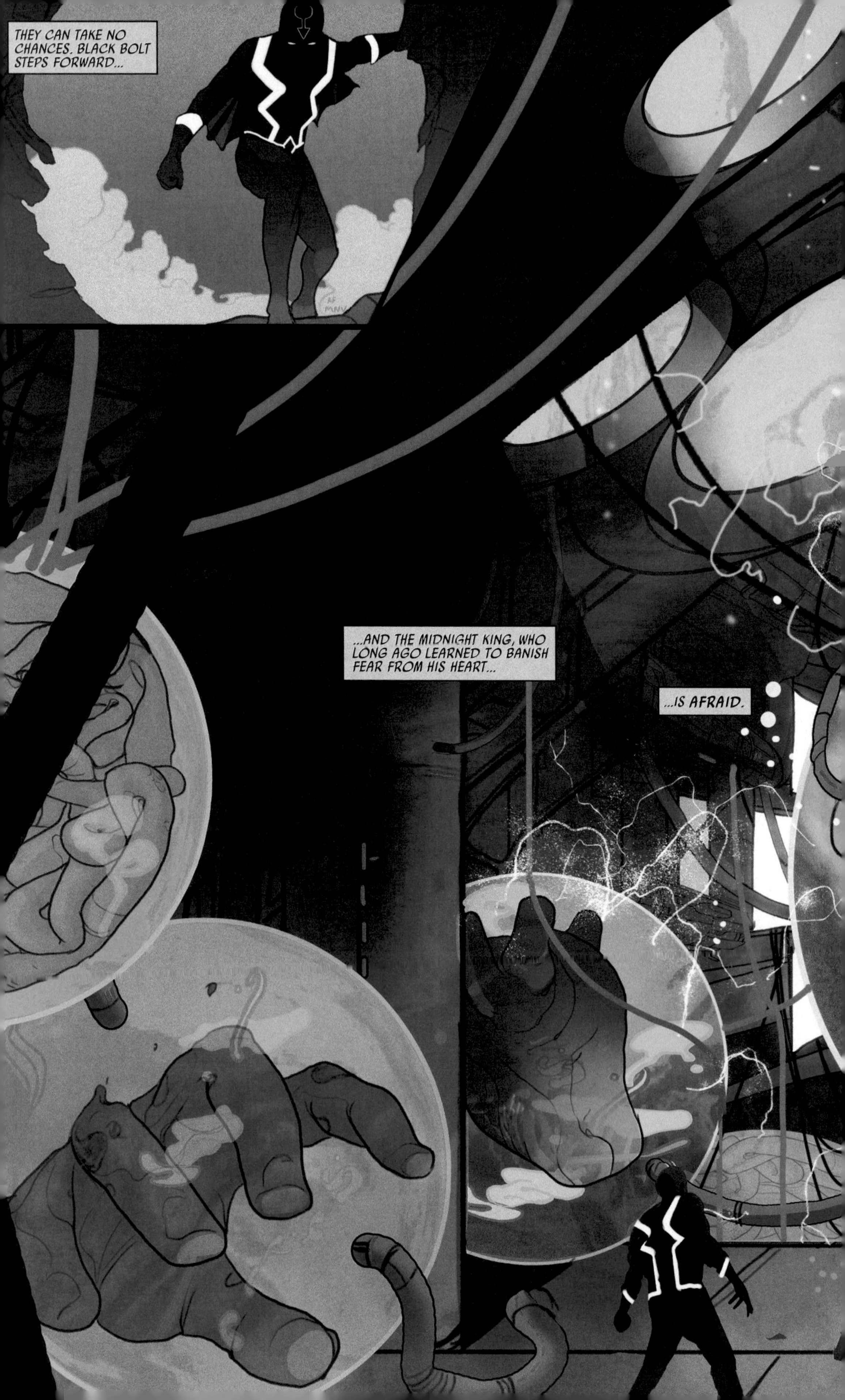
THEY CAN TAKE NO CHANCES. BLACK BOLT STEPS FORWARD...
...AND THE MIDNIGHT KING, WHO LONG AGO LEARNED TO BANISH FEAR FROM HIS HEART...
...IS AFRAID.

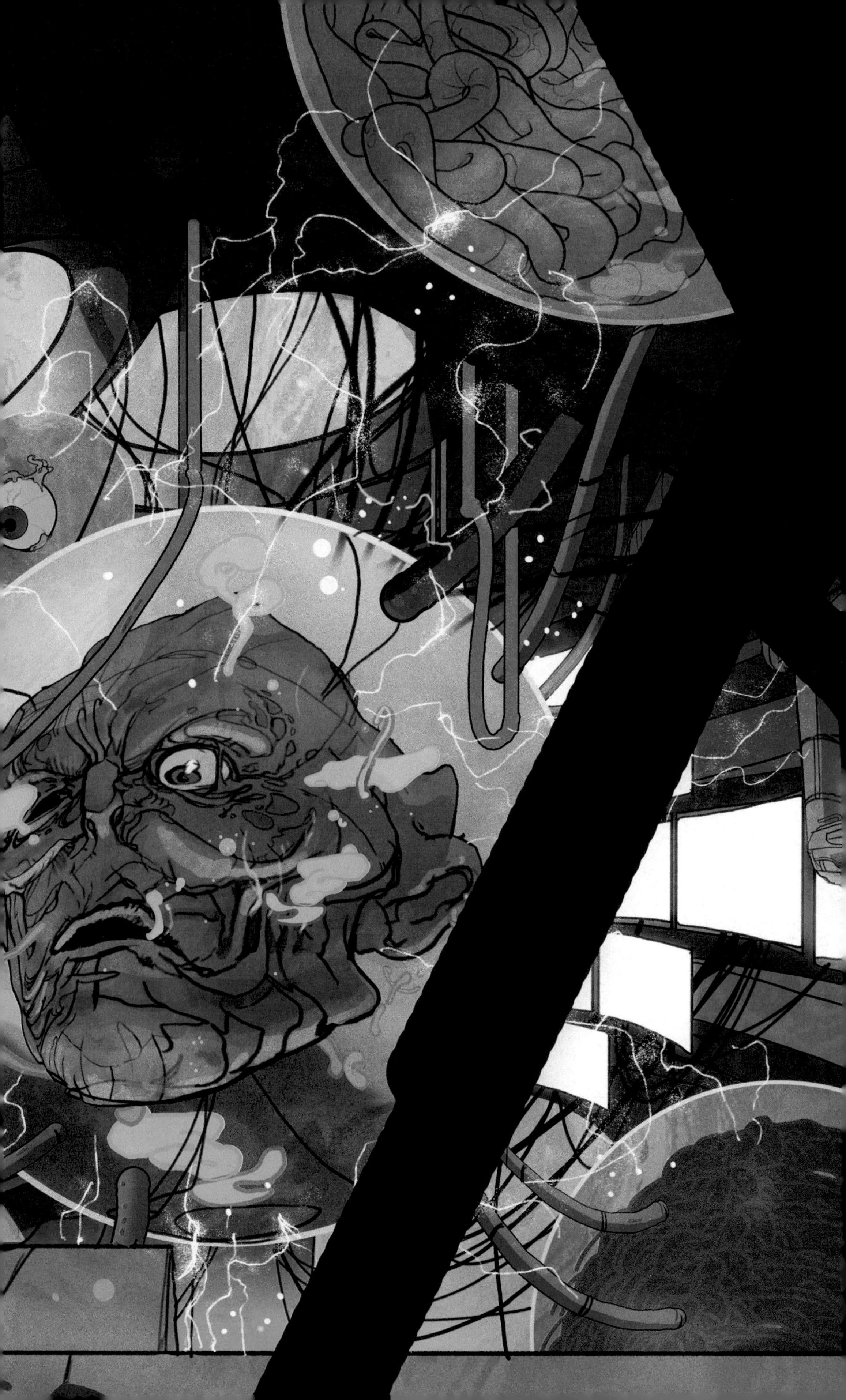

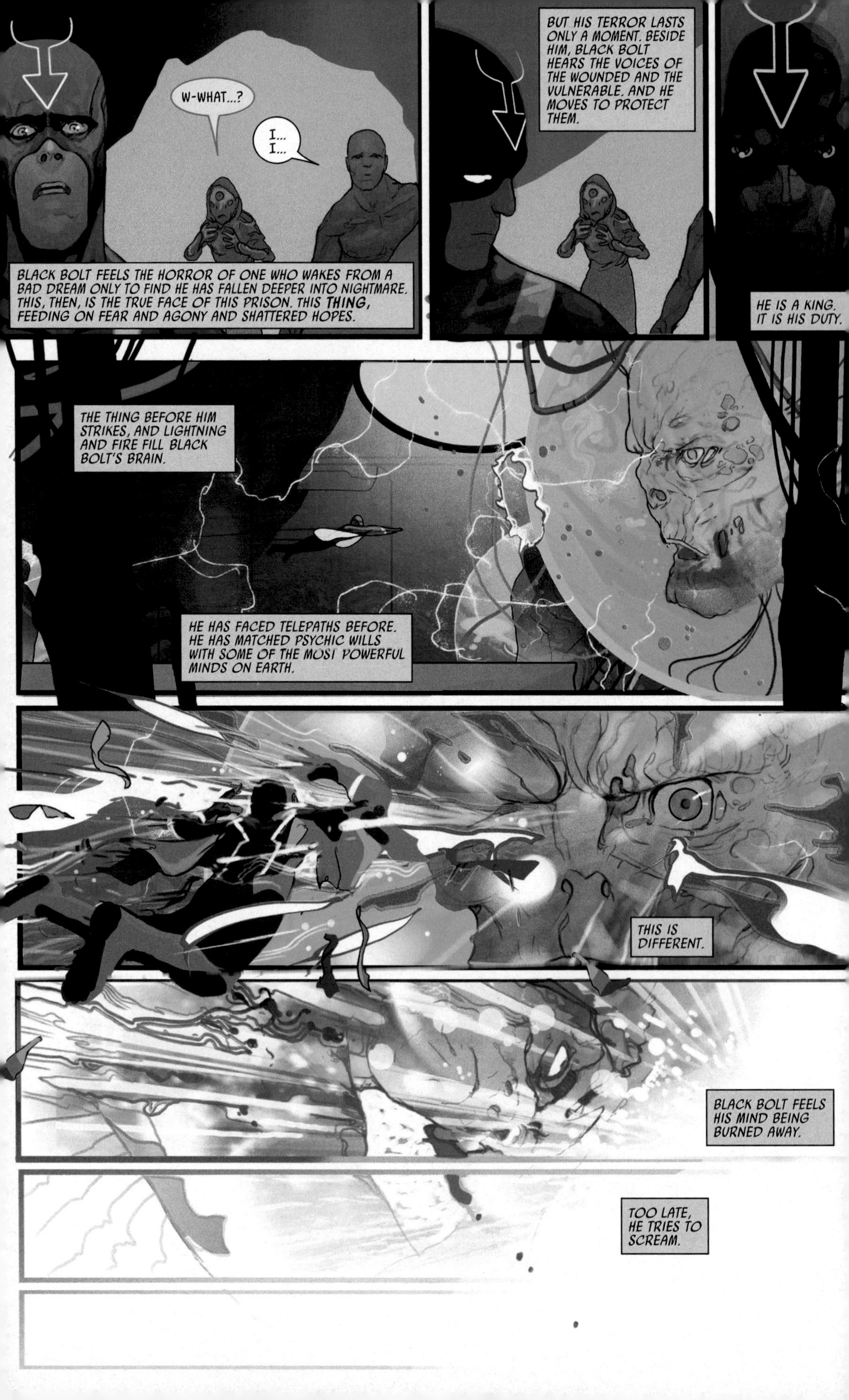

W-WHAT...?
I... I...
BLACK BOLT FEELS THE HORROR OF ONE WHO WAKES FROM A BAD DREAM ONLY TO FIND HE HAS FALLEN DEEPER INTO NIGHTMARE. THIS, THEN, IS THE TRUE FACE OF THIS PRISON. THIS THING, FEEDING ON FEAR AND AGONY AND SHATTERED HOPES.
BUT HIS TERROR LASTS ONLY A MOMENT. BESIDE HIM, BLACK BOLT HEARS THE VOICES OF THE WOUNDED AND THE VULNERABLE. AND HE MOVES TO PROTECT THEM.
HE IS A KING. IT IS HIS DUTY.
THE THING BEFORE HIM STRIKES, AND LIGHTNING AND FIRE FILL BLACK BOLT'S BRAIN.
HE HAS FACED TELEPATHS BEFORE. HE HAS MATCHED PSYCHIC WILLS WITH SOME OF THE MOST POWERFUL MINDS ON EARTH.
THIS IS DIFFERENT.
BLACK BOLT FEELS HIS MIND BEING BURNED AWAY.
TOO LATE, HE TRIES TO SCREAM.

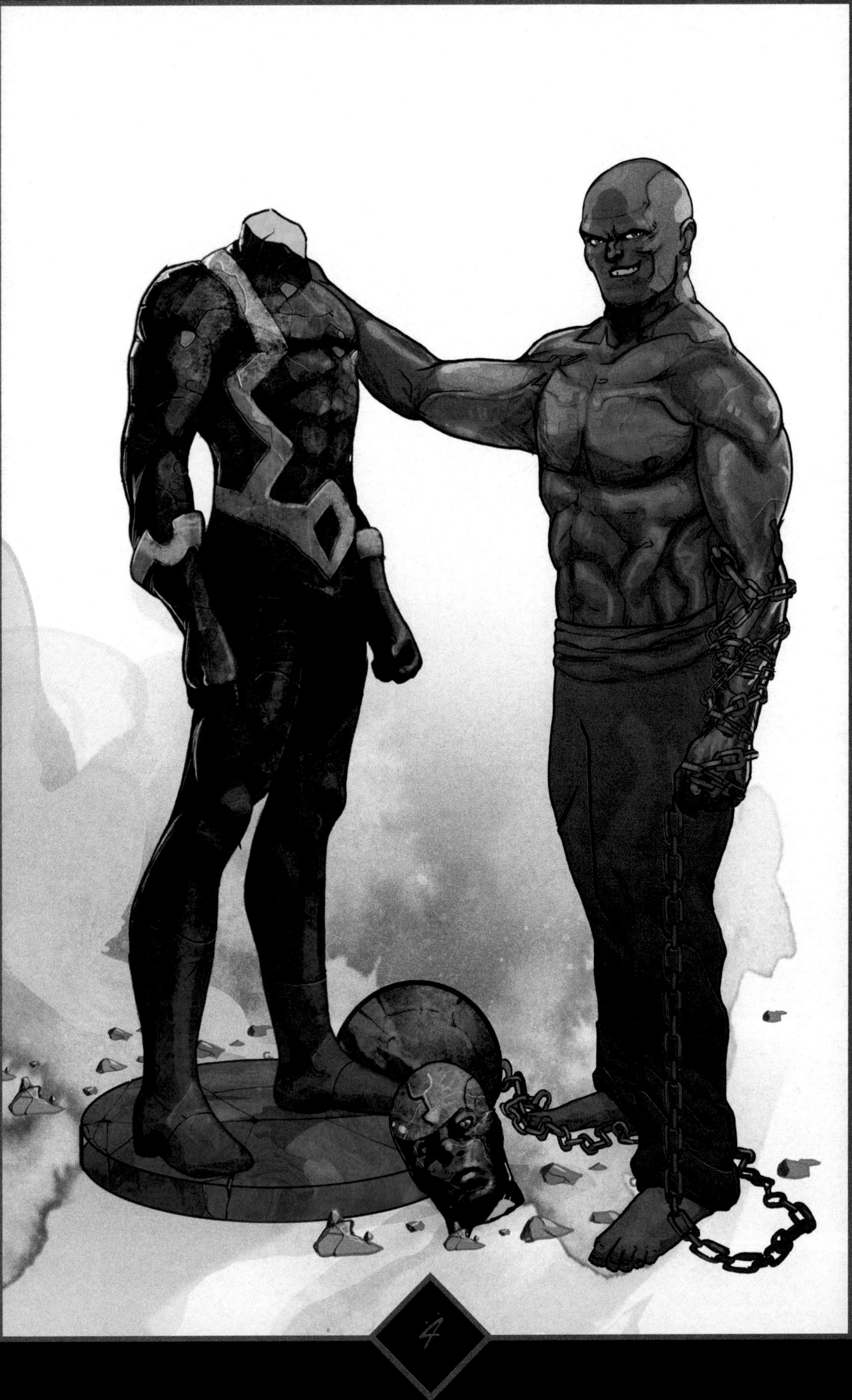
4

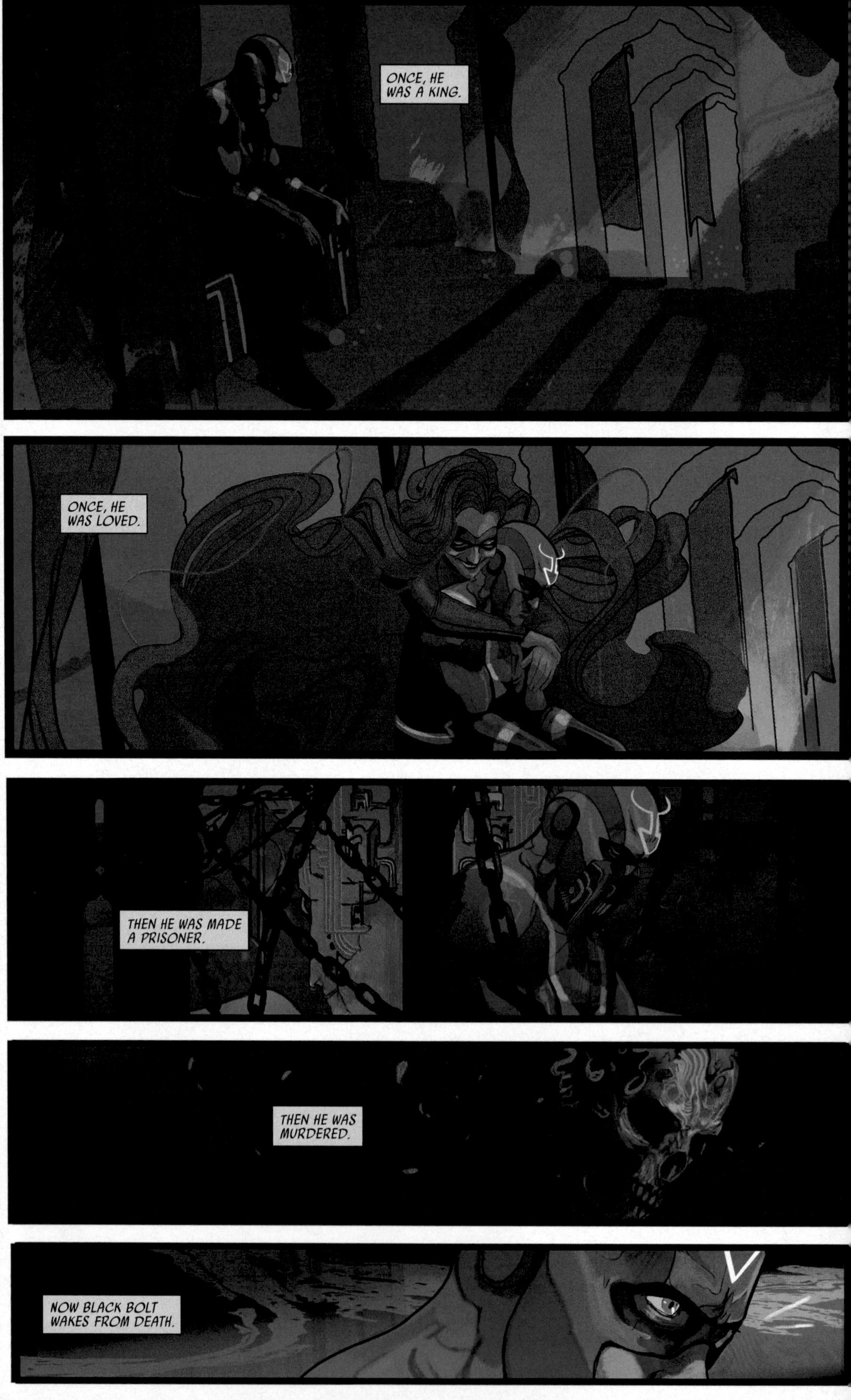
ONCE, HE WAS A KING.
ONCE, HE WAS LOVED.
THEN HE WAS MADE A PRISONER.
THEN HE WAS MURDERED.
NOW BLACK BOLT WAKES FROM DEATH.

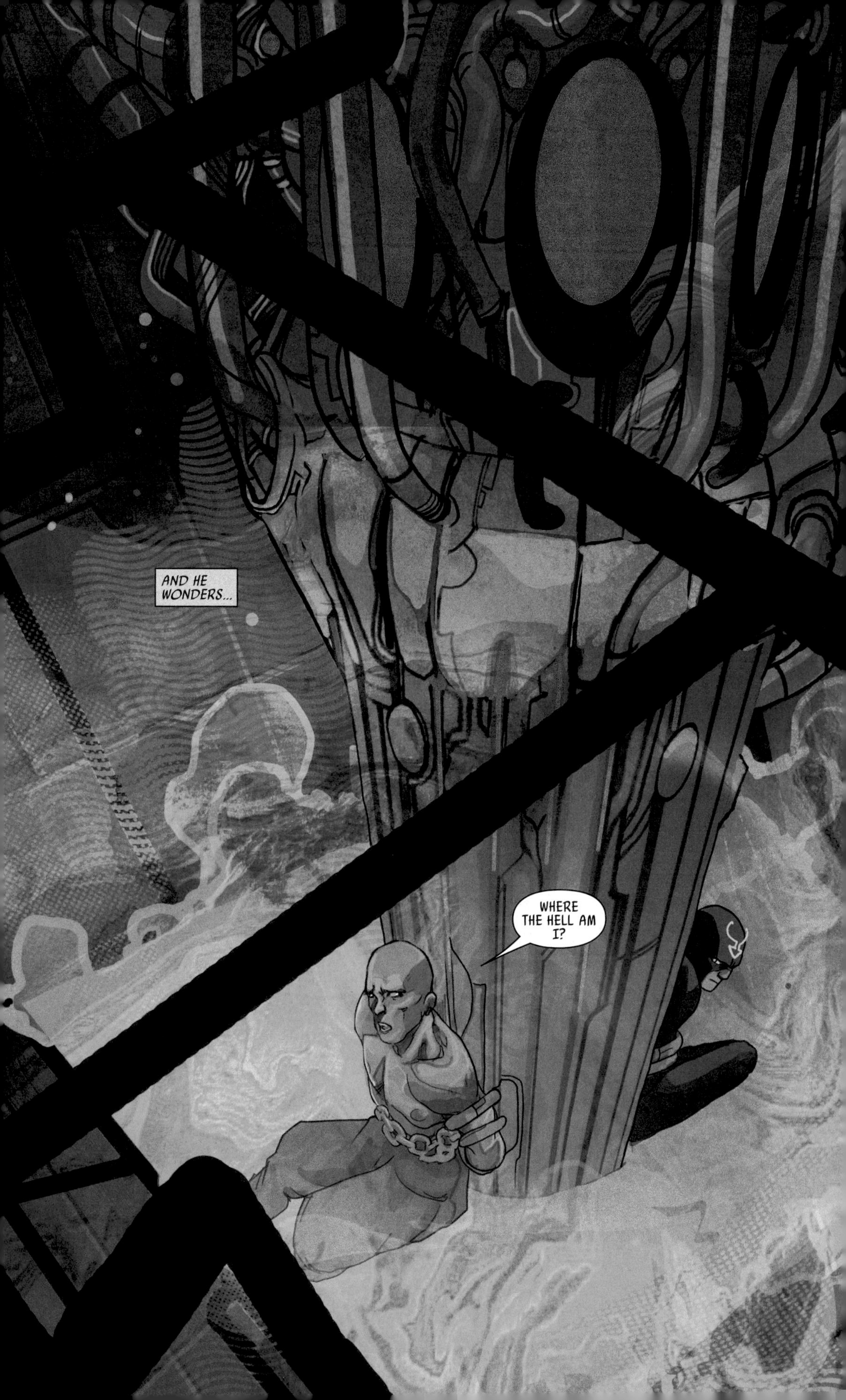
AND HE WONDERS...
WHERE THE HELL AM I?

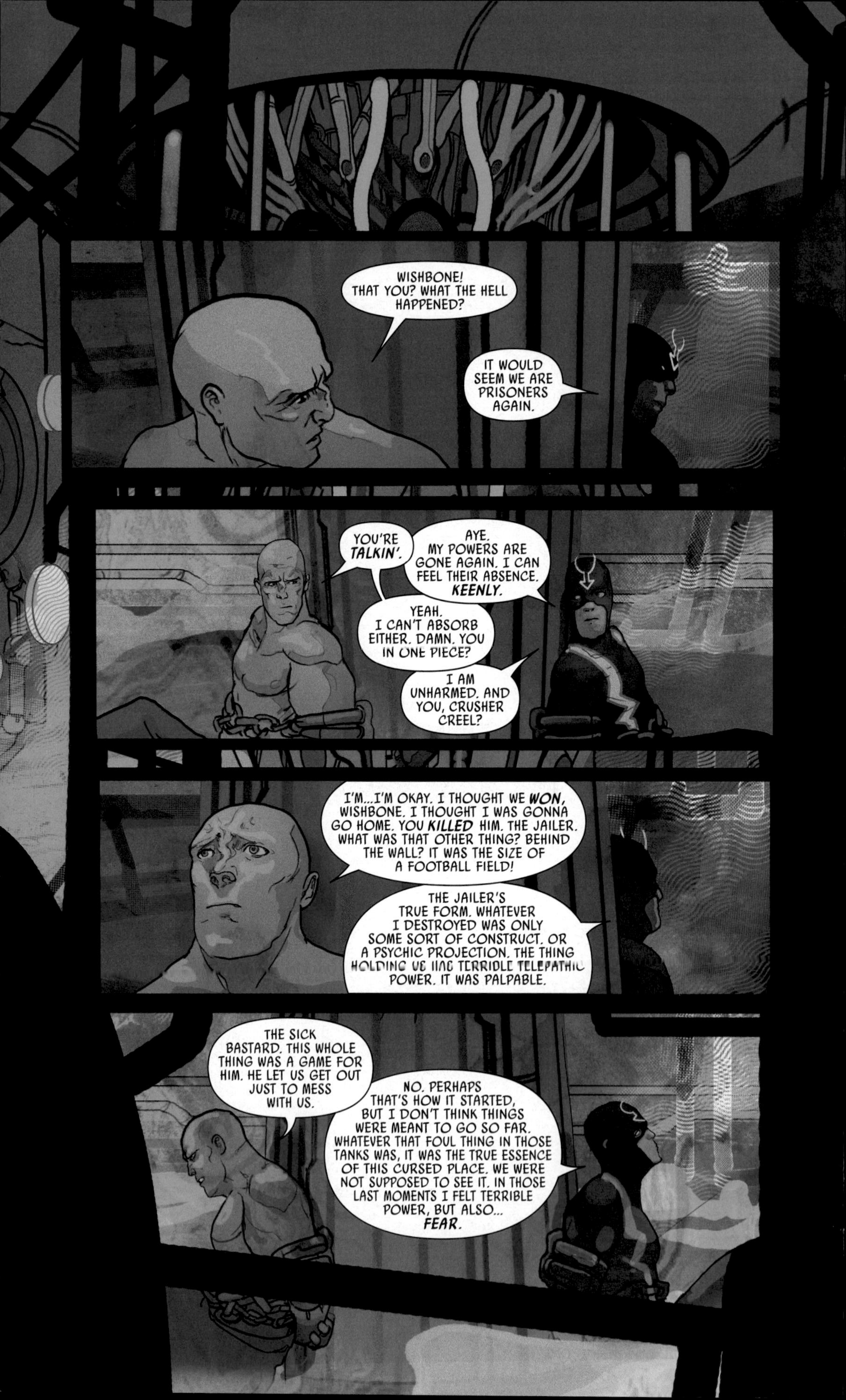
WISHBONE! THAT YOU? WHAT THE HELL HAPPENED?
IT WOULD SEEM WE ARE PRISONERS AGAIN.
YOU'RE *TALKIN'.*
AYE. MY POWERS ARE GONE AGAIN. I CAN FEEL THEIR ABSENCE. ***KEENLY.***
YEAH. I CAN'T ABSORB EITHER. DAMN. YOU IN ONE PIECE?
I AM UNHARMED. AND YOU, CRUSHER CREEL?
I'M...I'M OKAY. I THOUGHT WE ***WON,*** WISHBONE. I THOUGHT I WAS GONNA GO HOME. YOU ***KILLED*** HIM. THE JAILER. WHAT WAS THAT OTHER THING? BEHIND THE WALL? IT WAS THE SIZE OF A FOOTBALL FIELD!
THE JAILER'S TRUE FORM. WHATEVER I DESTROYED WAS ONLY SOME SORT OF CONSTRUCT. OR A PSYCHIC PROJECTION. THE THING HOLDING US HAS TERRIBLE TELEPATHIC POWER. IT WAS PALPABLE.
THE SICK BASTARD. THIS WHOLE THING WAS A GAME FOR HIM. HE LET US GET OUT JUST TO MESS WITH US.
NO. PERHAPS THAT'S HOW IT STARTED, BUT I DON'T THINK THINGS WERE MEANT TO GO SO FAR. WHATEVER THAT FOUL THING IN THOSE TANKS WAS, IT WAS THE TRUE ESSENCE OF THIS CURSED PLACE. WE WERE NOT SUPPOSED TO SEE IT. IN THOSE LAST MOMENTS I FELT TERRIBLE POWER, BUT ALSO... ***FEAR.***

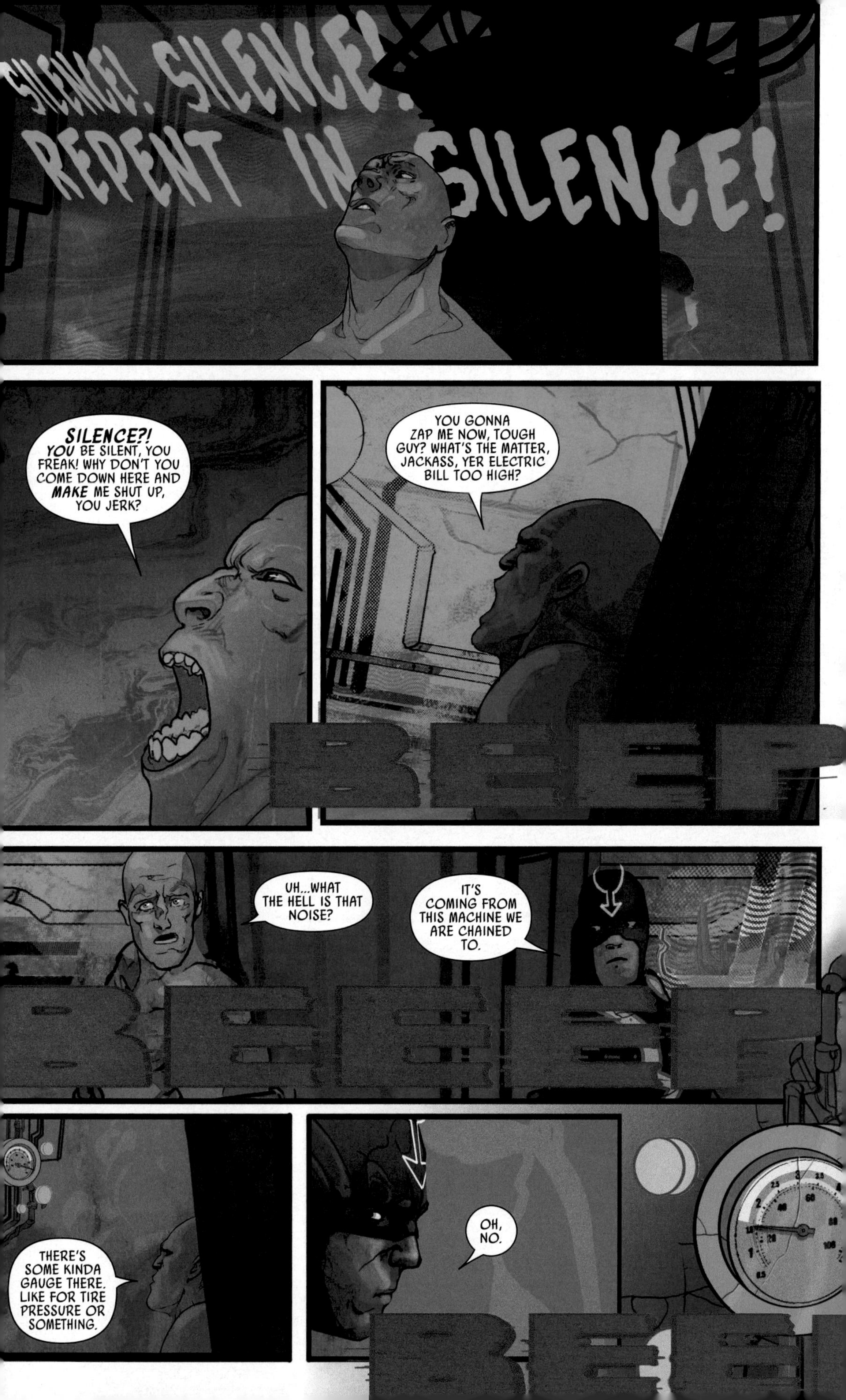
SILENCE! SILENCE!
REPENT IN SILENCE!
SILENCE?! YOU BE SILENT, YOU FREAK! WHY DON'T YOU COME DOWN HERE AND MAKE ME SHUT UP, YOU JERK?
YOU GONNA ZAP ME NOW, TOUGH GUY? WHAT'S THE MATTER, JACKASS, YER ELECTRIC BILL TOO HIGH?
BEEP
UH...WHAT THE HELL IS THAT NOISE?
IT'S COMING FROM THIS MACHINE WE ARE CHAINED TO.
BEEEEP
THERE'S SOME KINDA GAUGE THERE. LIKE FOR TIRE PRESSURE OR SOMETHING.
OH, NO.
BEEE

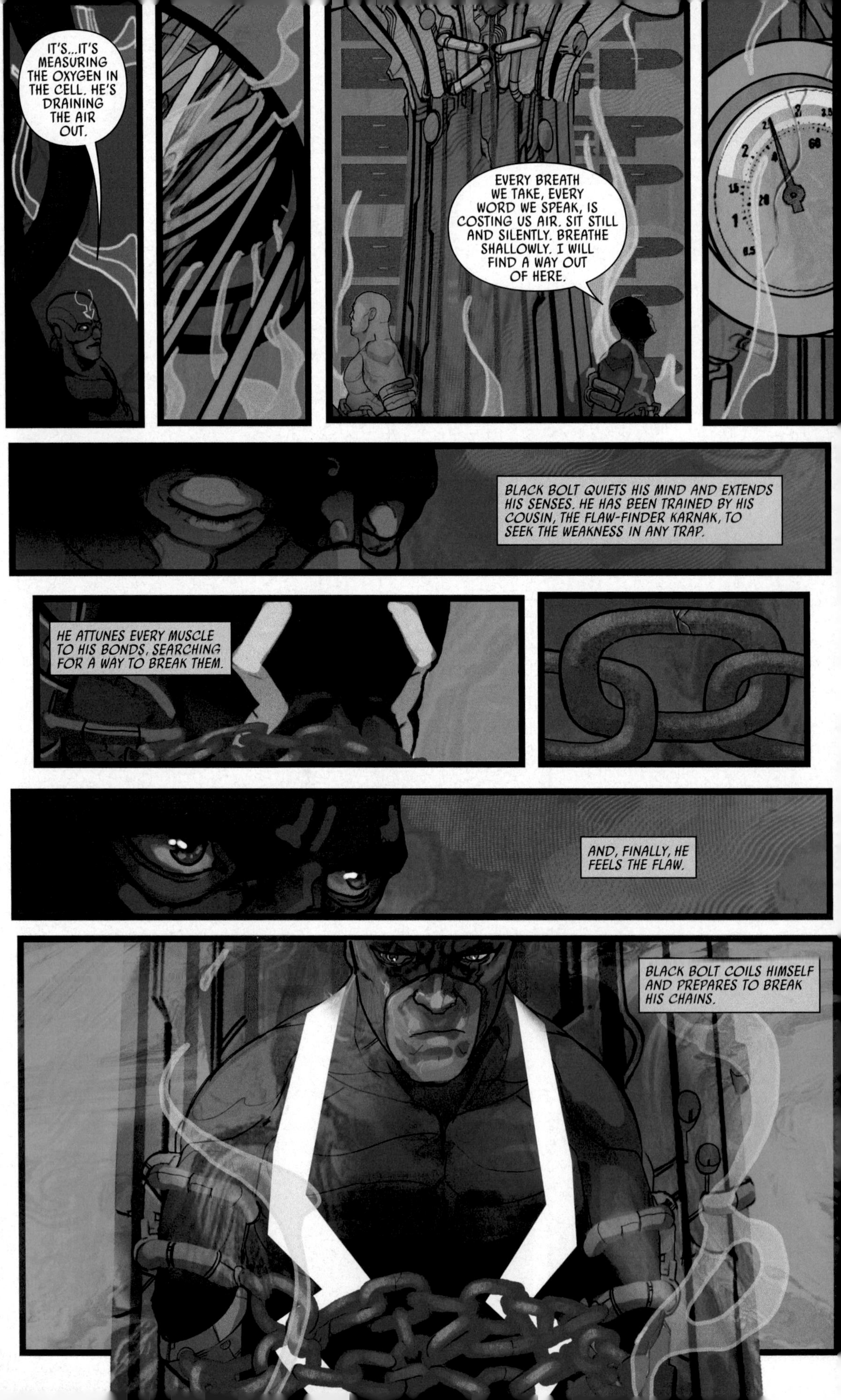
IT'S...IT'S MEASURING THE OXYGEN IN THE CELL. HE'S DRAINING THE AIR OUT.
EVERY BREATH WE TAKE, EVERY WORD WE SPEAK, IS COSTING US AIR. SIT STILL AND SILENTLY. BREATHE SHALLOWLY. I WILL FIND A WAY OUT OF HERE.
BLACK BOLT QUIETS HIS MIND AND EXTENDS HIS SENSES. HE HAS BEEN TRAINED BY HIS COUSIN, THE FLAW-FINDER KARNAK, TO SEEK THE WEAKNESS IN ANY TRAP.
HE ATTUNES EVERY MUSCLE TO HIS BONDS, SEARCHING FOR A WAY TO BREAK THEM.
AND, FINALLY, HE FEELS THE FLAW.
BLACK BOLT COILS HIMSELF AND PREPARES TO BREAK HIS CHAINS.

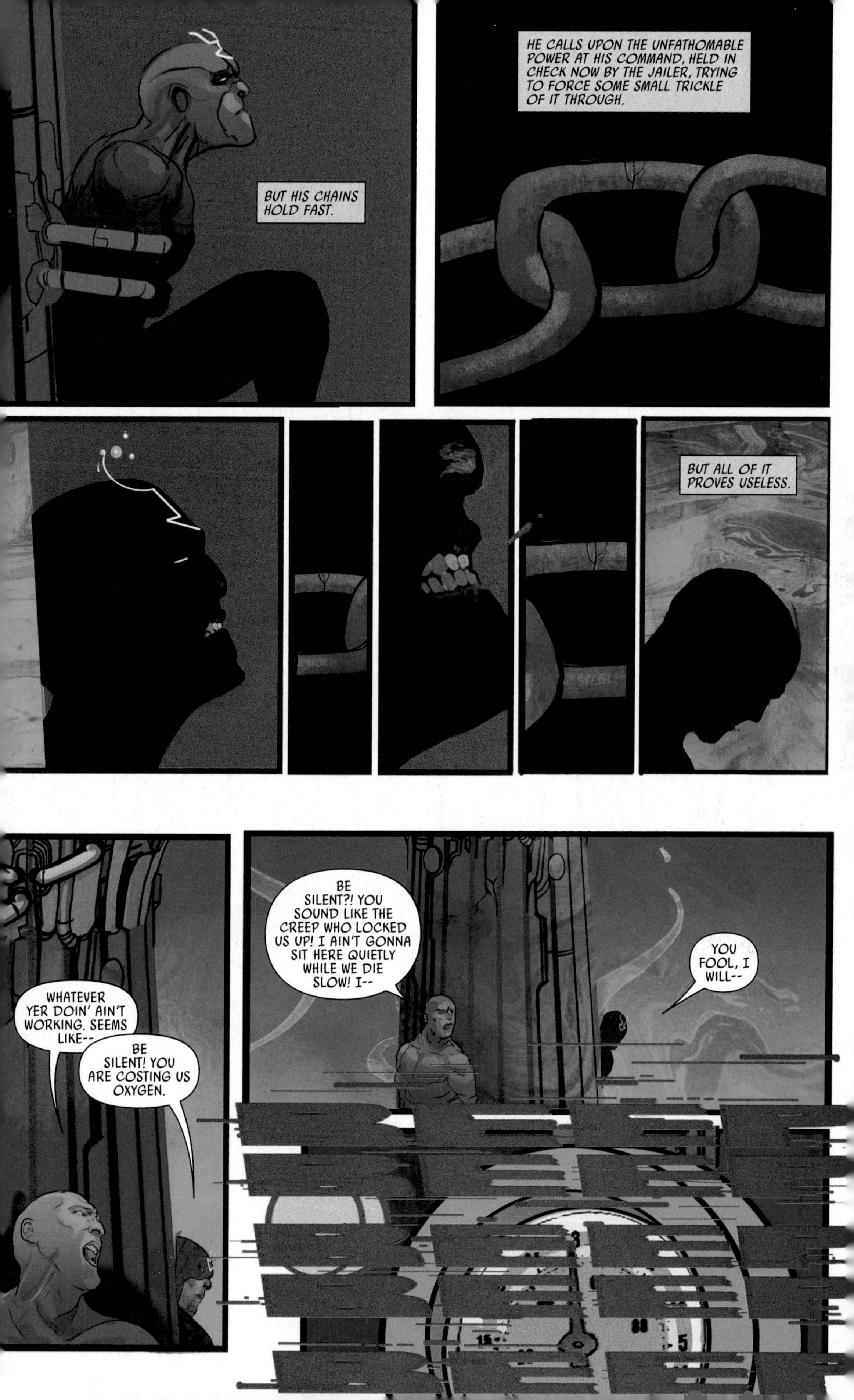
BUT HIS CHAINS HOLD FAST.
HE CALLS UPON THE UNFATHOMABLE POWER AT HIS COMMAND, HELD IN CHECK NOW BY THE JAILER, TRYING TO FORCE SOME SMALL TRICKLE OF IT THROUGH.
BUT ALL OF IT PROVES USELESS.
WHATEVER YER DOIN' AIN'T WORKING. SEEMS LIKE--
BE SILENT! YOU ARE COSTING US OXYGEN.
BE SILENT?! YOU SOUND LIKE THE CREEP WHO LOCKED US UP! I AIN'T GONNA SIT HERE QUIETLY WHILE WE DIE SLOW! I--
YOU FOOL, I WILL--

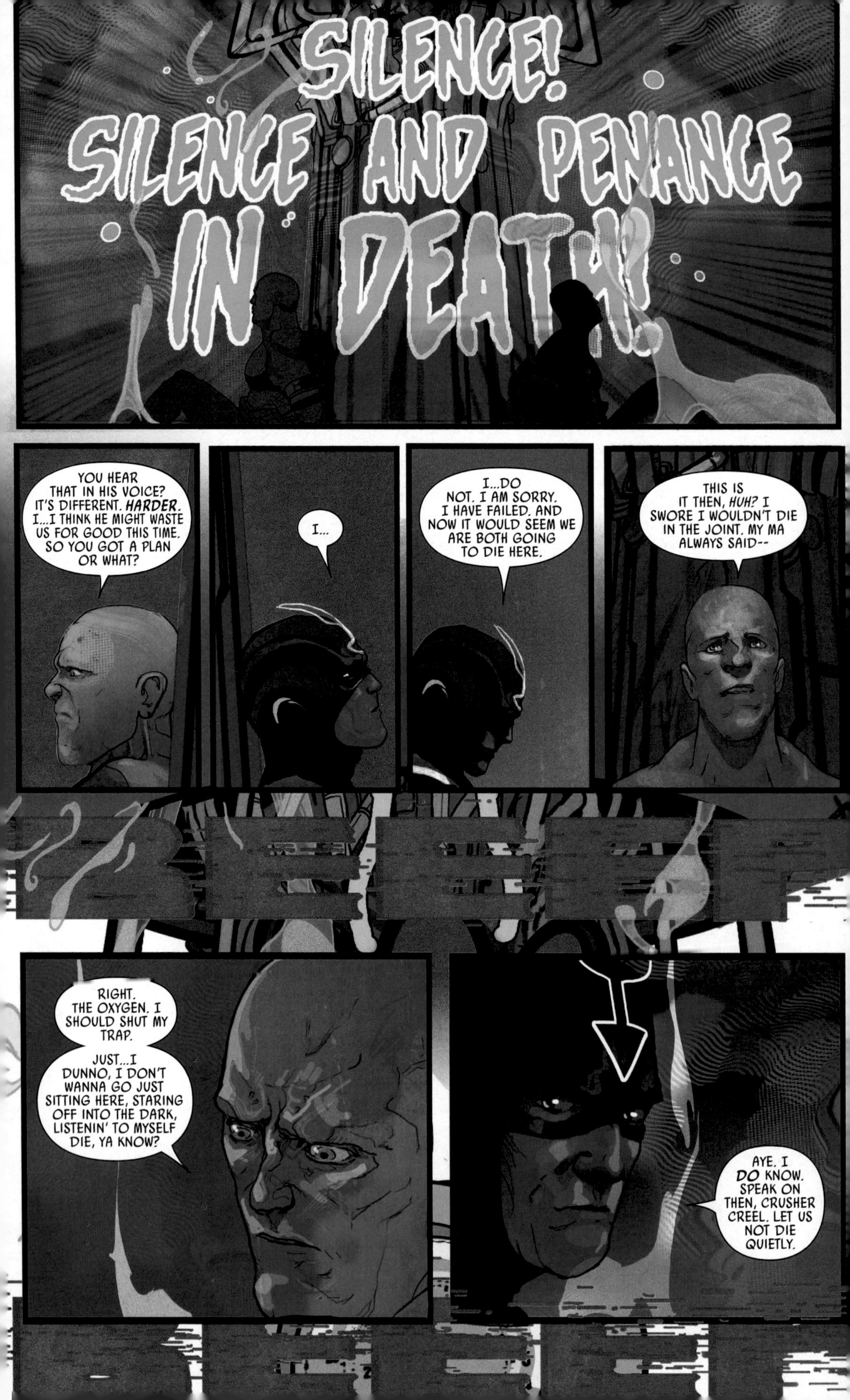
SILENCE! SILENCE AND PENANCE IN DEATH!
YOU HEAR THAT IN HIS VOICE? IT'S DIFFERENT. HARDER. I...I THINK HE MIGHT WASTE US FOR GOOD THIS TIME. SO YOU GOT A PLAN OR WHAT?
I...
I...DO NOT. I AM SORRY. I HAVE FAILED. AND NOW IT WOULD SEEM WE ARE BOTH GOING TO DIE HERE.
THIS IS IT THEN, HUH? I SWORE I WOULDN'T DIE IN THE JOINT. MY MA ALWAYS SAID--
BEEEP
RIGHT. THE OXYGEN. I SHOULD SHUT MY TRAP.
JUST...I DUNNO, I DON'T WANNA GO JUST SITTING HERE, STARING OFF INTO THE DARK, LISTENIN' TO MYSELF DIE, YA KNOW?
AYE. I DO KNOW. SPEAK ON THEN, CRUSHER CREEL. LET US NOT DIE QUIETLY.
BEEEP

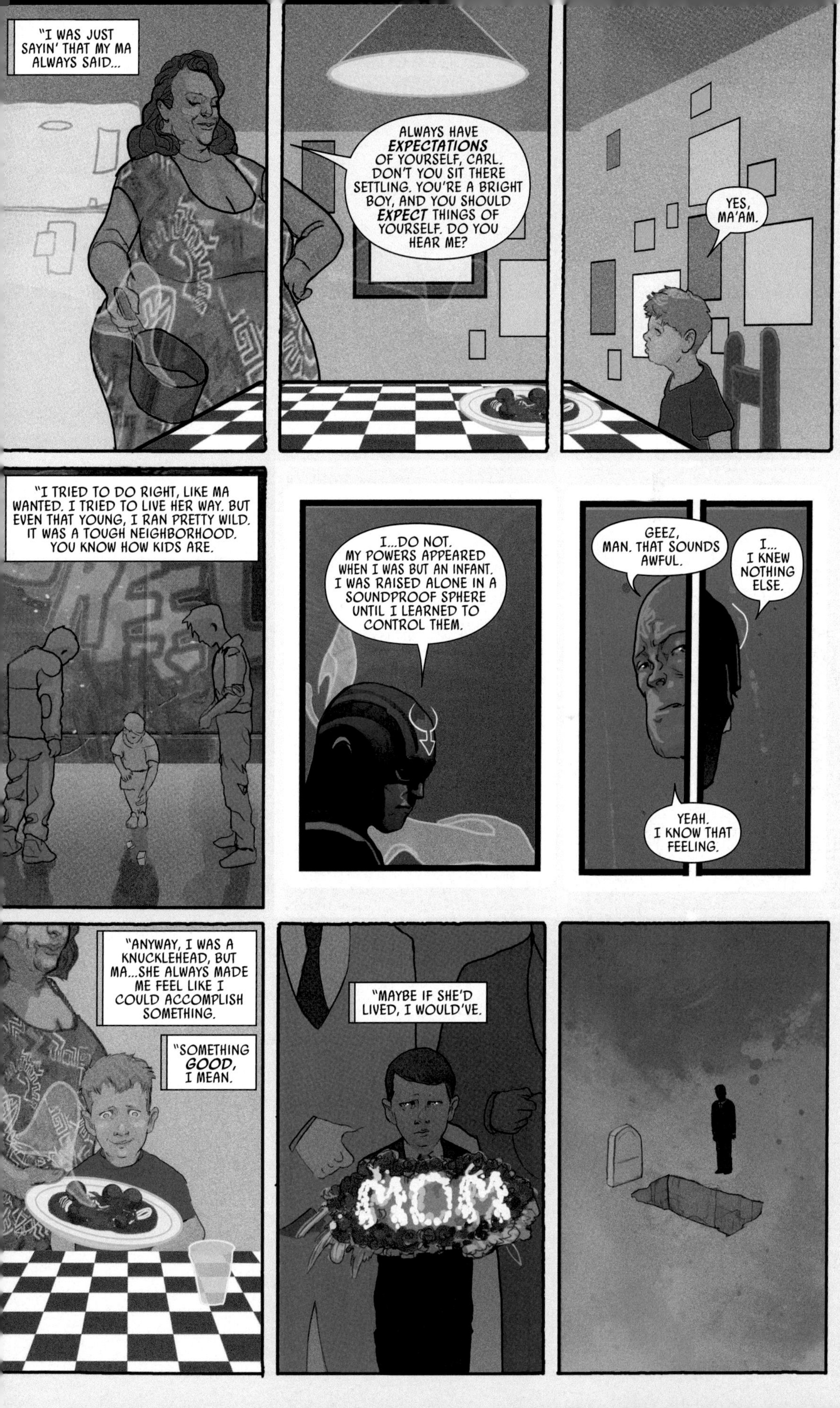
"I WAS JUST SAYIN' THAT MY MA ALWAYS SAID...
ALWAYS HAVE EXPECTATIONS OF YOURSELF, CARL. DON'T YOU SIT THERE SETTLING. YOU'RE A BRIGHT BOY, AND YOU SHOULD EXPECT THINGS OF YOURSELF. DO YOU HEAR ME?
YES, MA'AM.
"I TRIED TO DO RIGHT, LIKE MA WANTED. I TRIED TO LIVE HER WAY. BUT EVEN THAT YOUNG, I RAN PRETTY WILD. IT WAS A TOUGH NEIGHBORHOOD. YOU KNOW HOW KIDS ARE.
I...DO NOT. MY POWERS APPEARED WHEN I WAS BUT AN INFANT. I WAS RAISED ALONE IN A SOUNDPROOF SPHERE UNTIL I LEARNED TO CONTROL THEM.
GEEZ, MAN. THAT SOUNDS AWFUL.
I... I KNEW NOTHING ELSE.
YEAH. I KNOW THAT FEELING.
"ANYWAY, I WAS A KNUCKLEHEAD, BUT MA...SHE ALWAYS MADE ME FEEL LIKE I COULD ACCOMPLISH SOMETHING.
"SOMETHING GOOD, I MEAN.
"MAYBE IF SHE'D LIVED, I WOULD'VE.
MOM

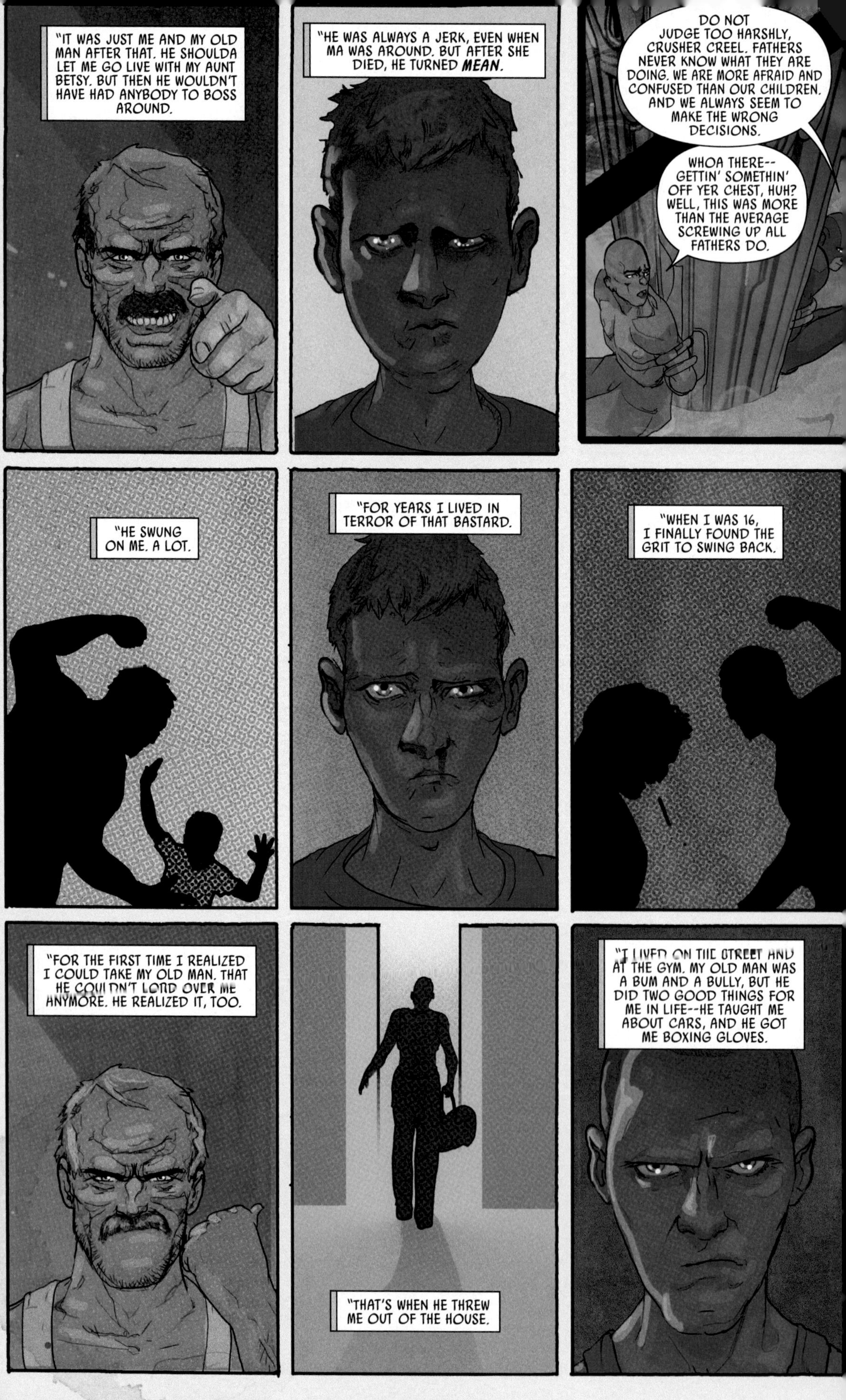
"IT WAS JUST ME AND MY OLD MAN AFTER THAT. HE SHOULDA LET ME GO LIVE WITH MY AUNT BETSY. BUT THEN HE WOULDN'T HAVE HAD ANYBODY TO BOSS AROUND.
"HE WAS ALWAYS A JERK, EVEN WHEN MA WAS AROUND. BUT AFTER SHE DIED, HE TURNED MEAN.
DO NOT JUDGE TOO HARSHLY, CRUSHER CREEL. FATHERS NEVER KNOW WHAT THEY ARE DOING. WE ARE MORE AFRAID AND CONFUSED THAN OUR CHILDREN. AND WE ALWAYS SEEM TO MAKE THE WRONG DECISIONS.
WHOA THERE--GETTIN' SOMETHIN' OFF YER CHEST, HUH? WELL, THIS WAS MORE THAN THE AVERAGE SCREWING UP ALL FATHERS DO.
"HE SWUNG ON ME. A LOT.
"FOR YEARS I LIVED IN TERROR OF THAT BASTARD.
"WHEN I WAS 16, I FINALLY FOUND THE GRIT TO SWING BACK.
"FOR THE FIRST TIME I REALIZED I COULD TAKE MY OLD MAN. THAT HE COULDN'T LORD OVER ME ANYMORE. HE REALIZED IT, TOO.
"THAT'S WHEN HE THREW ME OUT OF THE HOUSE.
"I LIVED ON THE STREET AND AT THE GYM. MY OLD MAN WAS A BUM AND A BULLY, BUT HE DID TWO GOOD THINGS FOR ME IN LIFE--HE TAUGHT ME ABOUT CARS, AND HE GOT ME BOXING GLOVES.

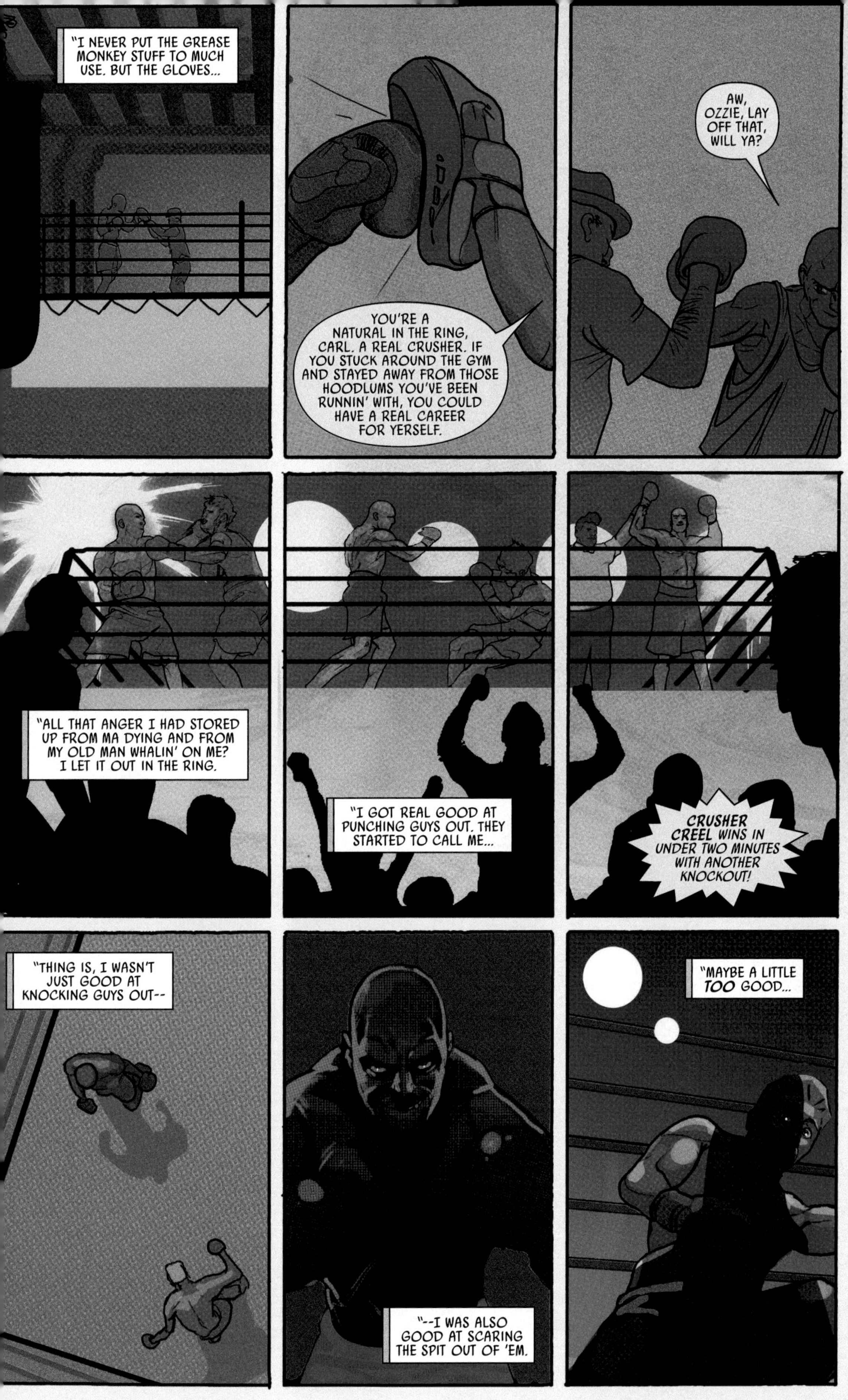
"I NEVER PUT THE GREASE MONKEY STUFF TO MUCH USE. BUT THE GLOVES...
YOU'RE A NATURAL IN THE RING, CARL. A REAL CRUSHER. IF YOU STUCK AROUND THE GYM AND STAYED AWAY FROM THOSE HOODLUMS YOU'VE BEEN RUNNIN' WITH, YOU COULD HAVE A REAL CAREER FOR YERSELF.
AW, OZZIE, LAY OFF THAT, WILL YA?
"ALL THAT ANGER I HAD STORED UP FROM MA DYING AND FROM MY OLD MAN WHALIN' ON ME? I LET IT OUT IN THE RING.
"I GOT REAL GOOD AT PUNCHING GUYS OUT. THEY STARTED TO CALL ME...
CRUSHER CREEL WINS IN UNDER TWO MINUTES WITH ANOTHER KNOCKOUT!
"THING IS, I WASN'T JUST GOOD AT KNOCKING GUYS OUT--
"--I WAS ALSO GOOD AT SCARING THE SPIT OUT OF 'EM.
"MAYBE A LITTLE TOO GOOD...

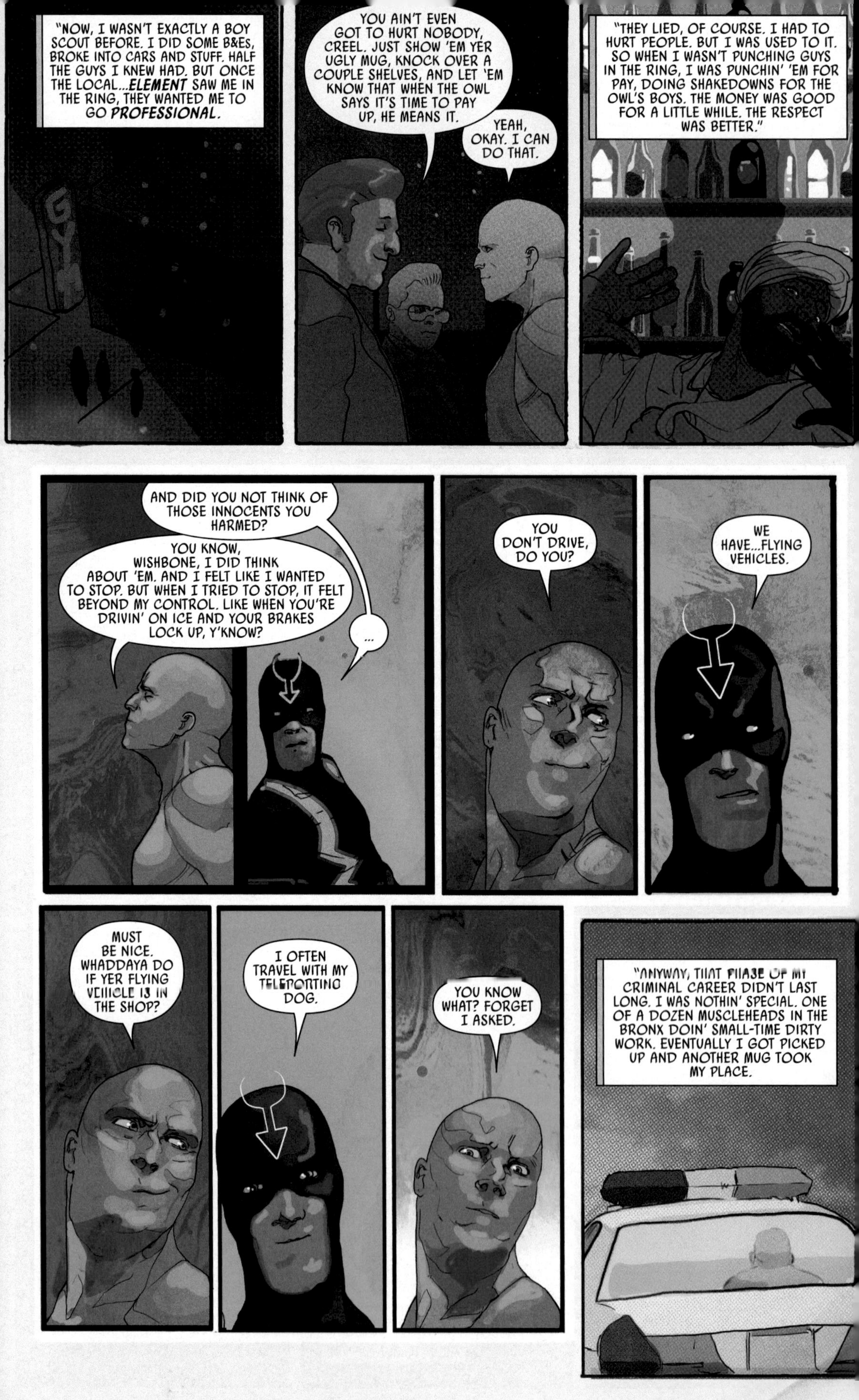
"NOW, I WASN'T EXACTLY A BOY SCOUT BEFORE. I DID SOME B&ES, BROKE INTO CARS AND STUFF. HALF THE GUYS I KNEW HAD. BUT ONCE THE LOCAL...ELEMENT SAW ME IN THE RING, THEY WANTED ME TO GO PROFESSIONAL.
GYM
YOU AIN'T EVEN GOT TO HURT NOBODY, CREEL. JUST SHOW 'EM YER UGLY MUG, KNOCK OVER A COUPLE SHELVES, AND LET 'EM KNOW THAT WHEN THE OWL SAYS IT'S TIME TO PAY UP, HE MEANS IT.
YEAH, OKAY. I CAN DO THAT.
"THEY LIED, OF COURSE. I HAD TO HURT PEOPLE. BUT I WAS USED TO IT. SO WHEN I WASN'T PUNCHING GUYS IN THE RING, I WAS PUNCHIN' 'EM FOR PAY, DOING SHAKEDOWNS FOR THE OWL'S BOYS. THE MONEY WAS GOOD FOR A LITTLE WHILE. THE RESPECT WAS BETTER."
AND DID YOU NOT THINK OF THOSE INNOCENTS YOU HARMED?
YOU KNOW, WISHBONE, I DID THINK ABOUT 'EM. AND I FELT LIKE I WANTED TO STOP. BUT WHEN I TRIED TO STOP, IT FELT BEYOND MY CONTROL. LIKE WHEN YOU'RE DRIVIN' ON ICE AND YOUR BRAKES LOCK UP, Y'KNOW?
...
YOU DON'T DRIVE, DO YOU?
WE HAVE...FLYING VEHICLES.
MUST BE NICE. WHADDAYA DO IF YER FLYING VEHICLE IS IN THE SHOP?
I OFTEN TRAVEL WITH MY TELEPORTING DOG.
YOU KNOW WHAT? FORGET I ASKED.
"ANYWAY, THAT PHASE OF MY CRIMINAL CAREER DIDN'T LAST LONG. I WAS NOTHIN' SPECIAL. ONE OF A DOZEN MUSCLEHEADS IN THE BRONX DOIN' SMALL-TIME DIRTY WORK. EVENTUALLY I GOT PICKED UP AND ANOTHER MUG TOOK MY PLACE.

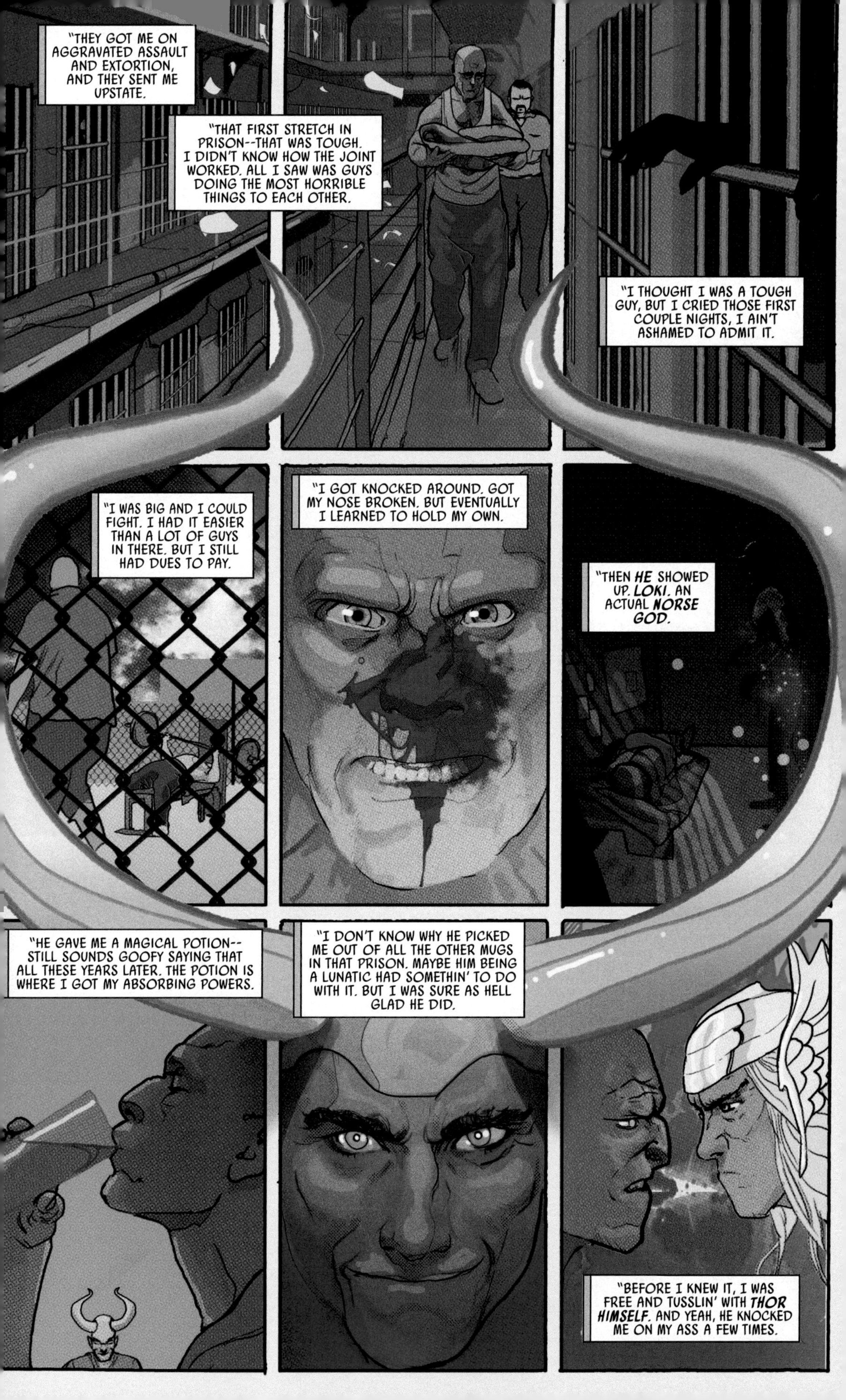
"THEY GOT ME ON AGGRAVATED ASSAULT AND EXTORTION, AND THEY SENT ME UPSTATE.
"THAT FIRST STRETCH IN PRISON--THAT WAS TOUGH. I DIDN'T KNOW HOW THE JOINT WORKED. ALL I SAW WAS GUYS DOING THE MOST HORRIBLE THINGS TO EACH OTHER.
"I THOUGHT I WAS A TOUGH GUY, BUT I CRIED THOSE FIRST COUPLE NIGHTS, I AIN'T ASHAMED TO ADMIT IT.
"I WAS BIG AND I COULD FIGHT. I HAD IT EASIER THAN A LOT OF GUYS IN THERE. BUT I STILL HAD DUES TO PAY.
"I GOT KNOCKED AROUND. GOT MY NOSE BROKEN. BUT EVENTUALLY I LEARNED TO HOLD MY OWN.
"THEN **HE** SHOWED UP. **LOKI**. AN ACTUAL **NORSE GOD**.
"HE GAVE ME A MAGICAL POTION--STILL SOUNDS GOOFY SAYING THAT ALL THESE YEARS LATER. THE POTION IS WHERE I GOT MY ABSORBING POWERS.
"I DON'T KNOW WHY HE PICKED ME OUT OF ALL THE OTHER MUGS IN THAT PRISON. MAYBE HIM BEING A LUNATIC HAD SOMETHIN' TO DO WITH IT. BUT I WAS SURE AS HELL GLAD HE DID.
"BEFORE I KNEW IT, I WAS FREE AND TUSSLIN' WITH **THOR HIMSELF**. AND YEAH, HE KNOCKED ME ON MY ASS A FEW TIMES.

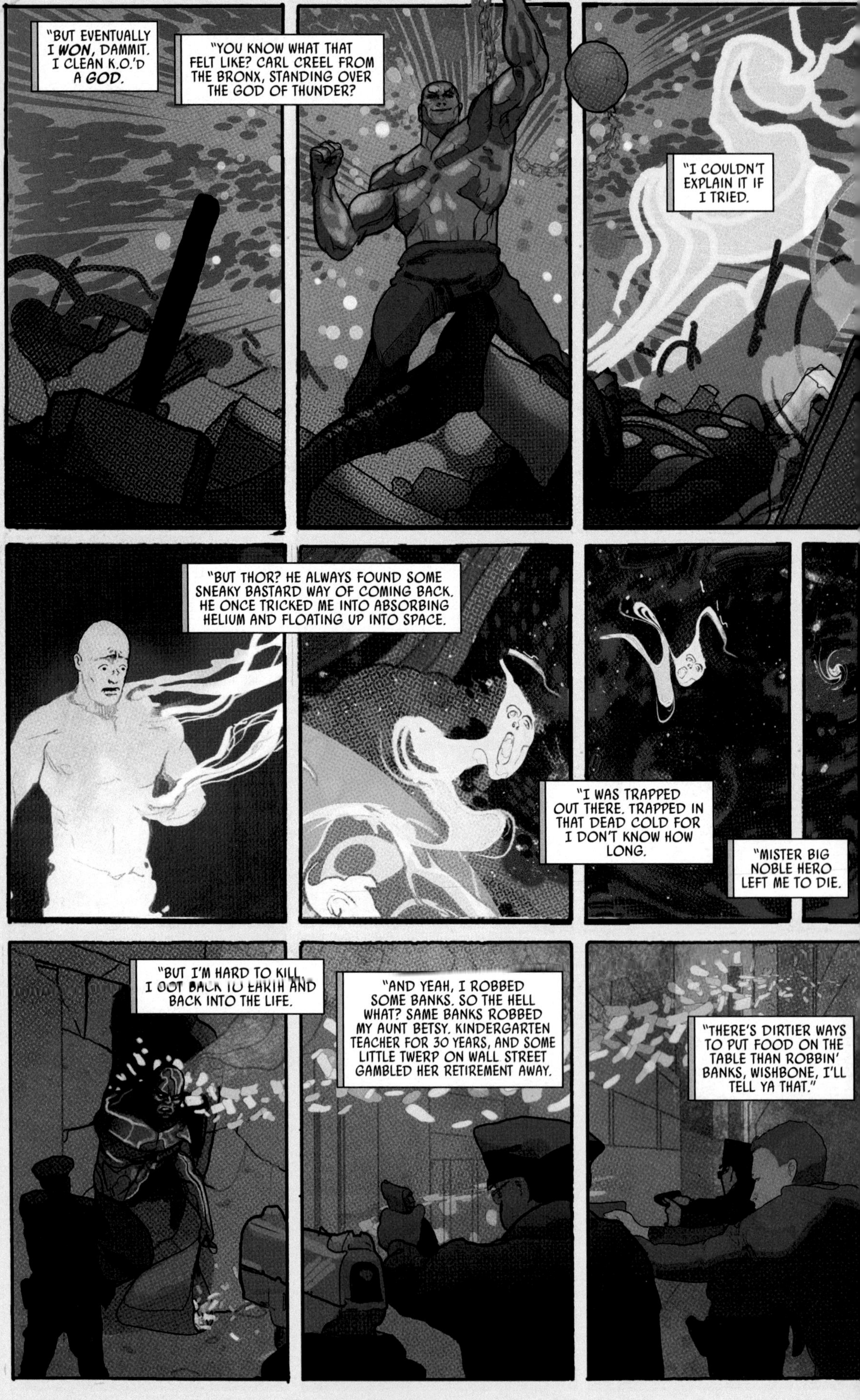
"BUT EVENTUALLY I *WON*, DAMMIT. I CLEAN K.O.'D A *GOD*.
"YOU KNOW WHAT THAT FELT LIKE? CARL CREEL FROM THE BRONX, STANDING OVER THE GOD OF THUNDER?
"I COULDN'T EXPLAIN IT IF I TRIED.
"BUT THOR? HE ALWAYS FOUND SOME SNEAKY BASTARD WAY OF COMING BACK. HE ONCE TRICKED ME INTO ABSORBING HELIUM AND FLOATING UP INTO SPACE.
"I WAS TRAPPED OUT THERE. TRAPPED IN THAT DEAD COLD FOR I DON'T KNOW HOW LONG.
"MISTER BIG NOBLE HERO LEFT ME TO DIE.
"BUT I'M HARD TO KILL. I GOT BACK TO EARTH AND BACK INTO THE LIFE.
"AND YEAH, I ROBBED SOME BANKS. SO THE HELL WHAT? SAME BANKS ROBBED MY AUNT BETSY. KINDERGARTEN TEACHER FOR 30 YEARS, AND SOME LITTLE TWERP ON WALL STREET GAMBLED HER RETIREMENT AWAY.
"THERE'S DIRTIER WAYS TO PUT FOOD ON THE TABLE THAN ROBBIN' BANKS, WISHBONE, I'LL TELL YA THAT."

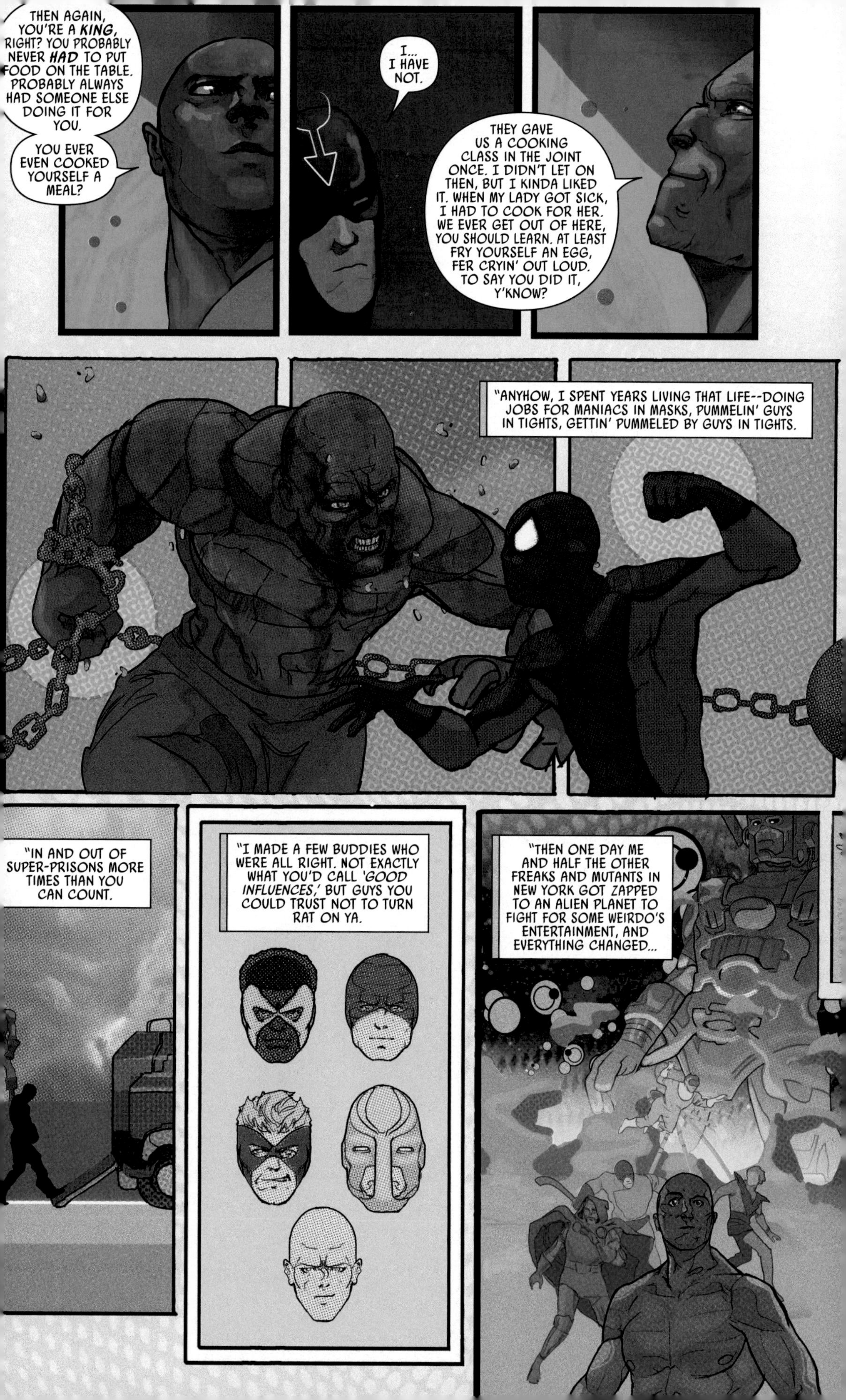
THEN AGAIN, YOU'RE A KING, RIGHT? YOU PROBABLY NEVER HAD TO PUT FOOD ON THE TABLE. PROBABLY ALWAYS HAD SOMEONE ELSE DOING IT FOR YOU.
YOU EVER EVEN COOKED YOURSELF A MEAL?
I... I HAVE NOT.
THEY GAVE US A COOKING CLASS IN THE JOINT ONCE. I DIDN'T LET ON THEN, BUT I KINDA LIKED IT. WHEN MY LADY GOT SICK, I HAD TO COOK FOR HER. WE EVER GET OUT OF HERE, YOU SHOULD LEARN. AT LEAST FRY YOURSELF AN EGG, FER CRYIN' OUT LOUD. TO SAY YOU DID IT, Y'KNOW?
"ANYHOW, I SPENT YEARS LIVING THAT LIFE--DOING JOBS FOR MANIACS IN MASKS, PUMMELIN' GUYS IN TIGHTS, GETTIN' PUMMELED BY GUYS IN TIGHTS.
"IN AND OUT OF SUPER-PRISONS MORE TIMES THAN YOU CAN COUNT.
"I MADE A FEW BUDDIES WHO WERE ALL RIGHT. NOT EXACTLY WHAT YOU'D CALL 'GOOD INFLUENCES,' BUT GUYS YOU COULD TRUST NOT TO TURN RAT ON YA.
"THEN ONE DAY ME AND HALF THE OTHER FREAKS AND MUTANTS IN NEW YORK GOT ZAPPED TO AN ALIEN PLANET TO FIGHT FOR SOME WEIRDO'S ENTERTAINMENT, AND EVERYTHING CHANGED...

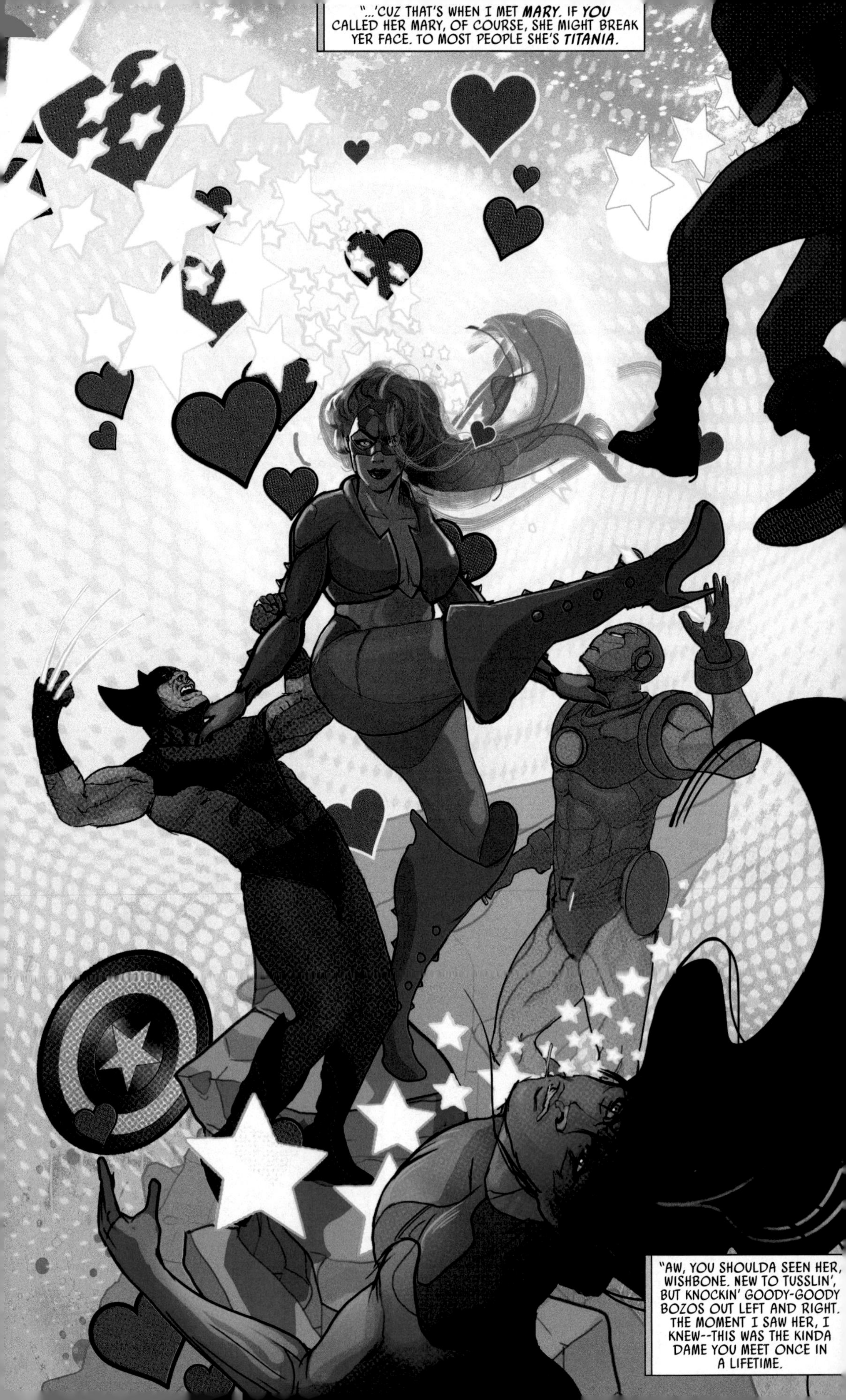
"...'CUZ THAT'S WHEN I MET MARY. IF YOU CALLED HER MARY, OF COURSE, SHE MIGHT BREAK YER FACE. TO MOST PEOPLE SHE'S TITANIA.
"AW, YOU SHOULDA SEEN HER, WISHBONE. NEW TO TUSSLIN', BUT KNOCKIN' GOODY-GOODY BOZOS OUT LEFT AND RIGHT. THE MOMENT I SAW HER, I KNEW--THIS WAS THE KINDA DAME YOU MEET ONCE IN A LIFETIME.

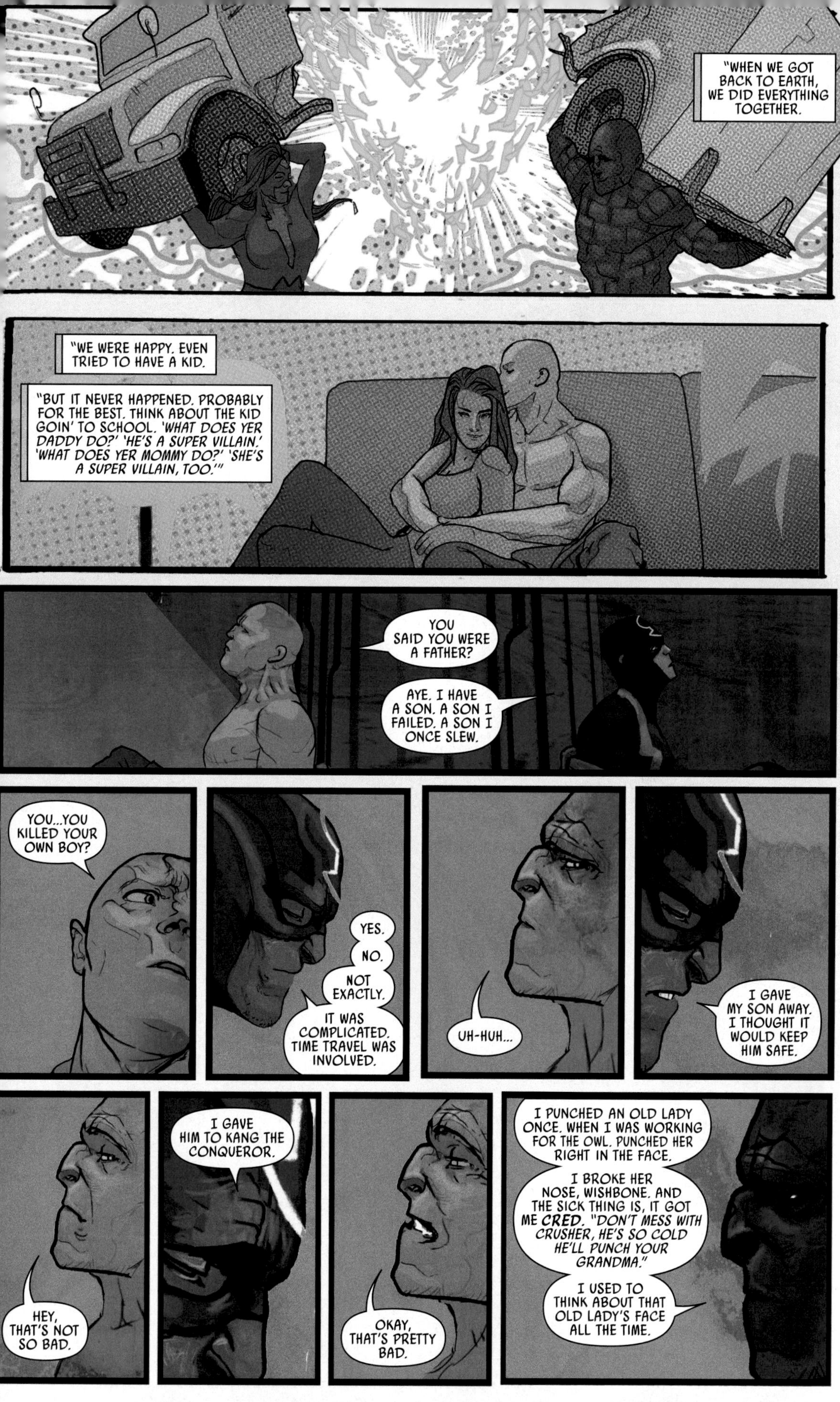
"WHEN WE GOT BACK TO EARTH, WE DID EVERYTHING TOGETHER.
"WE WERE HAPPY. EVEN TRIED TO HAVE A KID.
"BUT IT NEVER HAPPENED. PROBABLY FOR THE BEST. THINK ABOUT THE KID GOIN' TO SCHOOL. '*WHAT DOES YER DADDY DO?*' '*HE'S A SUPER VILLAIN.*' '*WHAT DOES YER MOMMY DO?*' '*SHE'S A SUPER VILLAIN, TOO.*'"
YOU SAID YOU WERE A FATHER?
AYE. I HAVE A SON. A SON I FAILED. A SON I ONCE SLEW.
YOU...YOU KILLED YOUR OWN BOY?
YES.
NO.
NOT EXACTLY.
IT WAS COMPLICATED. TIME TRAVEL WAS INVOLVED.
UH-HUH...
I GAVE MY SON AWAY. I THOUGHT IT WOULD KEEP HIM SAFE.
I GAVE HIM TO KANG THE CONQUEROR.
HEY, THAT'S NOT SO BAD.
OKAY, THAT'S PRETTY BAD.
I PUNCHED AN OLD LADY ONCE. WHEN I WAS WORKING FOR THE OWL. PUNCHED HER RIGHT IN THE FACE.
I BROKE HER NOSE, WISHBONE. AND THE SICK THING IS, IT GOT ME **CRED**. "*DON'T MESS WITH CRUSHER, HE'S SO COLD HE'LL PUNCH YOUR GRANDMA.*"
I USED TO THINK ABOUT THAT OLD LADY'S FACE ALL THE TIME.

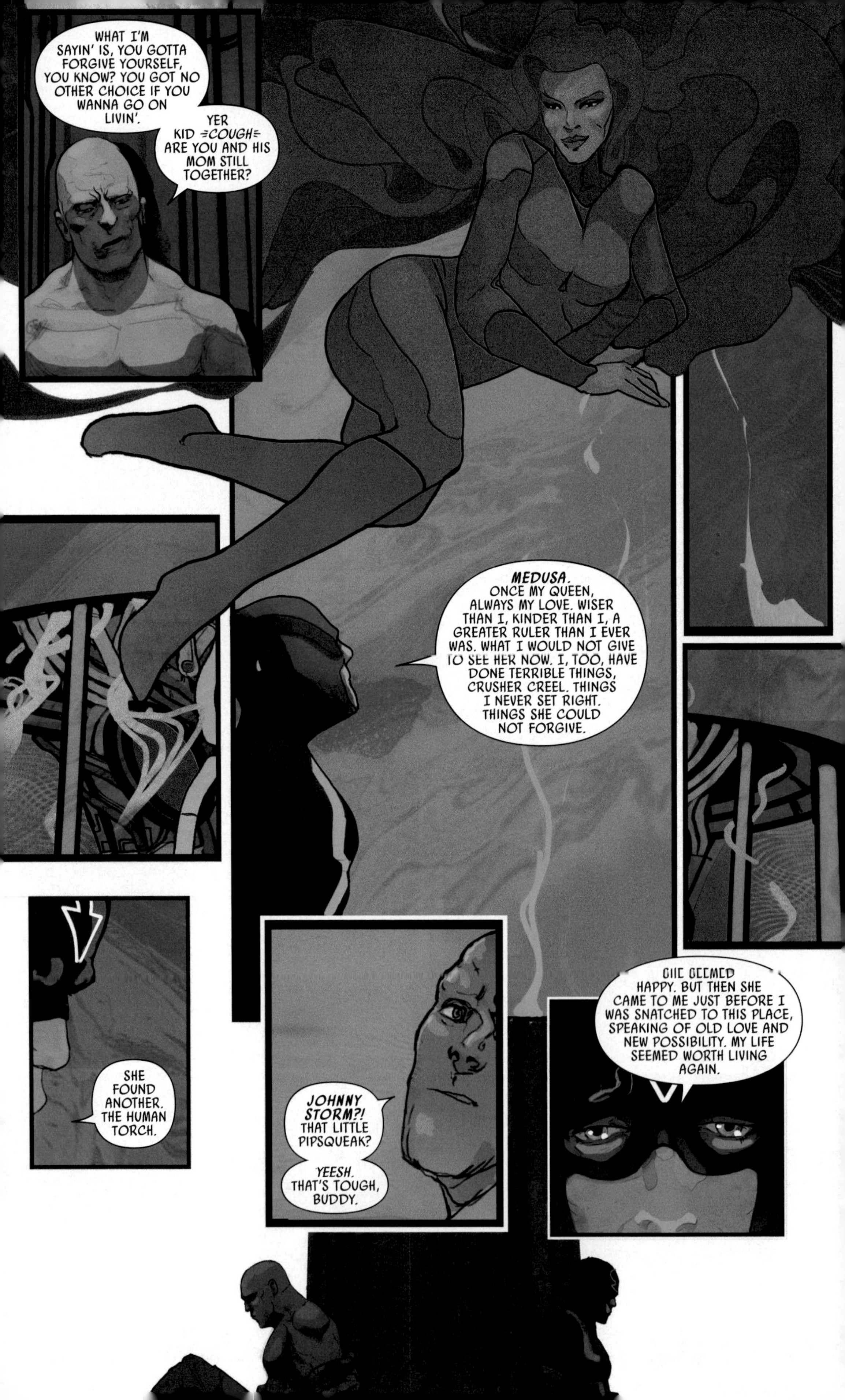
WHAT I'M SAYIN' IS, YOU GOTTA FORGIVE YOURSELF, YOU KNOW? YOU GOT NO OTHER CHOICE IF YOU WANNA GO ON LIVIN'.
YER KID =COUGH= ARE YOU AND HIS MOM STILL TOGETHER?
MEDUSA. ONCE MY QUEEN, ALWAYS MY LOVE. WISER THAN I, KINDER THAN I, A GREATER RULER THAN I EVER WAS. WHAT I WOULD NOT GIVE TO SEE HER NOW. I, TOO, HAVE DONE TERRIBLE THINGS, CRUSHER CREEL. THINGS I NEVER SET RIGHT. THINGS SHE COULD NOT FORGIVE.
SHE FOUND ANOTHER. THE HUMAN TORCH.
JOHNNY STORM?! THAT LITTLE PIPSQUEAK?
YEESH. THAT'S TOUGH, BUDDY.
HAPPY. BUT THEN SHE CAME TO ME JUST BEFORE I WAS SNATCHED TO THIS PLACE, SPEAKING OF OLD LOVE AND NEW POSSIBILITY. MY LIFE SEEMED WORTH LIVING AGAIN.

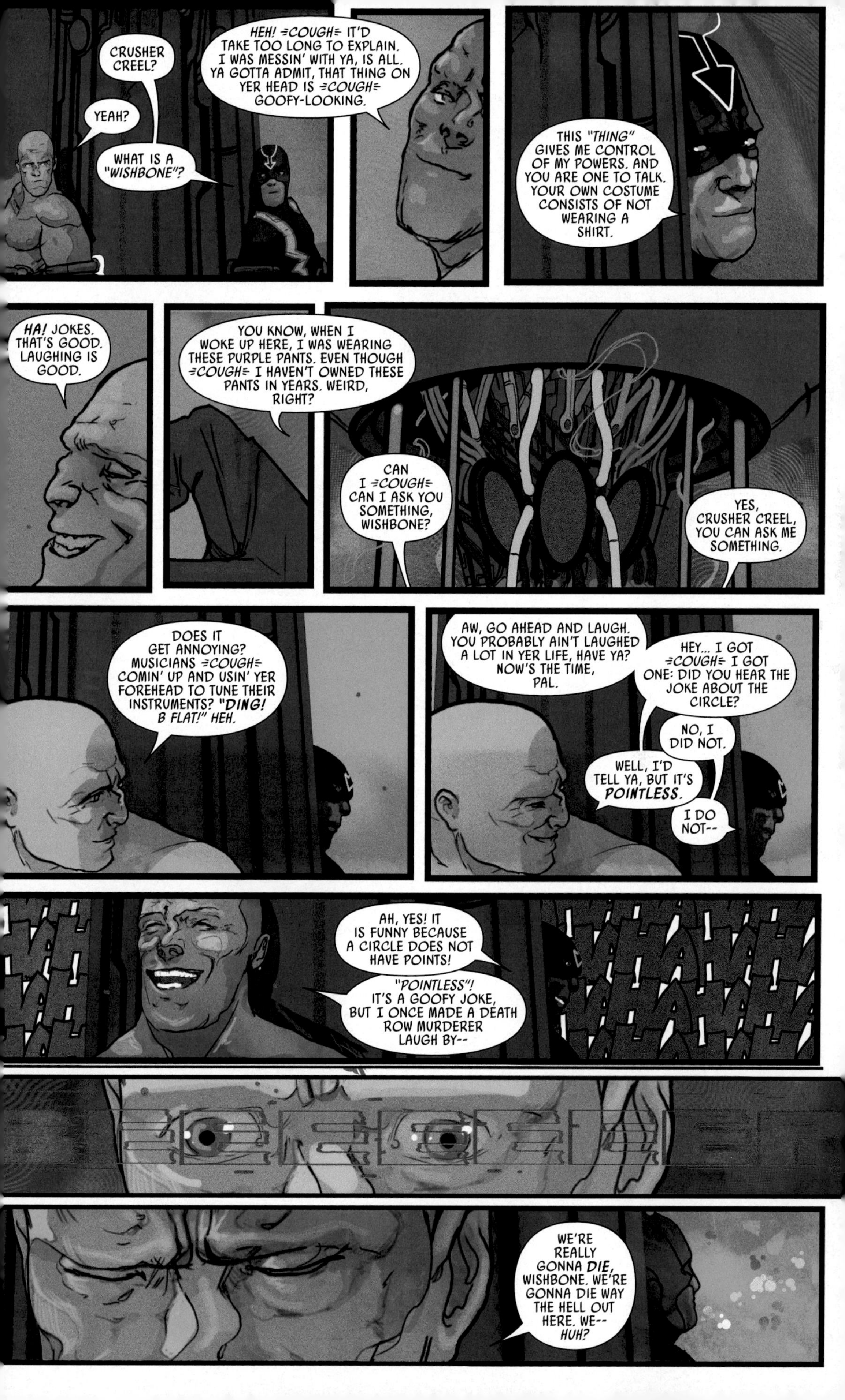
CRUSHER CREEL?
YEAH?
WHAT IS A "WISHBONE"?
HEH! =COUGH= IT'D TAKE TOO LONG TO EXPLAIN. I WAS MESSIN' WITH YA, IS ALL. YA GOTTA ADMIT, THAT THING ON YER HEAD IS =COUGH= GOOFY-LOOKING.
THIS "THING" GIVES ME CONTROL OF MY POWERS. AND YOU ARE ONE TO TALK. YOUR OWN COSTUME CONSISTS OF NOT WEARING A SHIRT.
HA! JOKES. THAT'S GOOD. LAUGHING IS GOOD.
YOU KNOW, WHEN I WOKE UP HERE, I WAS WEARING THESE PURPLE PANTS. EVEN THOUGH =COUGH= I HAVEN'T OWNED THESE PANTS IN YEARS. WEIRD, RIGHT?
CAN I =COUGH= CAN I ASK YOU SOMETHING, WISHBONE?
YES, CRUSHER CREEL, YOU CAN ASK ME SOMETHING.
DOES IT GET ANNOYING? MUSICIANS =COUGH= COMIN' UP AND USIN' YER FOREHEAD TO TUNE THEIR INSTRUMENTS? "DING! B FLAT!" HEH.
AW, GO AHEAD AND LAUGH. YOU PROBABLY AIN'T LAUGHED A LOT IN YER LIFE, HAVE YA? NOW'S THE TIME, PAL.
HEY... I GOT =COUGH= I GOT ONE: DID YOU HEAR THE JOKE ABOUT THE CIRCLE?
NO, I DID NOT.
WELL, I'D TELL YA, BUT IT'S POINTLESS.
I DO NOT--
AH, YES! IT IS FUNNY BECAUSE A CIRCLE DOES NOT HAVE POINTS!
"POINTLESS"! IT'S A GOOFY JOKE, BUT I ONCE MADE A DEATH ROW MURDERER LAUGH BY--
WE'RE REALLY GONNA DIE, WISHBONE. WE'RE GONNA DIE WAY THE HELL OUT HERE. WE-- HUH?

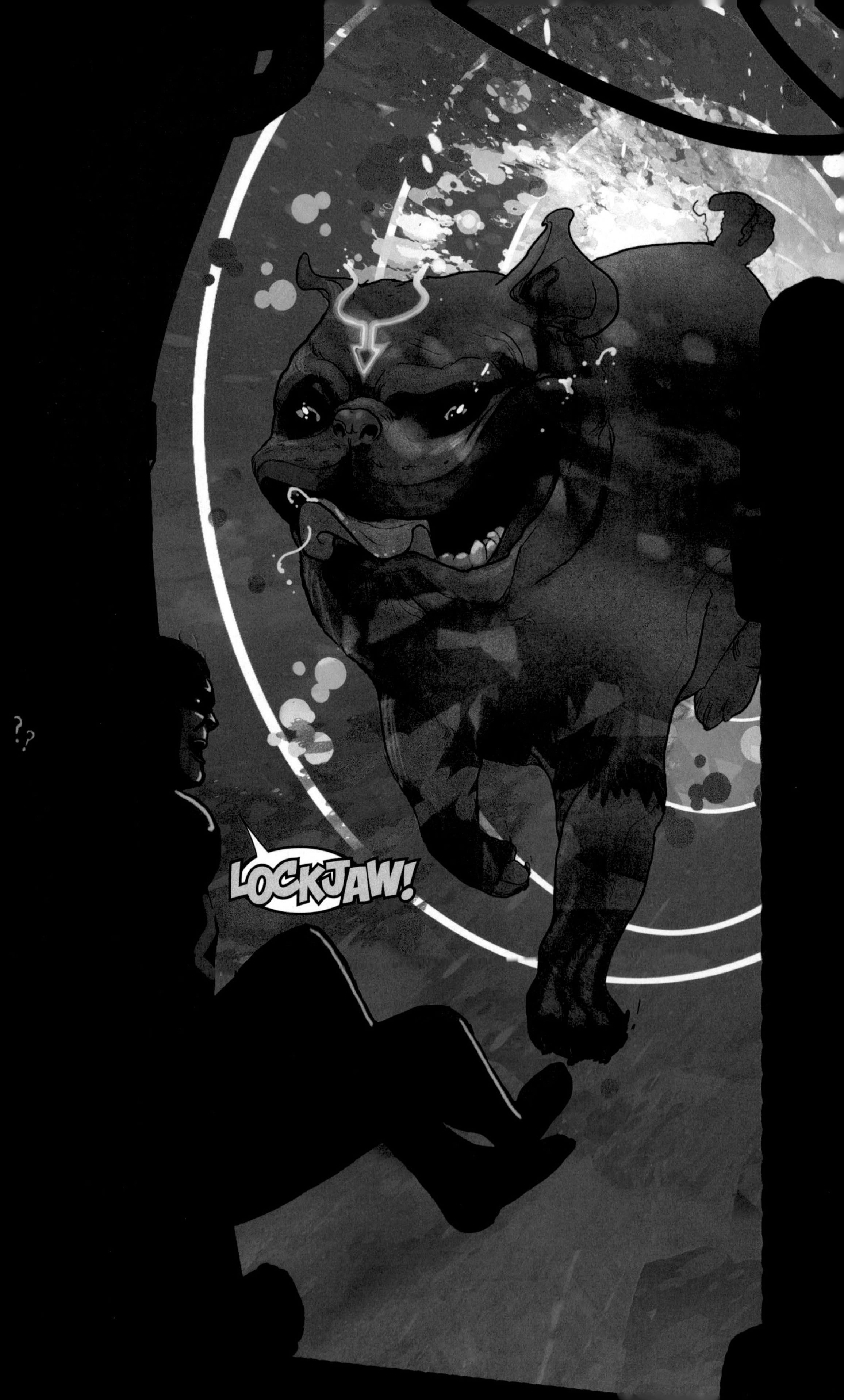
?
?
LOCKJAW!

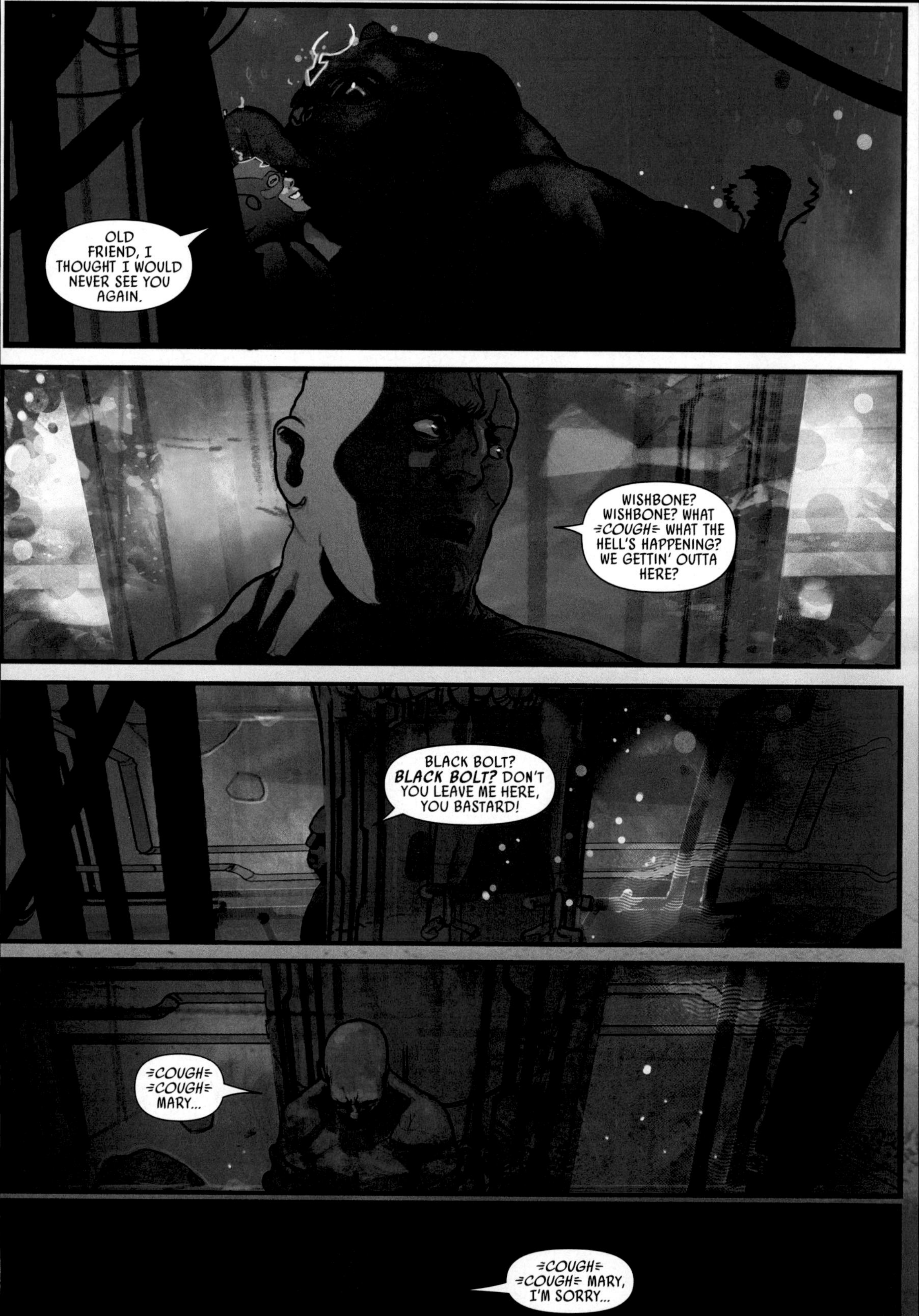
OLD FRIEND, I THOUGHT I WOULD NEVER SEE YOU AGAIN.
WISHBONE? WISHBONE? WHAT =COUGH= WHAT THE HELL'S HAPPENING? WE GETTIN' OUTTA HERE?
BLACK BOLT? **BLACK BOLT?** DON'T YOU LEAVE ME HERE, YOU BASTARD!
=COUGH= =COUGH= MARY...
=COUGH= =COUGH= MARY, I'M SORRY...

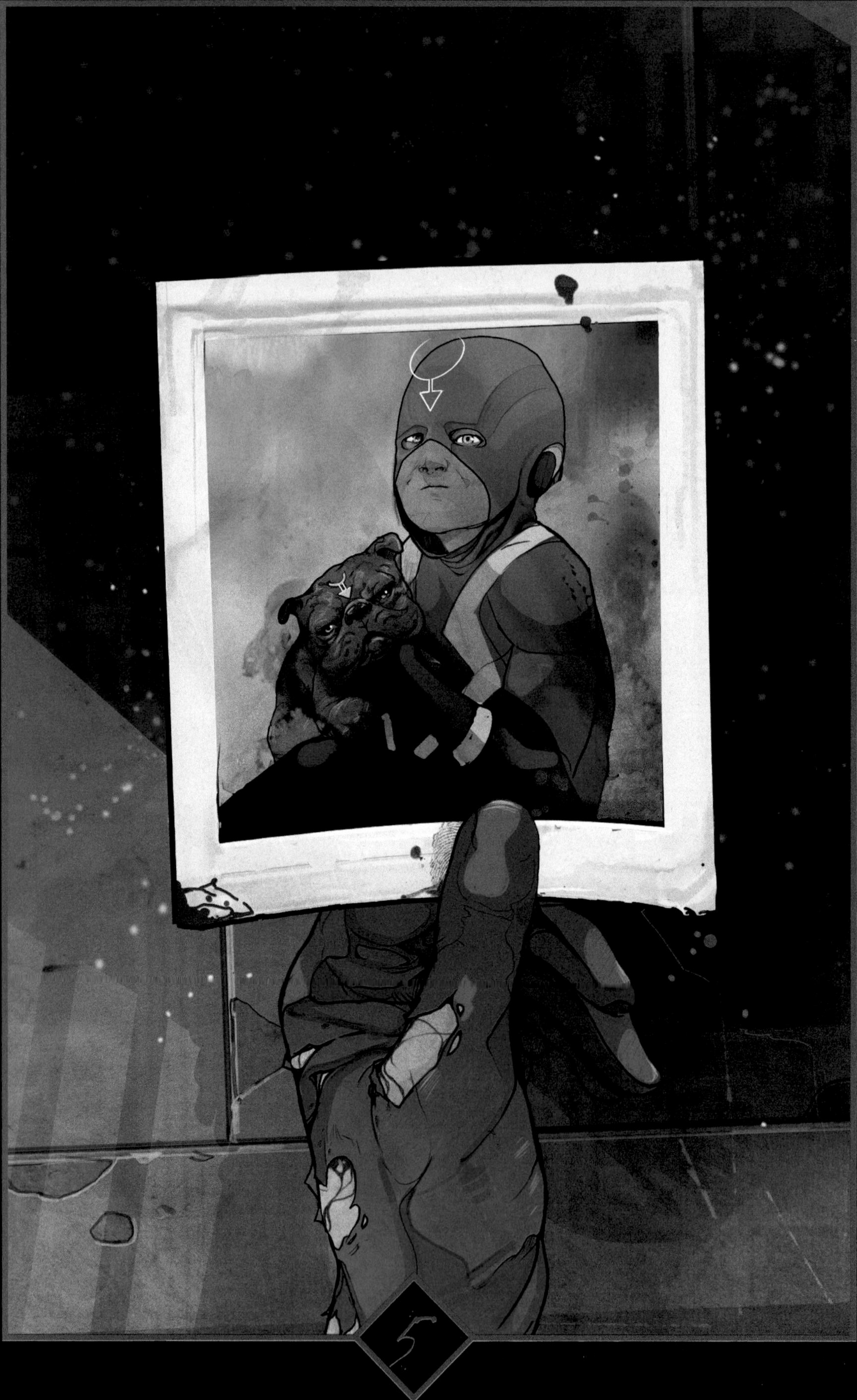
5

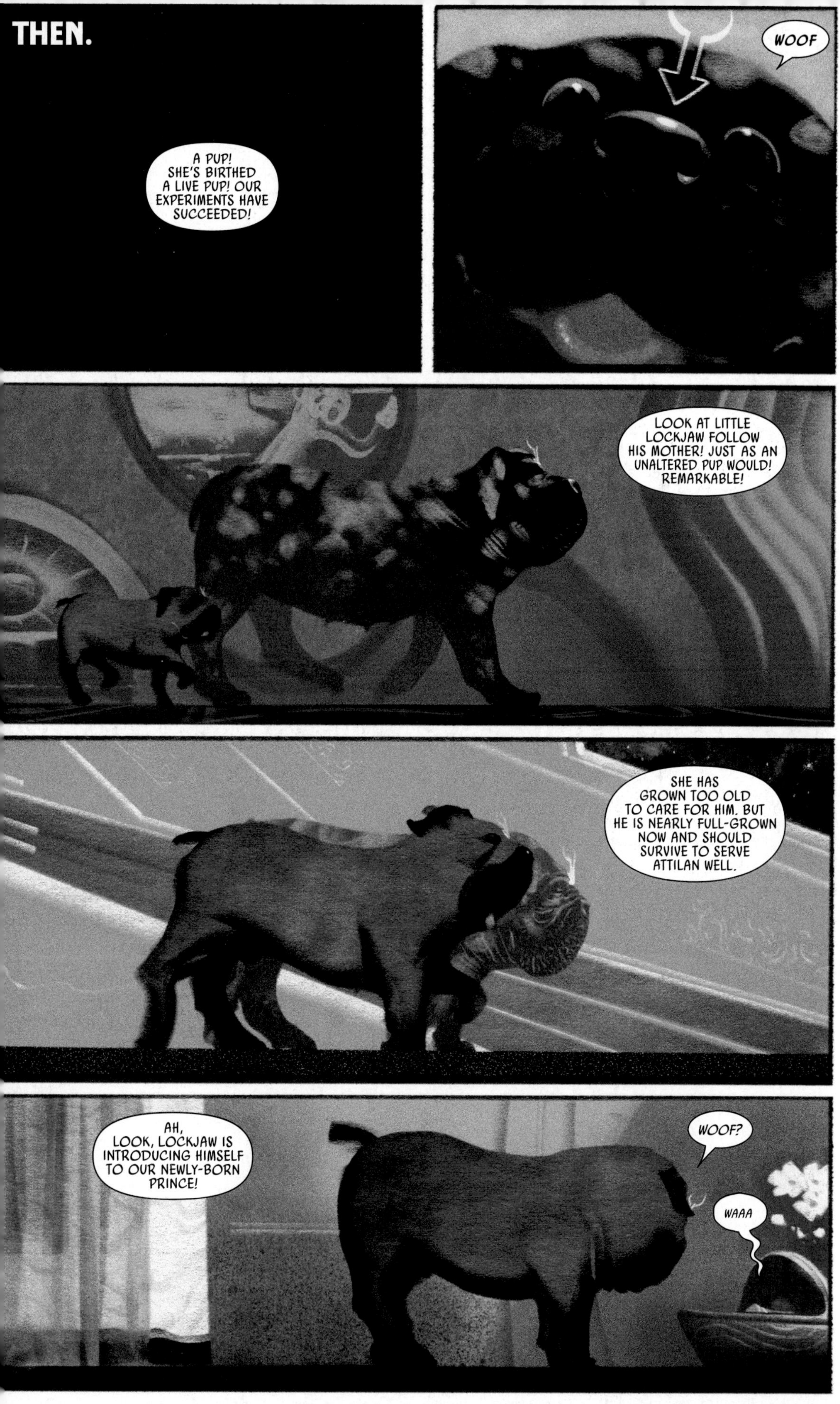
THEN.
A PUP! SHE'S BIRTHED A LIVE PUP! OUR EXPERIMENTS HAVE SUCCEEDED!
WOOF
LOOK AT LITTLE LOCKJAW FOLLOW HIS MOTHER! JUST AS AN UNALTERED PUP WOULD! REMARKABLE!
SHE HAS GROWN TOO OLD TO CARE FOR HIM. BUT HE IS NEARLY FULL-GROWN NOW AND SHOULD SURVIVE TO SERVE ATTILAN WELL.
AH, LOOK, LOCKJAW IS INTRODUCING HIMSELF TO OUR NEWLY-BORN PRINCE!
WOOF?
WAAA

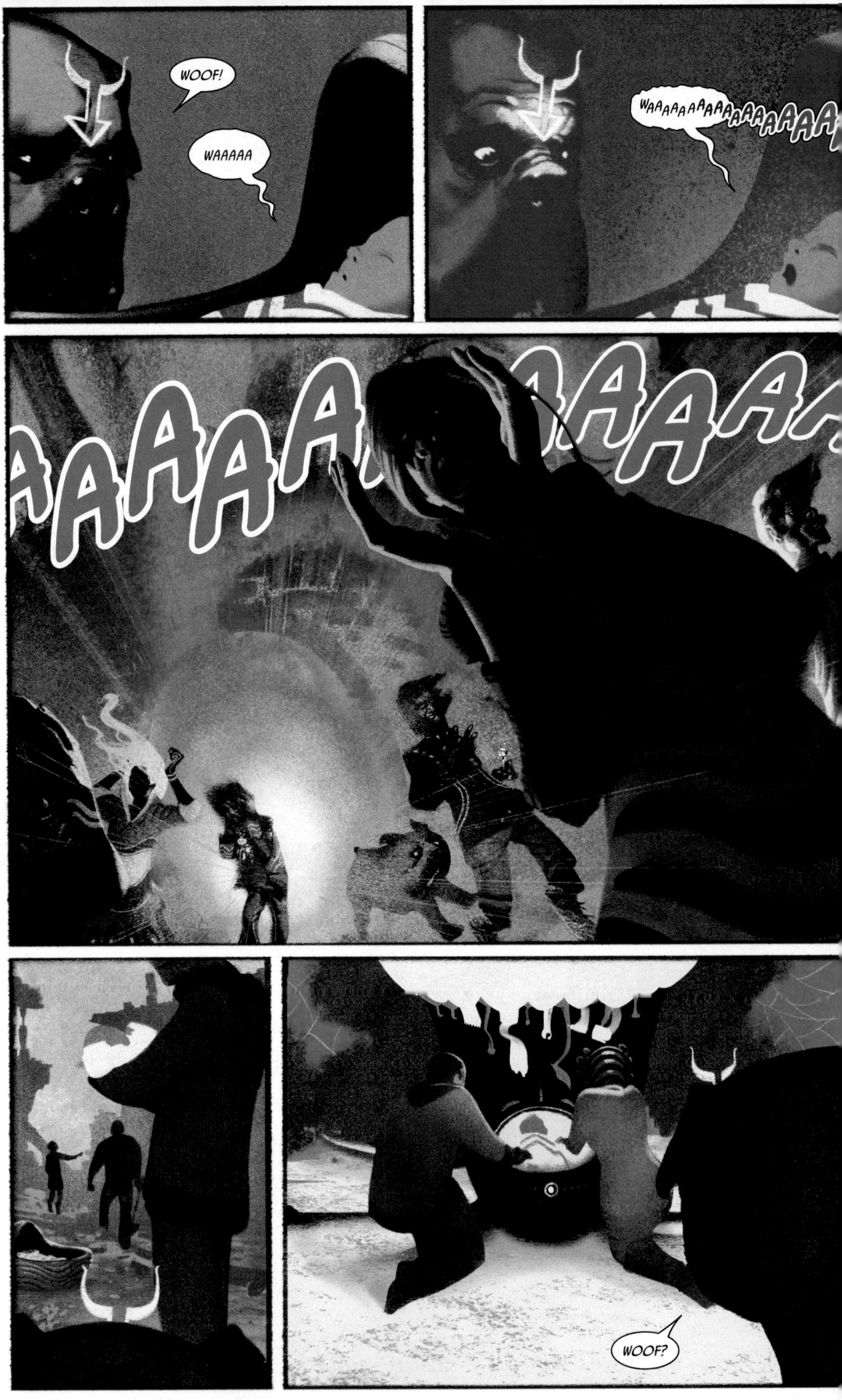
WOOF!
WAAAAA
WAAAAAAAAAAAAAAAAAAA
AAAAAAAAAAAAAAAA
WOOF?

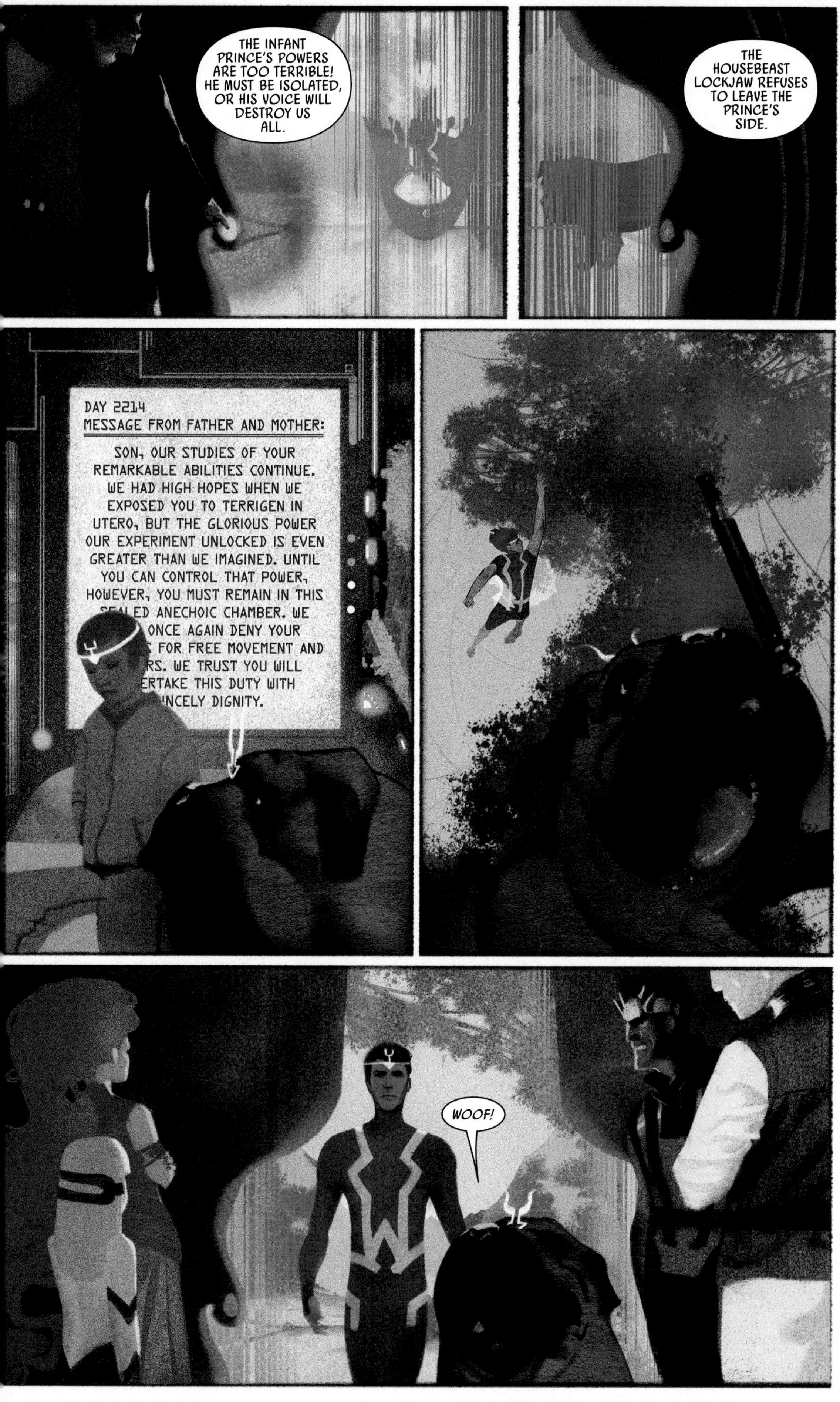
THE INFANT PRINCE'S POWERS ARE TOO TERRIBLE! HE MUST BE ISOLATED, OR HIS VOICE WILL DESTROY US ALL.
THE HOUSEBEAST LOCKJAW REFUSES TO LEAVE THE PRINCE'S SIDE.
DAY 2214
MESSAGE FROM FATHER AND MOTHER:
SON, OUR STUDIES OF YOUR REMARKABLE ABILITIES CONTINUE. WE HAD HIGH HOPES WHEN WE EXPOSED YOU TO TERRIGEN IN UTERO, BUT THE GLORIOUS POWER OUR EXPERIMENT UNLOCKED IS EVEN GREATER THAN WE IMAGINED. UNTIL YOU CAN CONTROL THAT POWER, HOWEVER, YOU MUST REMAIN IN THIS
ALED ANECHOIC CHAMBER. WE
ONCE AGAIN DENY YOUR
FOR FREE MOVEMENT AND
RS. WE TRUST YOU WILL
ERTAKE THIS DUTY WITH
INCELY DIGNITY.
WOOF!

WOOF!

WOOF!

WE PASS SENTENCE AGAINST YOU, *MAXIMUS BOLTAGON*--

WOOF?

--YOU WILL BE TAKEN *FAR* FROM HERE--

GRRRRRR!

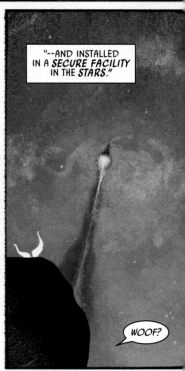

"--AND INSTALLED IN A *SECURE FACILITY* IN THE *STARS*."

WOOF?

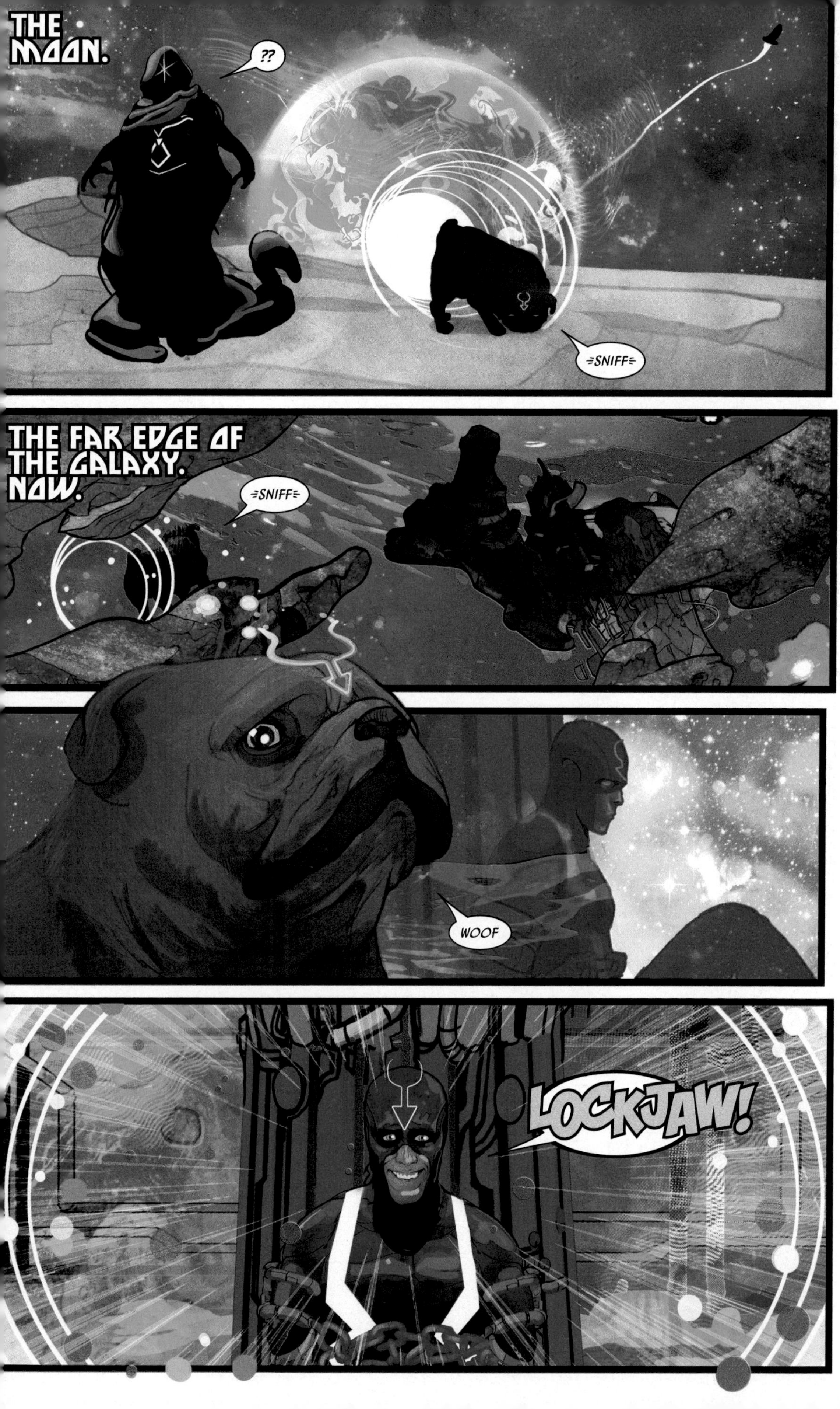
THE MOON.
??
SNIFF
THE FAR EDGE OF THE GALAXY. NOW.
SNIFF
WOOF
LOCKJAW!

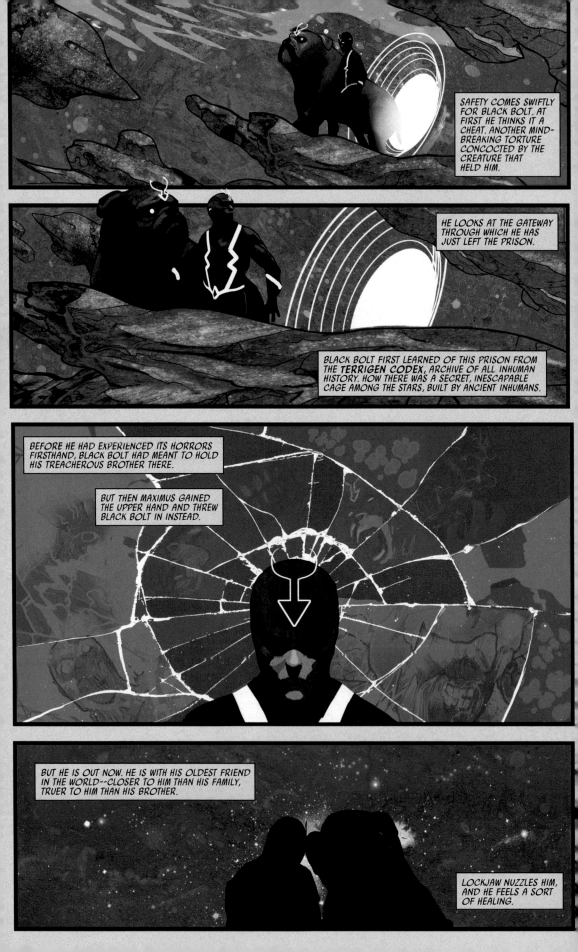

SAFETY COMES SWIFTLY FOR BLACK BOLT. AT FIRST HE THINKS IT A CHEAT. ANOTHER MIND-BREAKING TORTURE CONCOCTED BY THE CREATURE THAT HELD HIM.

HE LOOKS AT THE GATEWAY THROUGH WHICH HE HAS JUST LEFT THE PRISON.

BLACK BOLT FIRST LEARNED OF THIS PRISON FROM THE **TERRIGEN CODEX**, ARCHIVE OF ALL INHUMAN HISTORY. HOW THERE WAS A SECRET, INESCAPABLE CAGE AMONG THE STARS, BUILT BY ANCIENT INHUMANS.

BEFORE HE HAD EXPERIENCED ITS HORRORS FIRSTHAND, BLACK BOLT HAD MEANT TO HOLD HIS TREACHEROUS BROTHER THERE.

BUT THEN MAXIMUS GAINED THE UPPER HAND AND THREW BLACK BOLT IN INSTEAD.

BUT HE IS OUT NOW. HE IS WITH HIS OLDEST FRIEND IN THE WORLD--CLOSER TO HIM THAN HIS FAMILY, TRUER TO HIM THAN HIS BROTHER.

LOCKJAW NUZZLES HIM, AND HE FEELS A SORT OF HEALING.

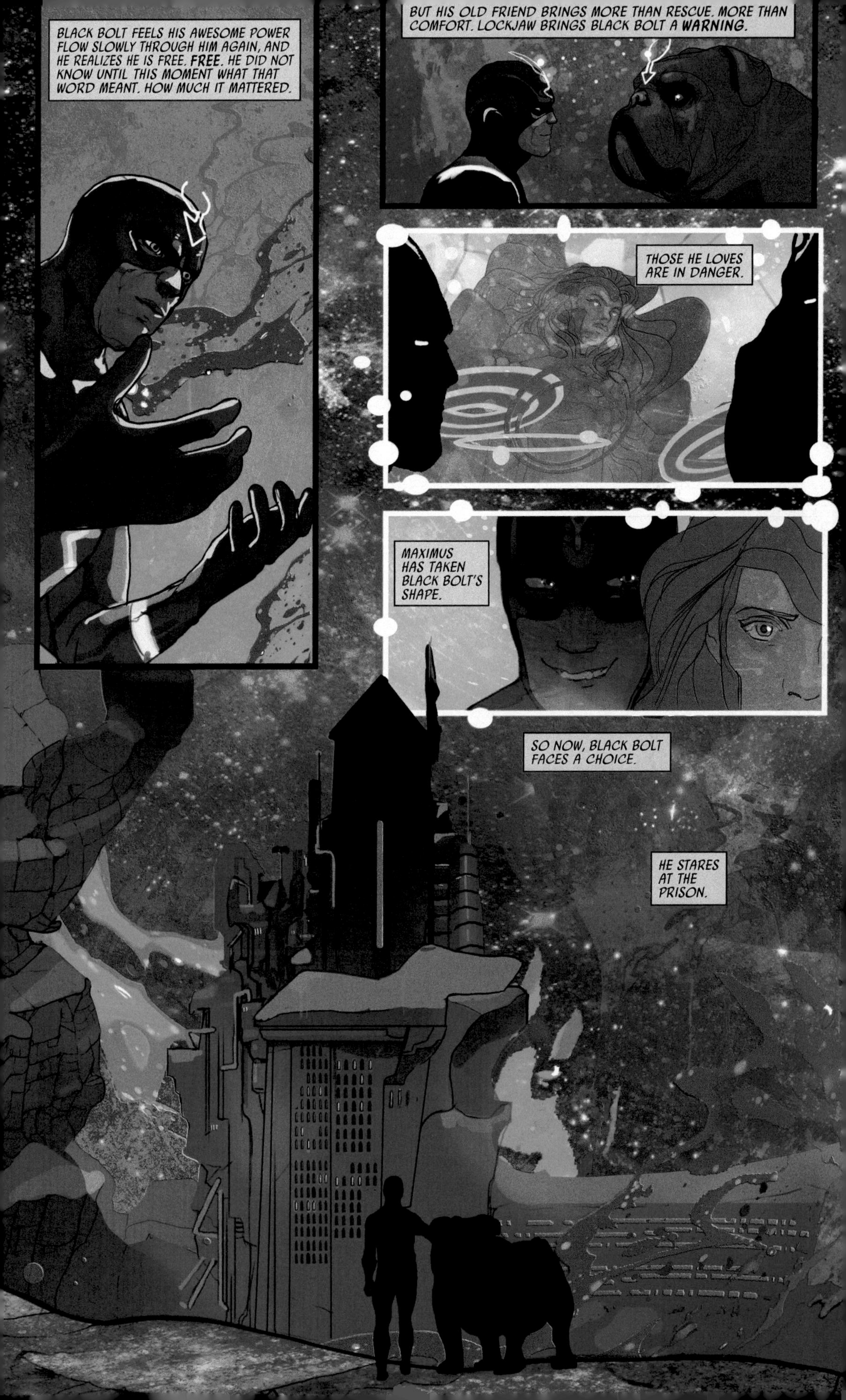
BLACK BOLT FEELS HIS AWESOME POWER FLOW SLOWLY THROUGH HIM AGAIN, AND HE REALIZES HE IS FREE. FREE. HE DID NOT KNOW UNTIL THIS MOMENT WHAT THAT WORD MEANT. HOW MUCH IT MATTERED.
BUT HIS OLD FRIEND BRINGS MORE THAN RESCUE. MORE THAN COMFORT. LOCKJAW BRINGS BLACK BOLT A WARNING.
THOSE HE LOVES ARE IN DANGER.
MAXIMUS HAS TAKEN BLACK BOLT'S SHAPE.
SO NOW, BLACK BOLT FACES A CHOICE.
HE STARES AT THE PRISON.

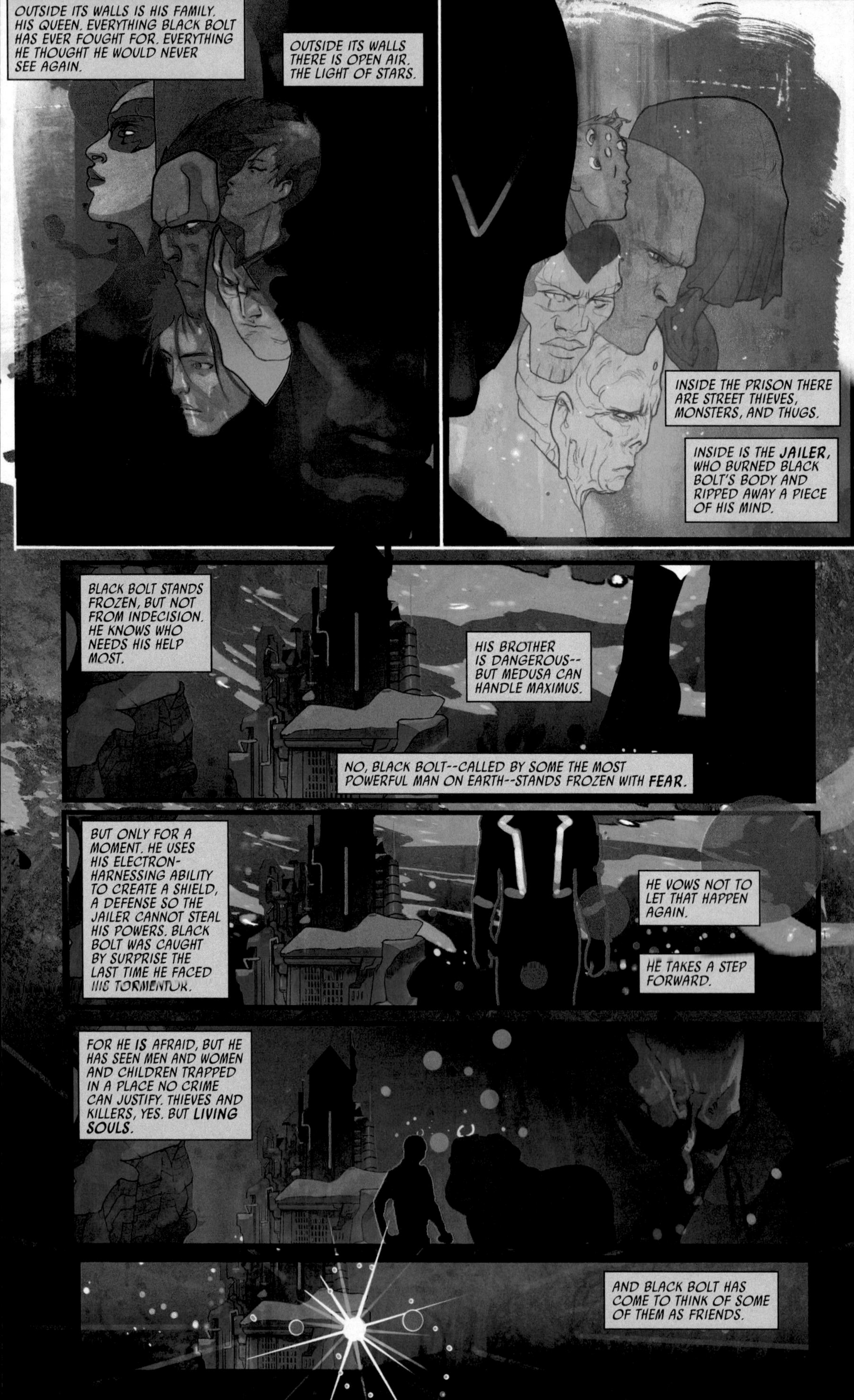
OUTSIDE ITS WALLS IS HIS FAMILY. HIS QUEEN. EVERYTHING BLACK BOLT HAS EVER FOUGHT FOR. EVERYTHING HE THOUGHT HE WOULD NEVER SEE AGAIN.
OUTSIDE ITS WALLS THERE IS OPEN AIR. THE LIGHT OF STARS.
INSIDE THE PRISON THERE ARE STREET THIEVES, MONSTERS, AND THUGS.
INSIDE IS THE JAILER, WHO BURNED BLACK BOLT'S BODY AND RIPPED AWAY A PIECE OF HIS MIND.
BLACK BOLT STANDS FROZEN, BUT NOT FROM INDECISION. HE KNOWS WHO NEEDS HIS HELP MOST.
HIS BROTHER IS DANGEROUS--BUT MEDUSA CAN HANDLE MAXIMUS.
NO, BLACK BOLT--CALLED BY SOME THE MOST POWERFUL MAN ON EARTH--STANDS FROZEN WITH FEAR.
BUT ONLY FOR A MOMENT. HE USES HIS ELECTRON-HARNESSING ABILITY TO CREATE A SHIELD, A DEFENSE SO THE JAILER CANNOT STEAL HIS POWERS. BLACK BOLT WAS CAUGHT BY SURPRISE THE LAST TIME HE FACED HIS TORMENTOR.
HE VOWS NOT TO LET THAT HAPPEN AGAIN.
HE TAKES A STEP FORWARD.
FOR HE IS AFRAID, BUT HE HAS SEEN MEN AND WOMEN AND CHILDREN TRAPPED IN A PLACE NO CRIME CAN JUSTIFY. THIEVES AND KILLERS, YES. BUT LIVING SOULS.
AND BLACK BOLT HAS COME TO THINK OF SOME OF THEM AS FRIENDS.

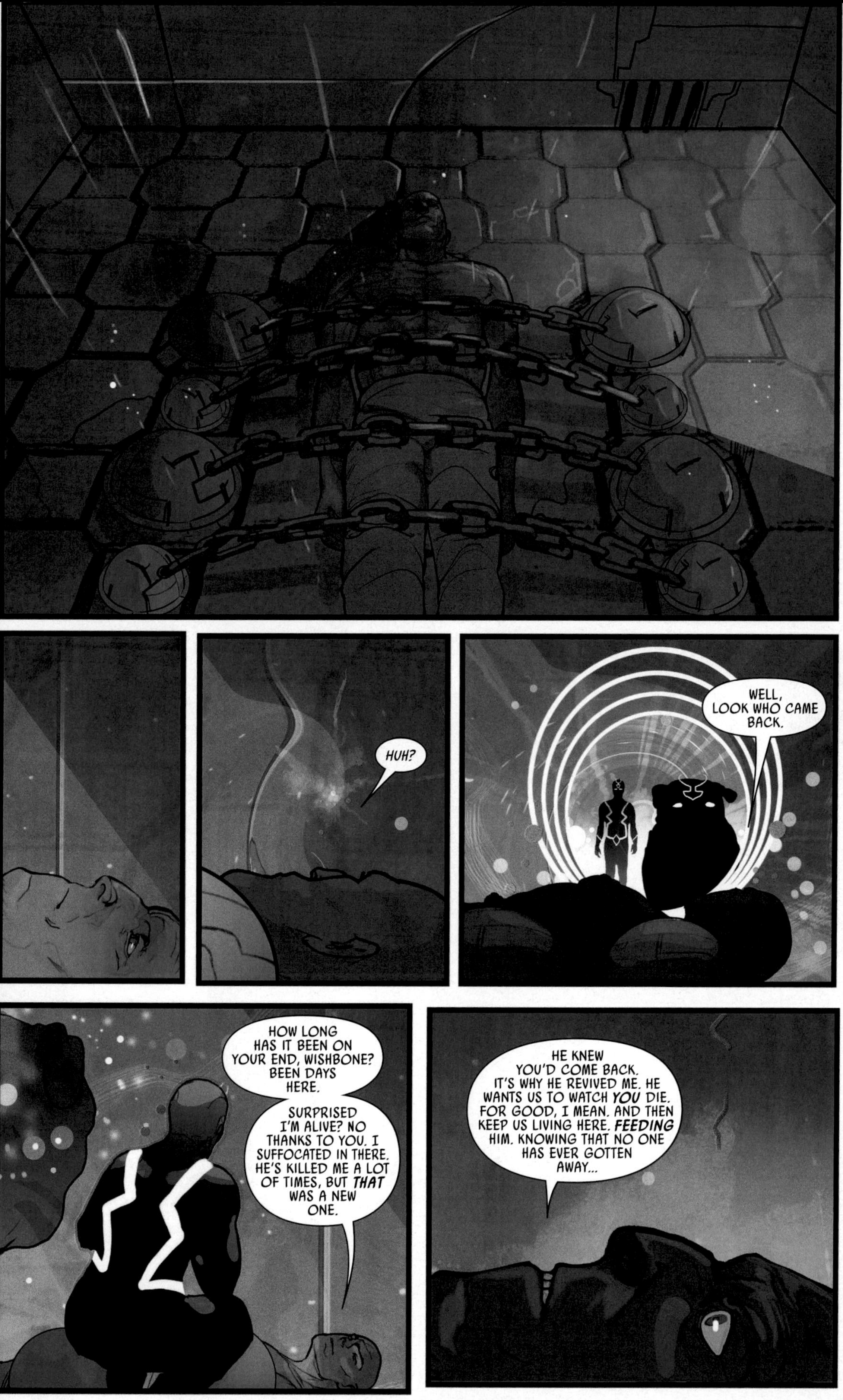
HUH?
WELL, LOOK WHO CAME BACK.
HOW LONG HAS IT BEEN ON YOUR END, WISHBONE? BEEN DAYS HERE.
SURPRISED I'M ALIVE? NO THANKS TO YOU. I SUFFOCATED IN THERE. HE'S KILLED ME A LOT OF TIMES, BUT *THAT* WAS A NEW ONE.
HE KNEW YOU'D COME BACK. IT'S WHY HE REVIVED ME. HE WANTS US TO WATCH *YOU* DIE. FOR GOOD, I MEAN. AND THEN KEEP US LIVING HERE. *FEEDING* HIM. KNOWING THAT NO ONE HAS EVER GOTTEN AWAY...

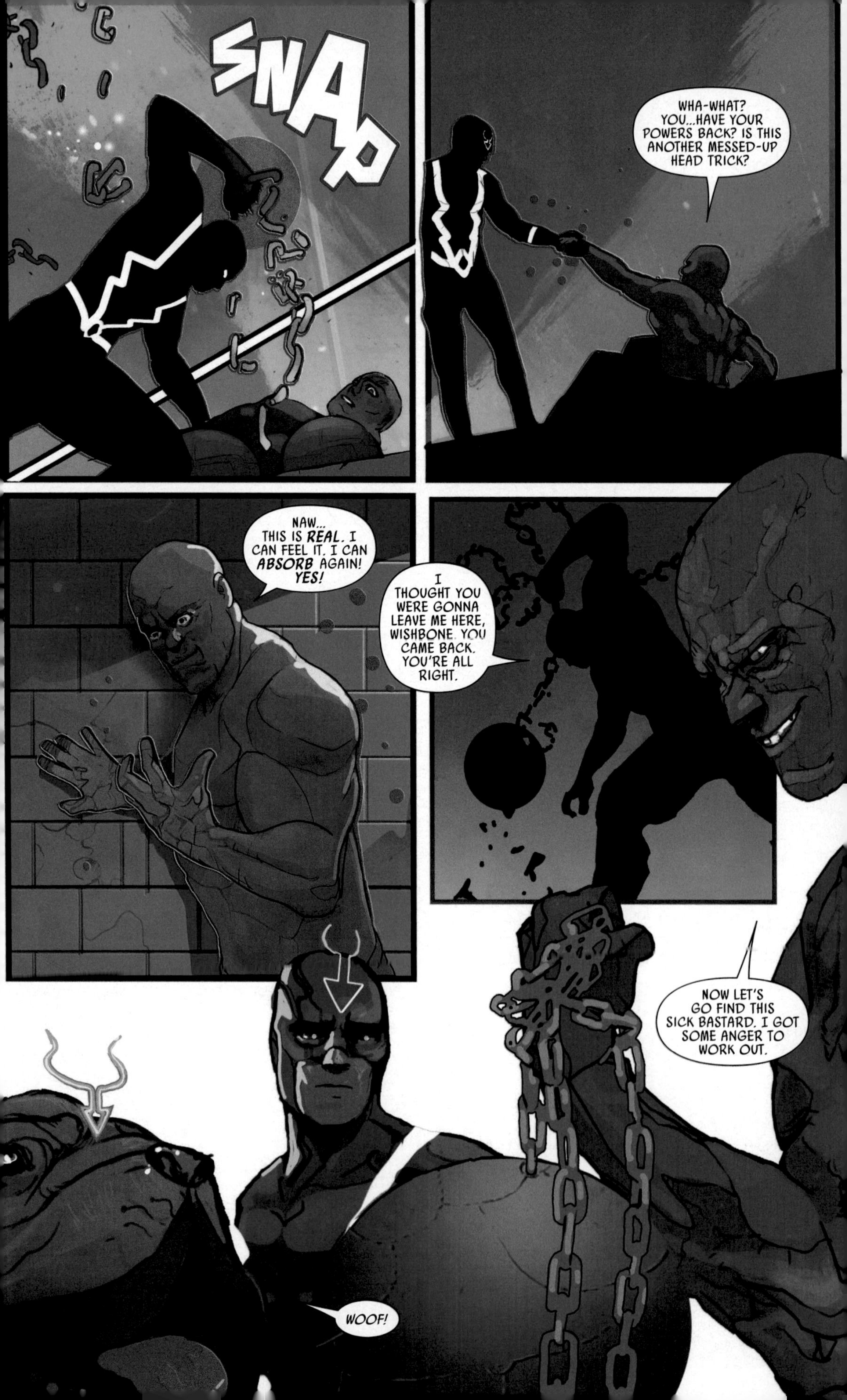
SNAP
WHA-WHAT? YOU...HAVE YOUR POWERS BACK? IS THIS ANOTHER MESSED-UP HEAD TRICK?
NAW... THIS IS REAL. I CAN FEEL IT. I CAN ABSORB AGAIN! YES!
I THOUGHT YOU WERE GONNA LEAVE ME HERE, WISHBONE. YOU CAME BACK. YOU'RE ALL RIGHT.
NOW LET'S GO FIND THIS SICK BASTARD. I GOT SOME ANGER TO WORK OUT.
WOOF!

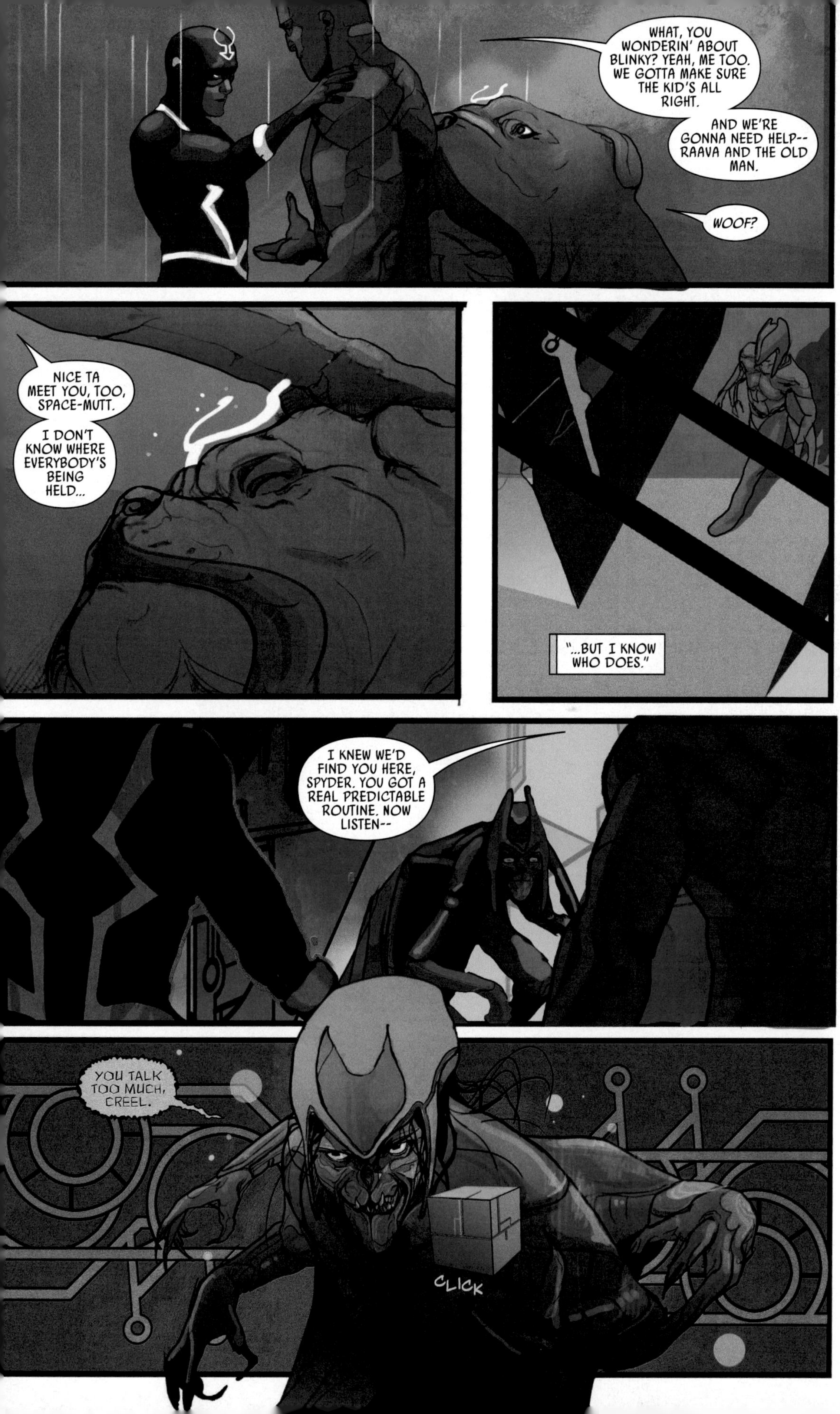
WHAT, YOU WONDERIN' ABOUT BLINKY? YEAH, ME TOO. WE GOTTA MAKE SURE THE KID'S ALL RIGHT.
AND WE'RE GONNA NEED HELP-- RAAVA AND THE OLD MAN.
WOOF?
NICE TA MEET YOU, TOO, SPACE-MUTT.
I DON'T KNOW WHERE EVERYBODY'S BEING HELD...
"...BUT I KNOW WHO DOES."
I KNEW WE'D FIND YOU HERE, SPYDER. YOU GOT A REAL PREDICTABLE ROUTINE. NOW LISTEN--
YOU TALK TOO MUCH, CREEL.
CLICK

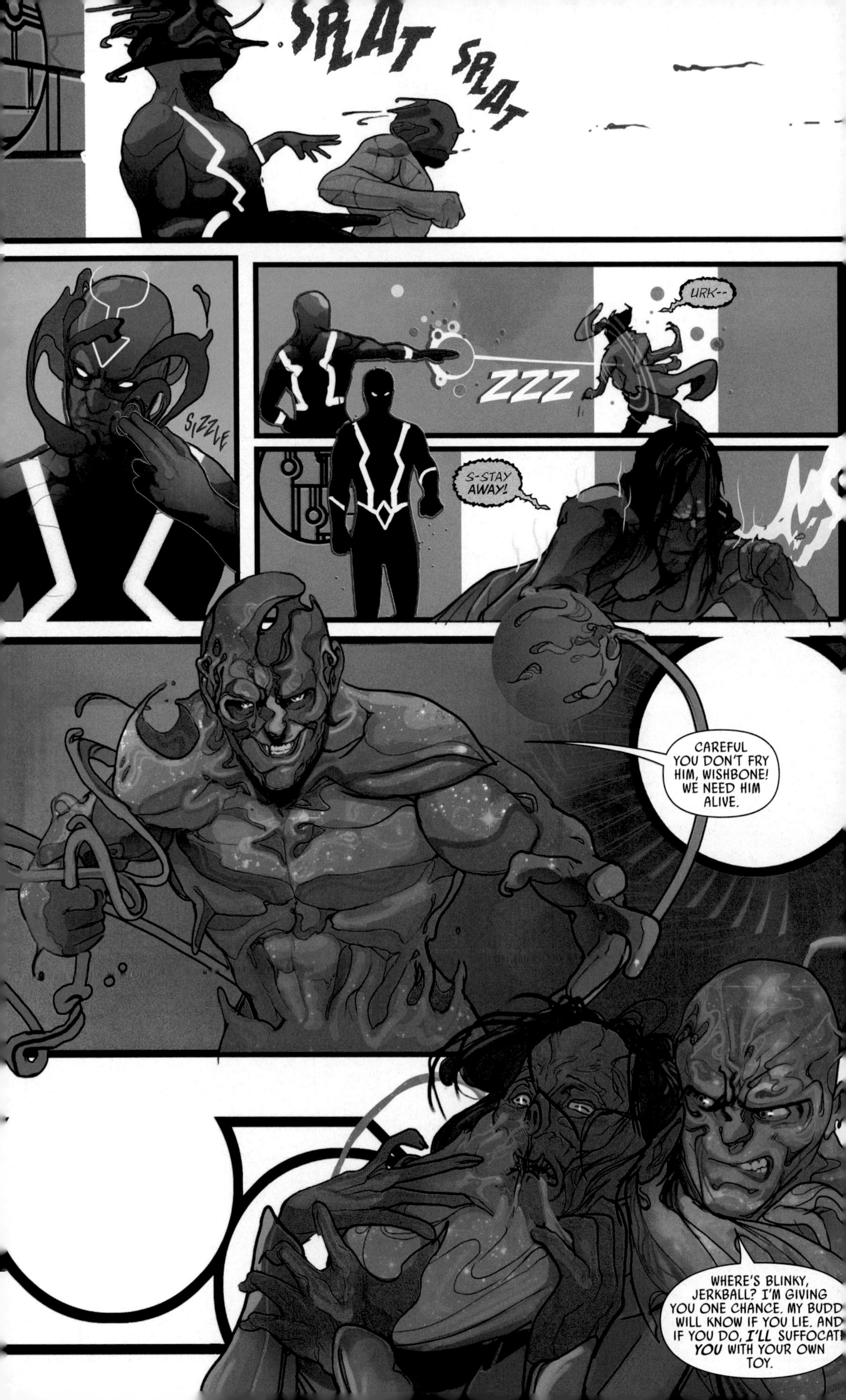
SRAT SRAT
SIZZLE
URK--
ZZZ
S-STAY AWAY!
CAREFUL YOU DON'T FRY HIM, WISHBONE! WE NEED HIM ALIVE.
WHERE'S BLINKY, JERKBALL? I'M GIVING YOU ONE CHANCE. MY BUDD WILL KNOW IF YOU LIE. AND IF YOU DO, I'LL SUFFOCAT YOU WITH YOUR OWN TOY.

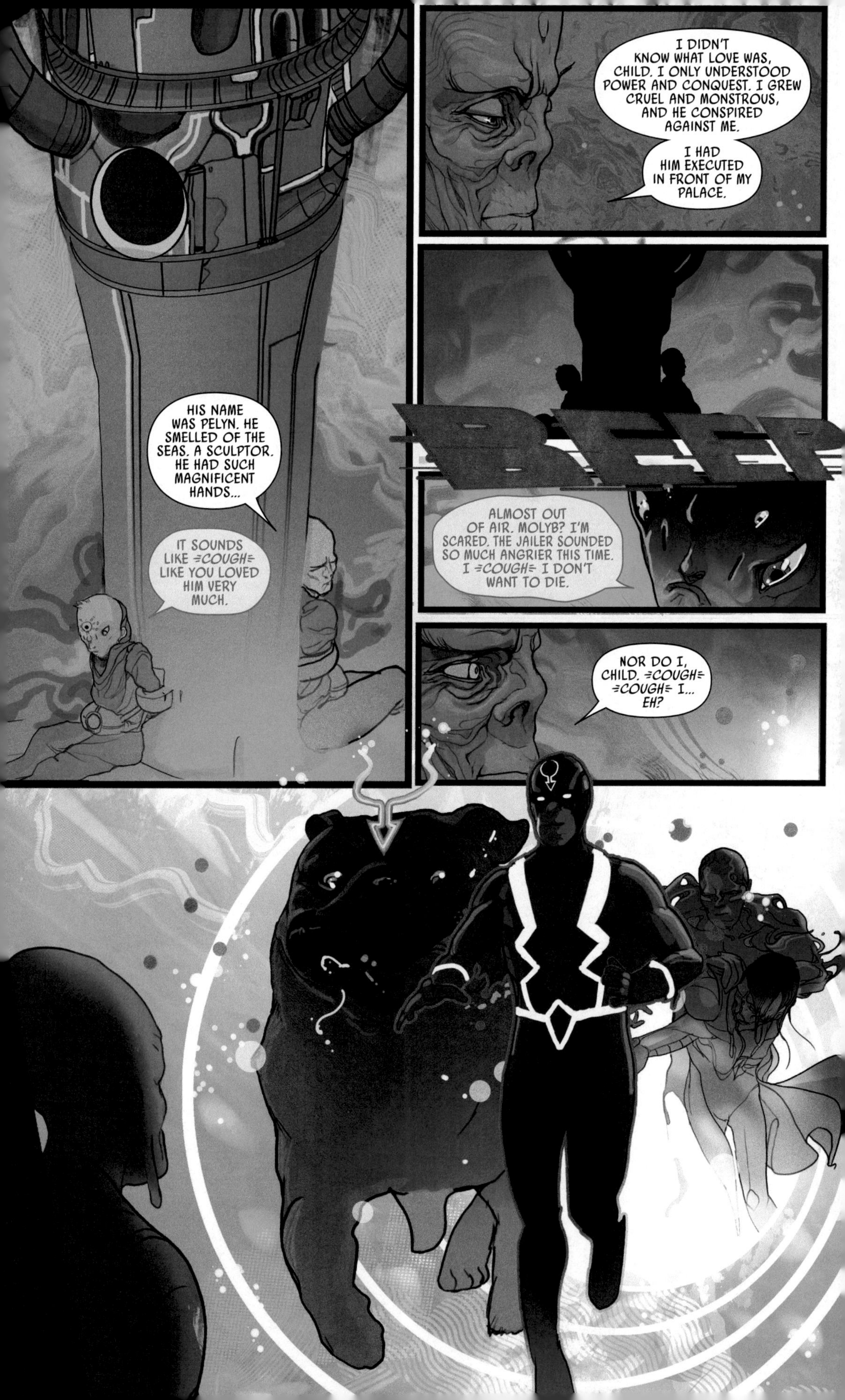
HIS NAME WAS PELYN. HE SMELLED OF THE SEAS. A SCULPTOR. HE HAD SUCH MAGNIFICENT HANDS...
IT SOUNDS LIKE =COUGH= LIKE YOU LOVED HIM VERY MUCH.
I DIDN'T KNOW WHAT LOVE WAS, CHILD. I ONLY UNDERSTOOD POWER AND CONQUEST. I GREW CRUEL AND MONSTROUS, AND HE CONSPIRED AGAINST ME.
I HAD HIM EXECUTED IN FRONT OF MY PALACE.
BEEP
ALMOST OUT OF AIR. MOLYB? I'M SCARED. THE JAILER SOUNDED SO MUCH ANGRIER THIS TIME. I =COUGH= I DON'T WANT TO DIE.
NOR DO I, CHILD. =COUGH= =COUGH= I... EH?

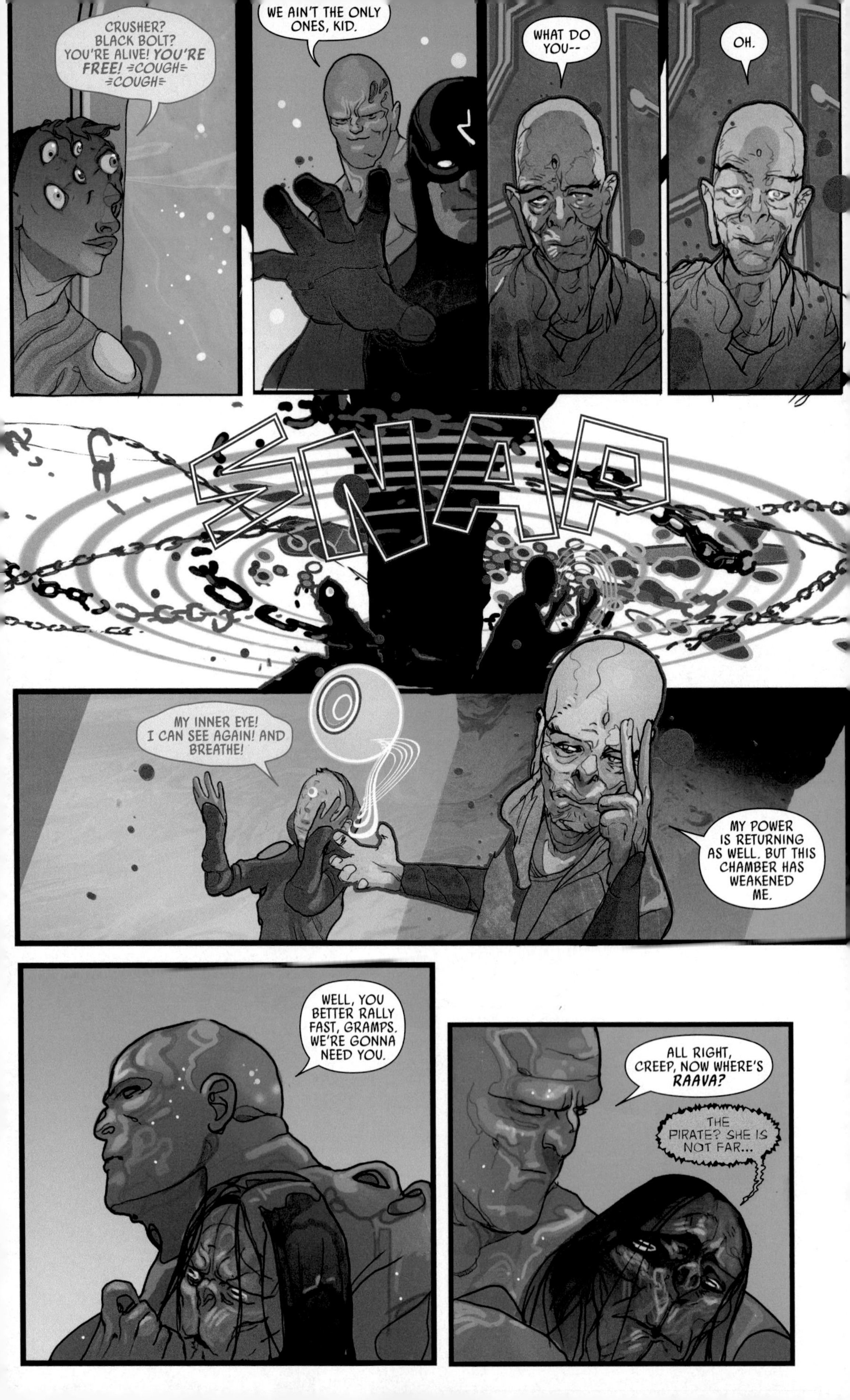
CRUSHER? BLACK BOLT? YOU'RE ALIVE! YOU'RE FREE! =COUGH= =COUGH=
WE AIN'T THE ONLY ONES, KID.
WHAT DO YOU--
OH.
SNAP
MY INNER EYE! I CAN SEE AGAIN! AND BREATHE!
MY POWER IS RETURNING AS WELL. BUT THIS CHAMBER HAS WEAKENED ME.
WELL, YOU BETTER RALLY FAST, GRAMPS. WE'RE GONNA NEED YOU.
ALL RIGHT, CREEP, NOW WHERE'S RAAVA?
THE PIRATE? SHE IS NOT FAR...

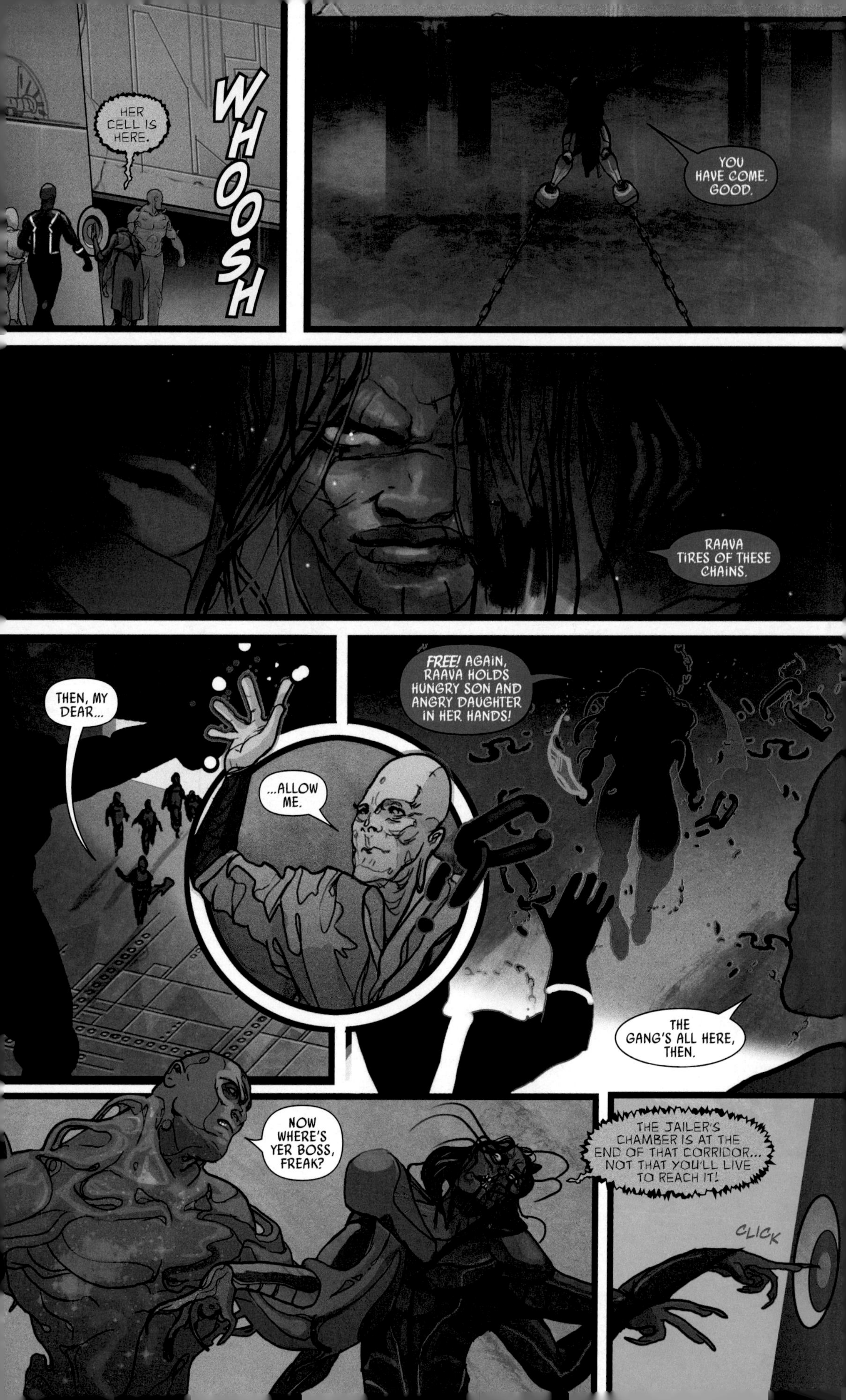
HER CELL IS HERE.
WHOOSH
YOU HAVE COME. GOOD.
RAAVA TIRES OF THESE CHAINS.
THEN, MY DEAR...
...ALLOW ME.
FREE! AGAIN, RAAVA HOLDS HUNGRY SON AND ANGRY DAUGHTER IN HER HANDS!
THE GANG'S ALL HERE, THEN.
NOW WHERE'S YER BOSS, FREAK?
THE JAILER'S CHAMBER IS AT THE END OF THAT CORRIDOR... NOT THAT YOU'LL LIVE TO REACH IT!
CLICK

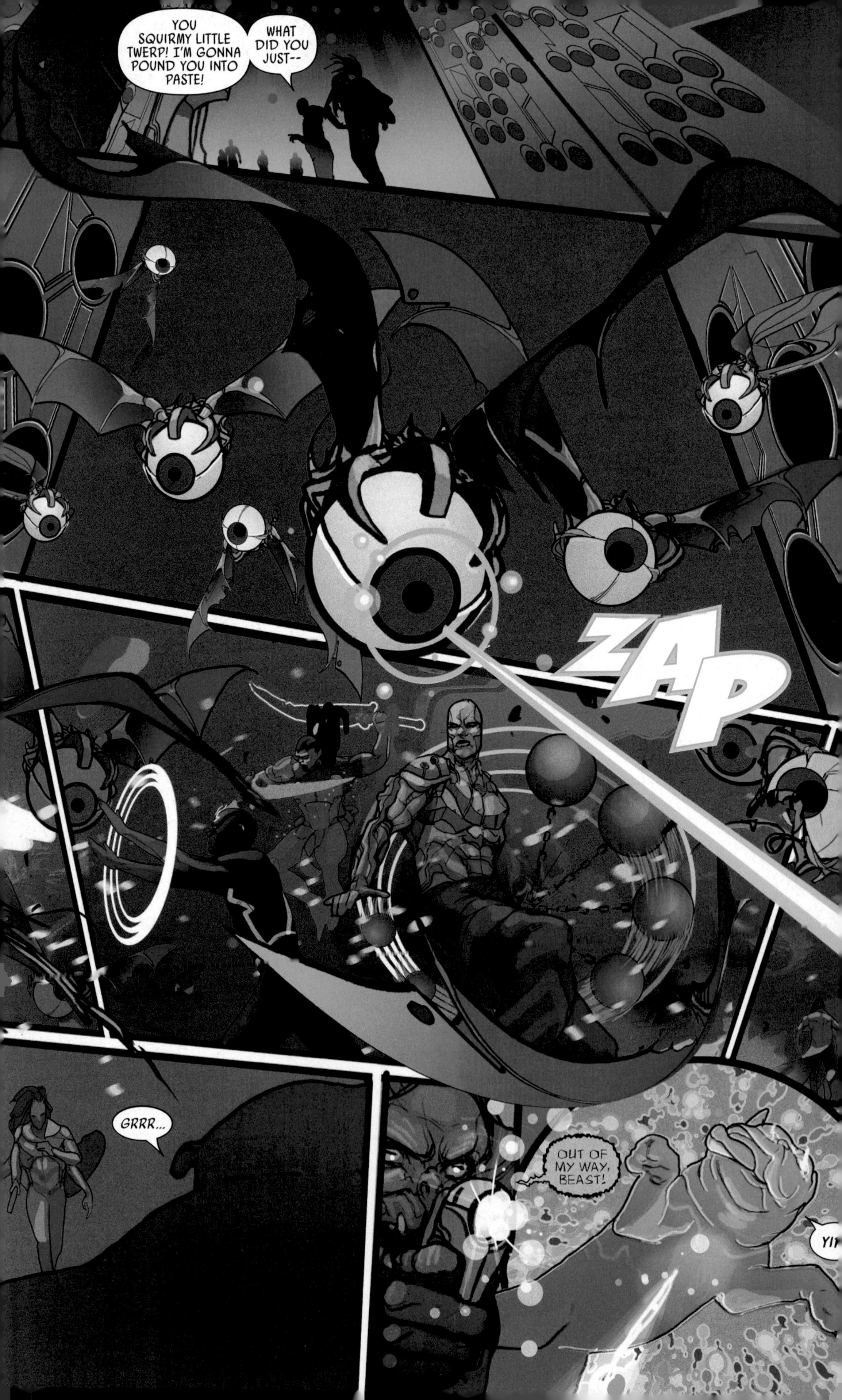
YOU SQUIRMY LITTLE TWERP! I'M GONNA POUND YOU INTO PASTE!
WHAT DID YOU JUST--
ZAP
GRRR...
OUT OF MY WAY, BEAST!

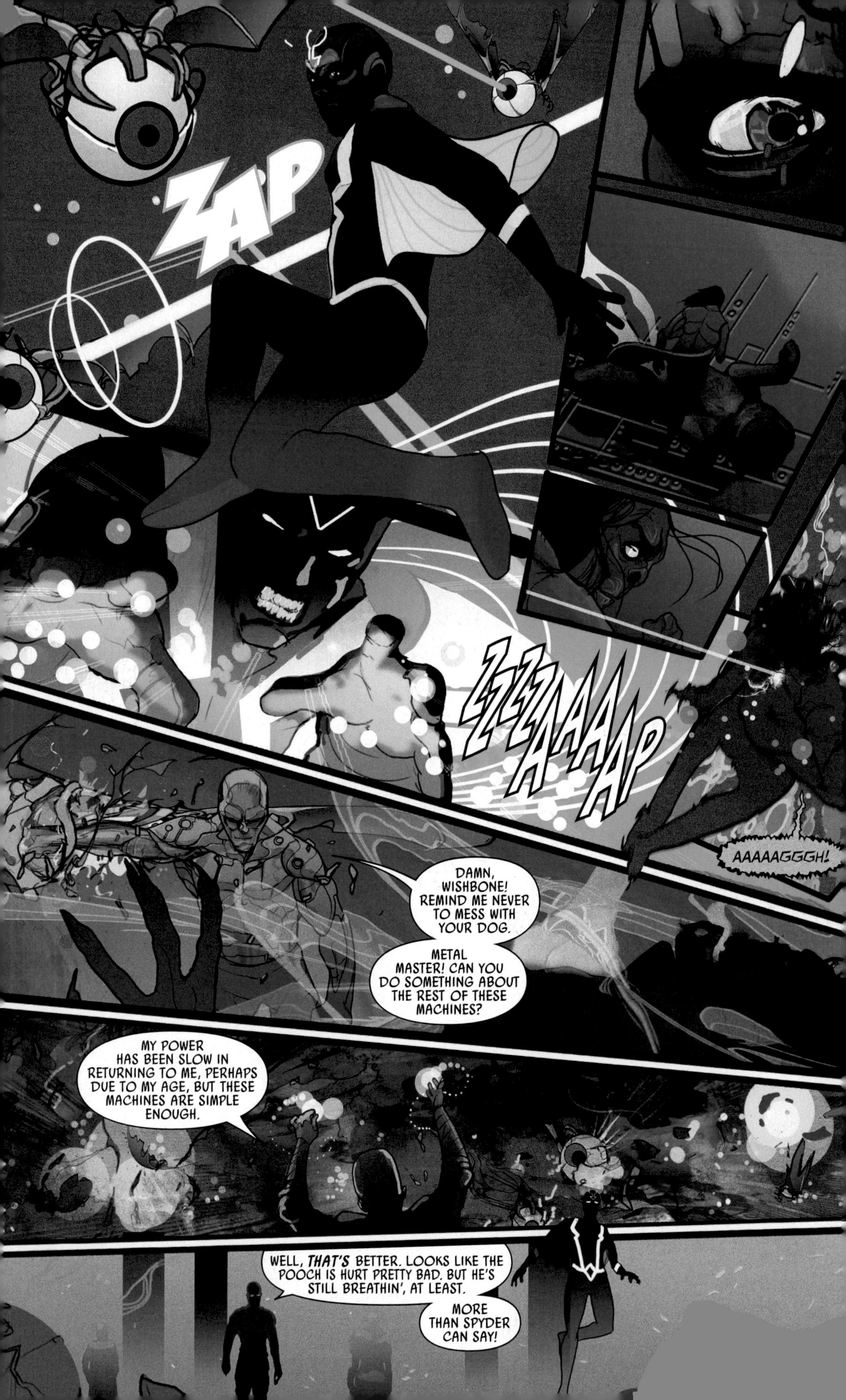
ZAP
ZZZAAAAAP
AAAAAGGGH!
DAMN, WISHBONE! REMIND ME NEVER TO MESS WITH YOUR DOG.
METAL MASTER! CAN YOU DO SOMETHING ABOUT THE REST OF THESE MACHINES?
MY POWER HAS BEEN SLOW IN RETURNING TO ME, PERHAPS DUE TO MY AGE, BUT THESE MACHINES ARE SIMPLE ENOUGH.
WELL, *THAT'S* BETTER. LOOKS LIKE THE POOCH IS HURT PRETTY BAD. BUT HE'S STILL BREATHIN', AT LEAST.
MORE THAN SPYDER CAN SAY!

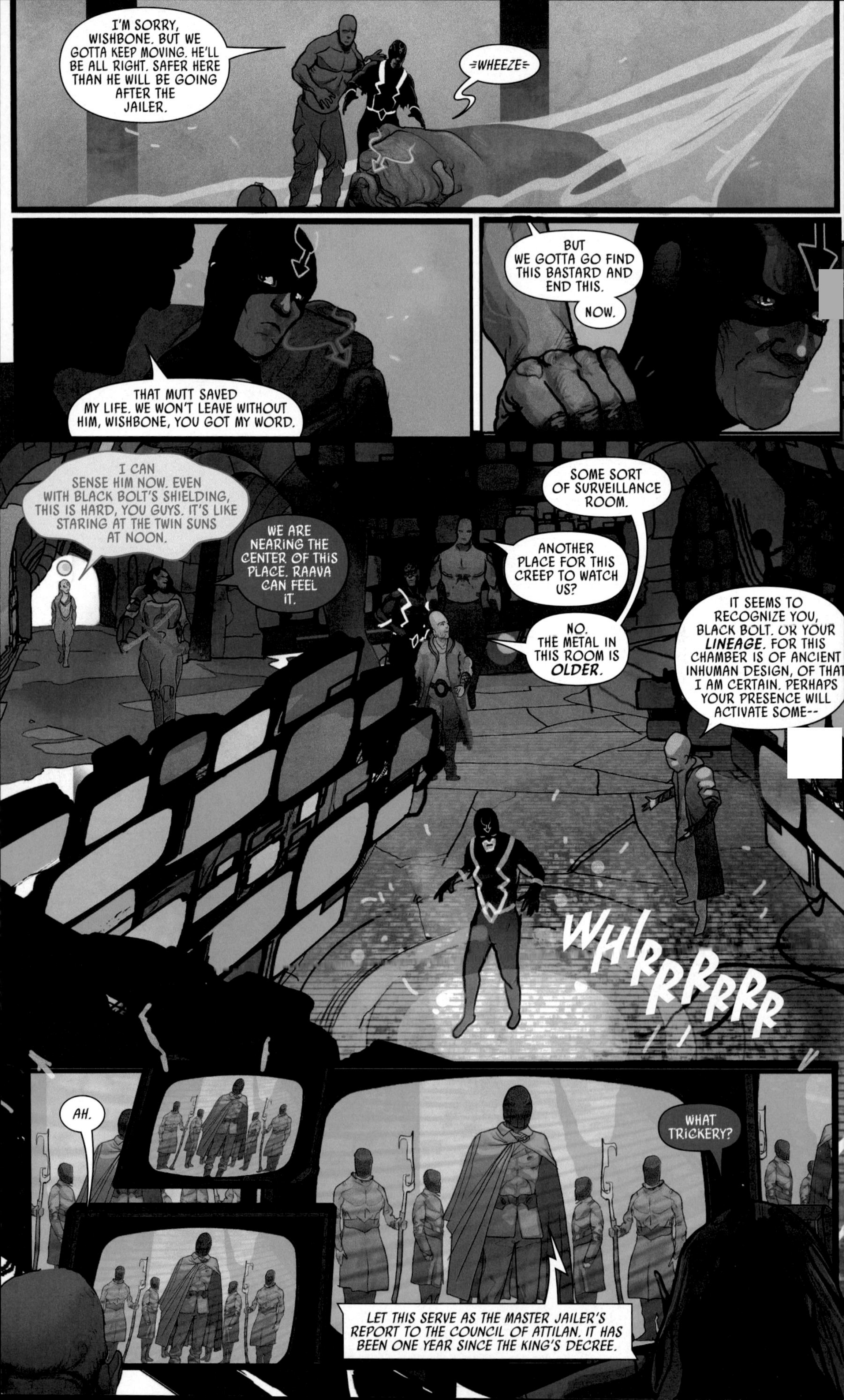
I'M SORRY, WISHBONE. BUT WE GOTTA KEEP MOVING. HE'LL BE ALL RIGHT. SAFER HERE THAN HE WILL BE GOING AFTER THE JAILER.
=WHEEZE=
THAT MUTT SAVED MY LIFE. WE WON'T LEAVE WITHOUT HIM, WISHBONE, YOU GOT MY WORD.
BUT WE GOTTA GO FIND THIS BASTARD AND END THIS.
NOW.
I CAN SENSE HIM NOW. EVEN WITH BLACK BOLT'S SHIELDING, THIS IS HARD, YOU GUYS. IT'S LIKE STARING AT THE TWIN SUNS AT NOON.
WE ARE NEARING THE CENTER OF THIS PLACE. RAAVA CAN FEEL IT.
SOME SORT OF SURVEILLANCE ROOM.
ANOTHER PLACE FOR THIS CREEP TO WATCH US?
NO. THE METAL IN THIS ROOM IS OLDER.
IT SEEMS TO RECOGNIZE YOU, BLACK BOLT. OR YOUR LINEAGE. FOR THIS CHAMBER IS OF ANCIENT INHUMAN DESIGN, OF THAT I AM CERTAIN. PERHAPS YOUR PRESENCE WILL ACTIVATE SOME--
WHIRRRRRR
AH.
WHAT TRICKERY?
LET THIS SERVE AS THE MASTER JAILER'S REPORT TO THE COUNCIL OF ATTILAN. IT HAS BEEN ONE YEAR SINCE THE KING'S DECREE.

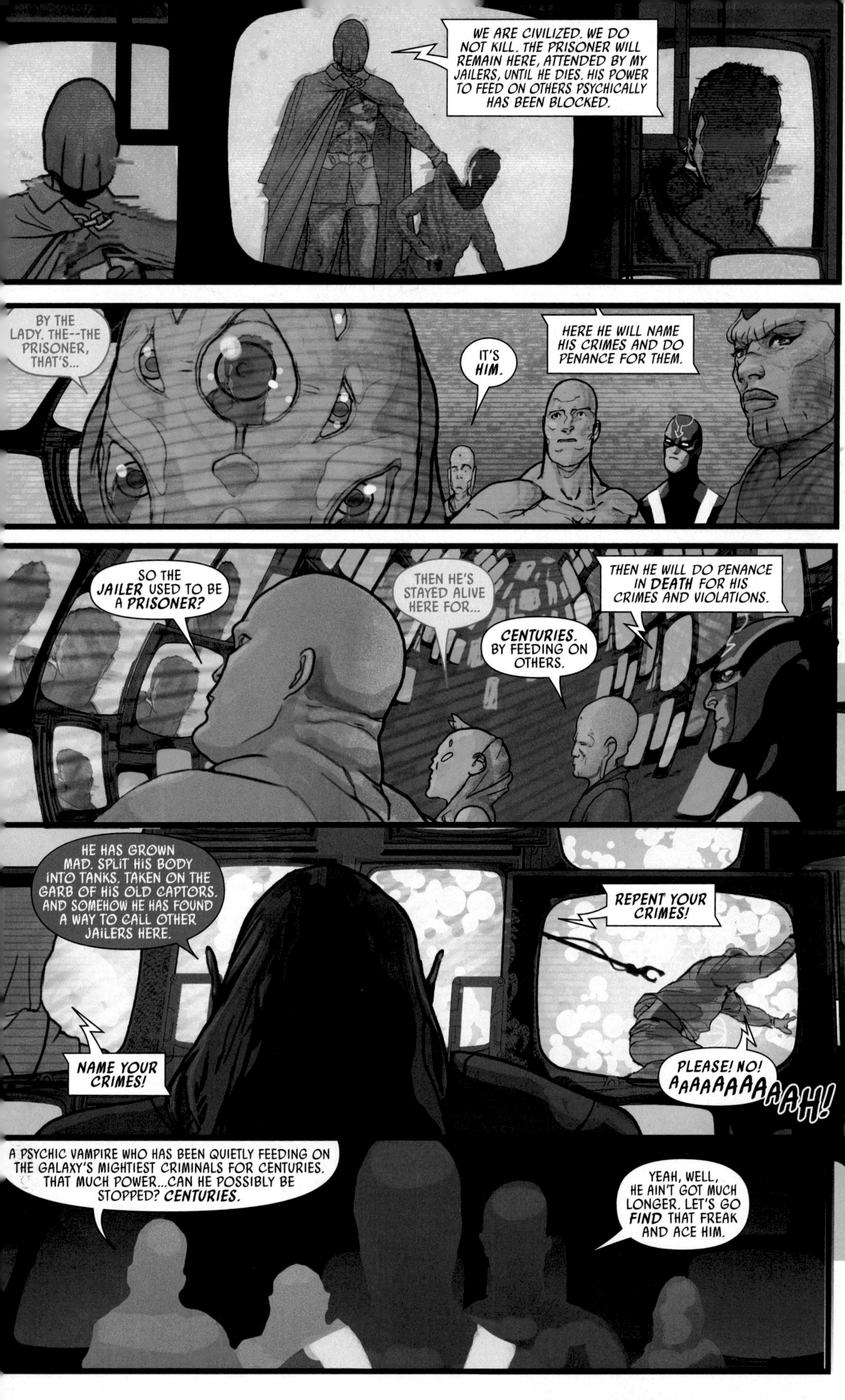
WE ARE CIVILIZED. WE DO NOT KILL. THE PRISONER WILL REMAIN HERE, ATTENDED BY MY JAILERS, UNTIL HE DIES. HIS POWER TO FEED ON OTHERS PSYCHICALLY HAS BEEN BLOCKED.
BY THE LADY. THE--THE PRISONER, THAT'S...
IT'S HIM.
HERE HE WILL NAME HIS CRIMES AND DO PENANCE FOR THEM.
SO THE JAILER USED TO BE A PRISONER?
THEN HE'S STAYED ALIVE HERE FOR...
CENTURIES. BY FEEDING ON OTHERS.
THEN HE WILL DO PENANCE IN DEATH FOR HIS CRIMES AND VIOLATIONS.
HE HAS GROWN MAD, SPLIT HIS BODY INTO TANKS, TAKEN ON THE GARB OF HIS OLD CAPTORS. AND SOMEHOW HE HAS FOUND A WAY TO CALL OTHER JAILERS HERE.
NAME YOUR CRIMES!
REPENT YOUR CRIMES!
PLEASE! NO! AAAAAAAAAAH!
A PSYCHIC VAMPIRE WHO HAS BEEN QUIETLY FEEDING ON THE GALAXY'S MIGHTIEST CRIMINALS FOR CENTURIES. THAT MUCH POWER...CAN HE POSSIBLY BE STOPPED? CENTURIES.
YEAH, WELL, HE AIN'T GOT MUCH LONGER. LET'S GO FIND THAT FREAK AND ACE HIM.

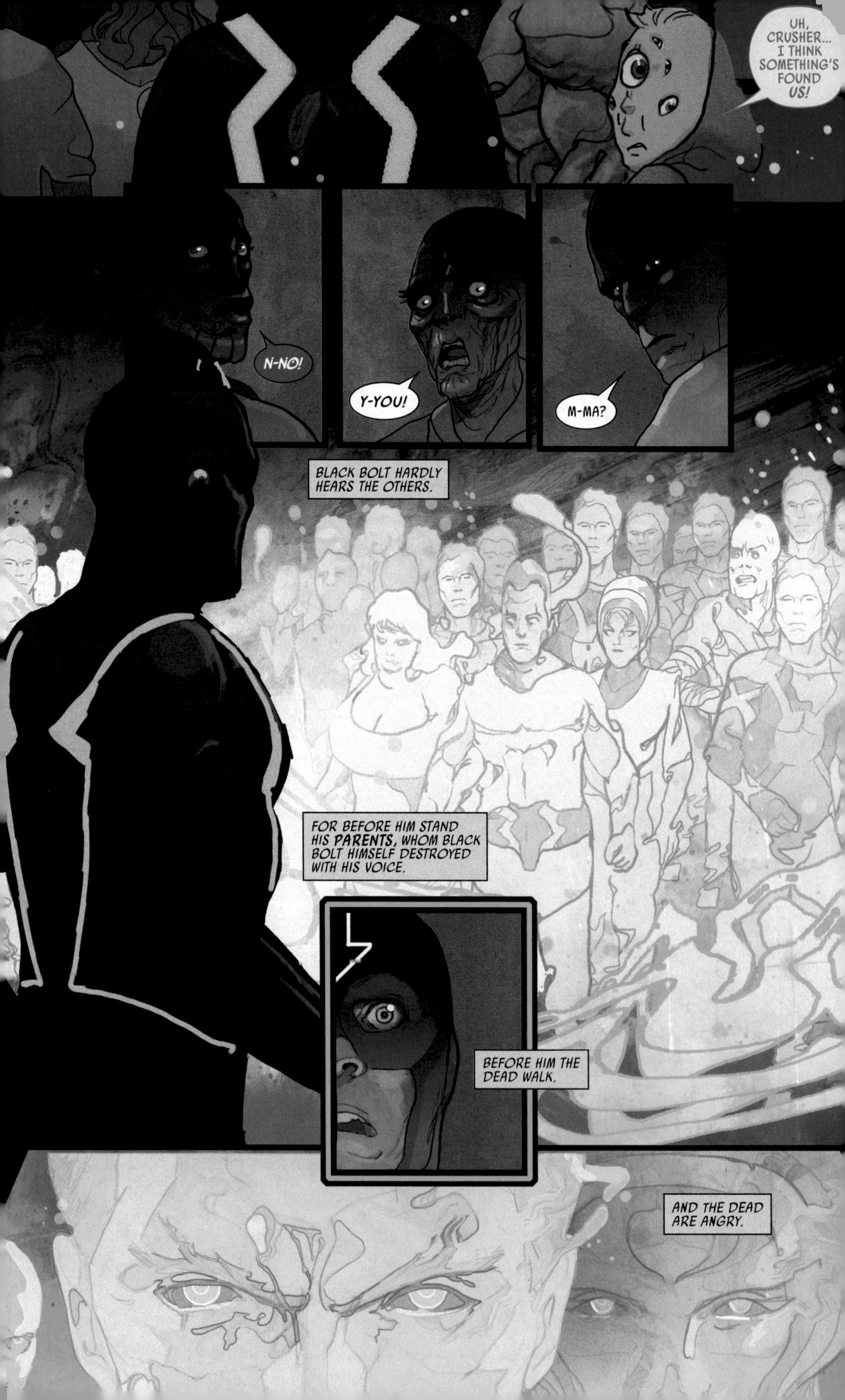
UH, CRUSHER... I THINK SOMETHING'S FOUND US!
N-NO!
Y-YOU!
M-MA?
BLACK BOLT HARDLY HEARS THE OTHERS.
FOR BEFORE HIM STAND HIS PARENTS, WHOM BLACK BOLT HIMSELF DESTROYED WITH HIS VOICE.
BEFORE HIM THE DEAD WALK.
AND THE DEAD ARE ANGRY.

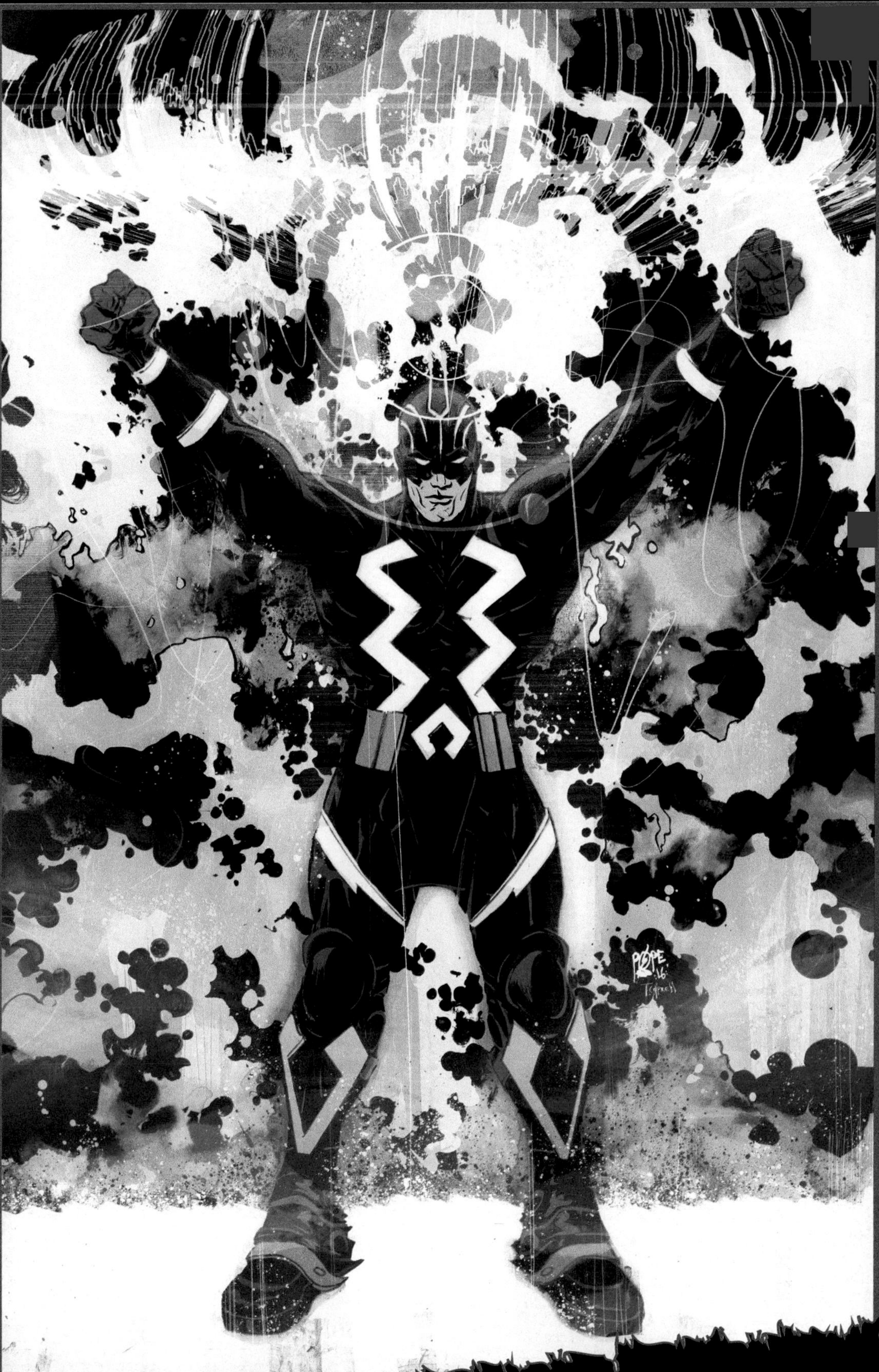

#1 VARIANT BY PAUL POPE & TOBY CYPRESS

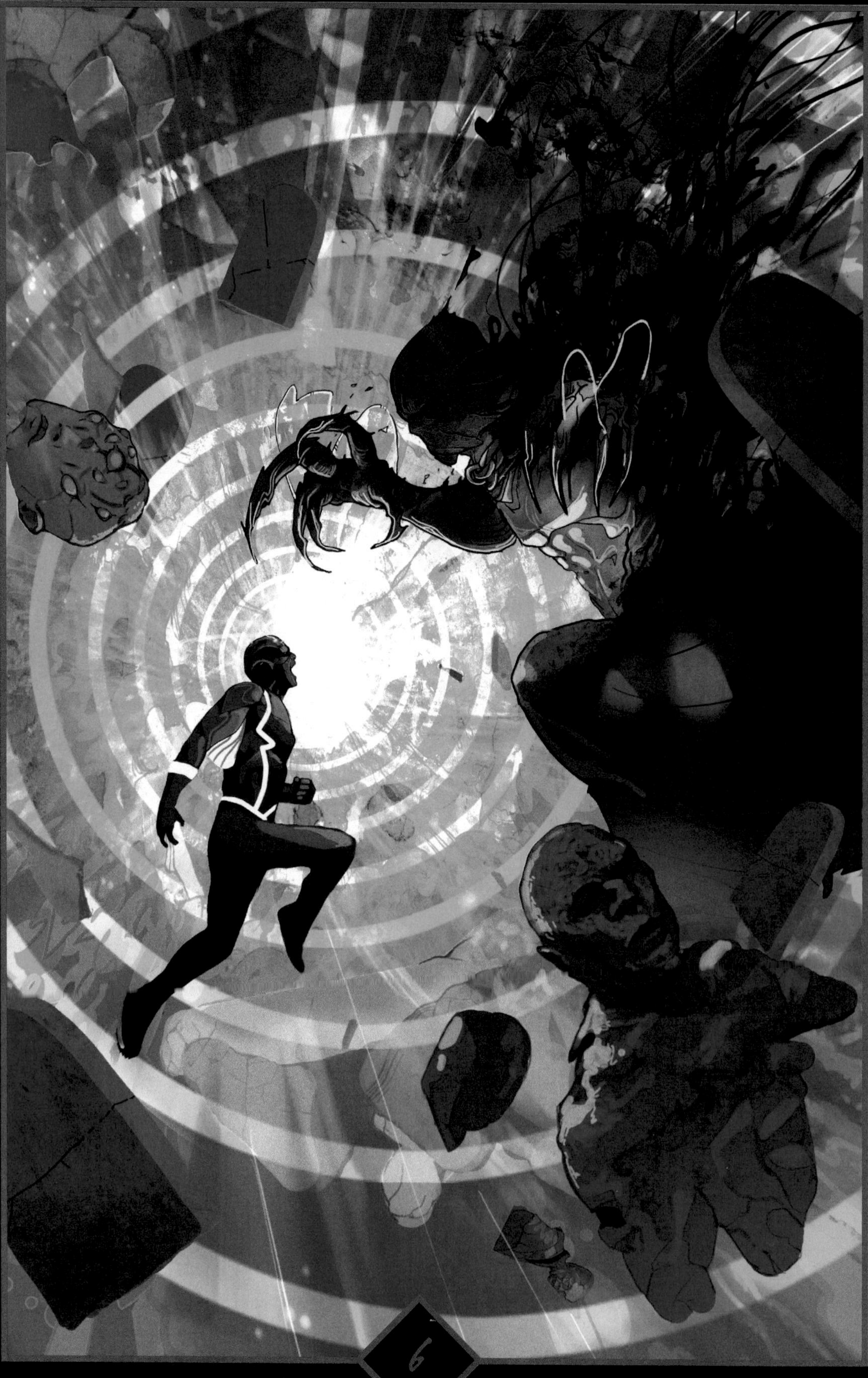

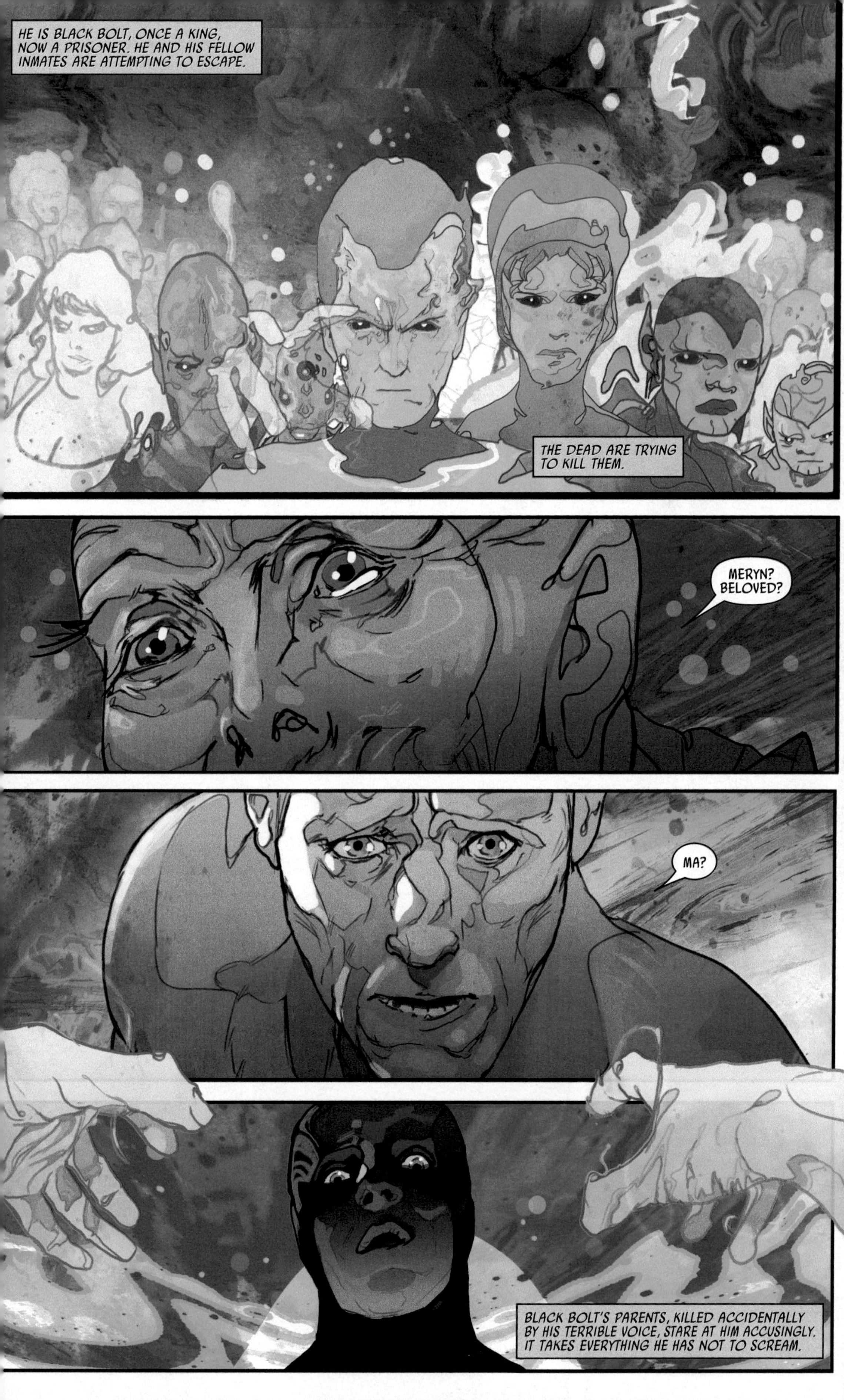
HE IS BLACK BOLT, ONCE A KING, NOW A PRISONER. HE AND HIS FELLOW INMATES ARE ATTEMPTING TO ESCAPE.
THE DEAD ARE TRYING TO KILL THEM.
MERYN? BELOVED?
MA?
BLACK BOLT'S PARENTS, KILLED ACCIDENTALLY BY HIS TERRIBLE VOICE, STARE AT HIM ACCUSINGLY. IT TAKES EVERYTHING HE HAS NOT TO SCREAM.

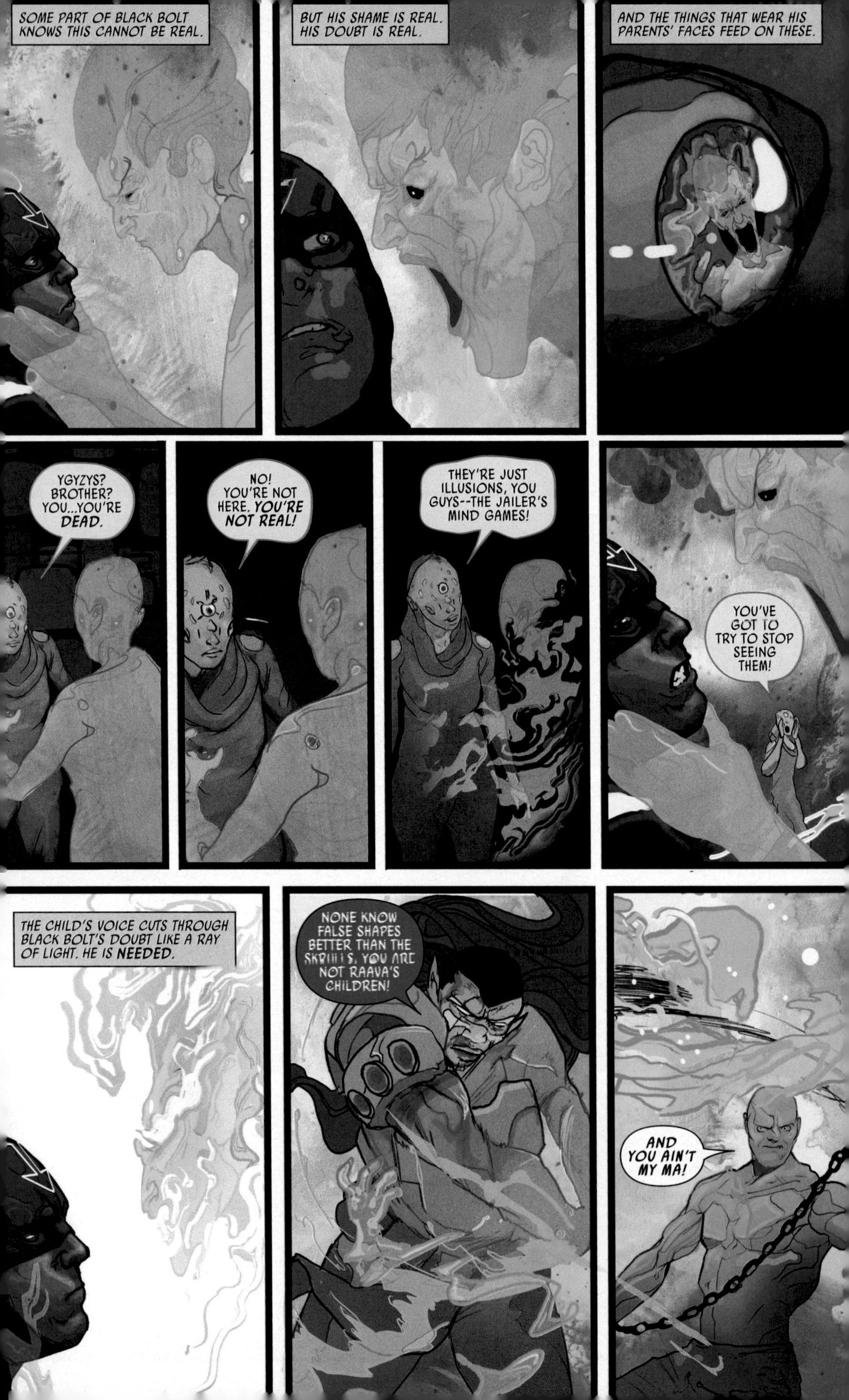
SOME PART OF BLACK BOLT KNOWS THIS CANNOT BE REAL.
BUT HIS SHAME IS REAL. HIS DOUBT IS REAL.
AND THE THINGS THAT WEAR HIS PARENTS' FACES FEED ON THESE.
YGYZYS? BROTHER? YOU...YOU'RE DEAD.
NO! YOU'RE NOT HERE. YOU'RE NOT REAL!
THEY'RE JUST ILLUSIONS, YOU GUYS--THE JAILER'S MIND GAMES!
YOU'VE GOT TO TRY TO STOP SEEING THEM!
THE CHILD'S VOICE CUTS THROUGH BLACK BOLT'S DOUBT LIKE A RAY OF LIGHT. HE IS NEEDED.
NONE KNOW FALSE SHAPES BETTER THAN THE SKRULLS. YOU ARE NOT RAAVA'S CHILDREN!
AND YOU AIN'T MY MA!

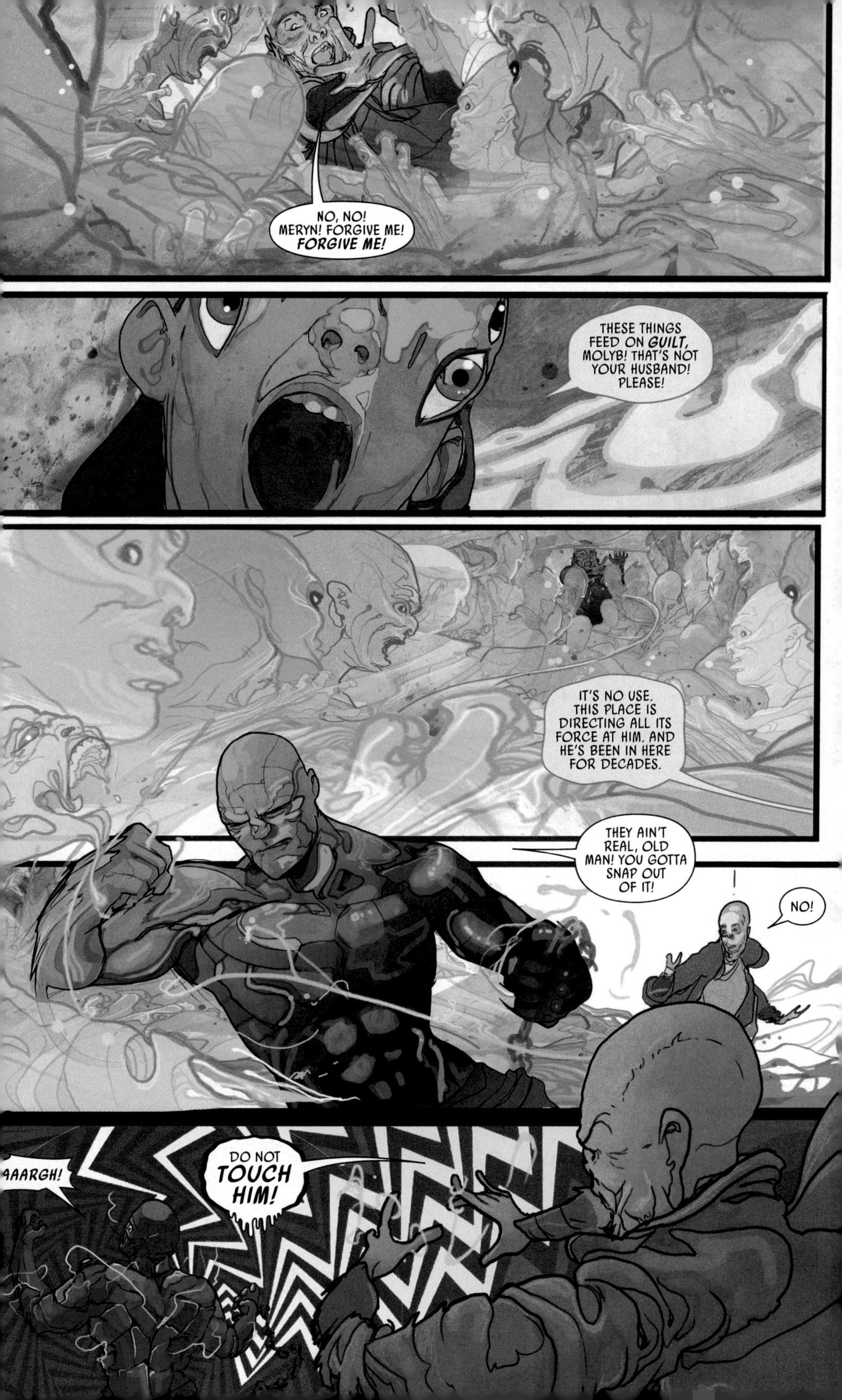
NO, NO!
MERYN! FORGIVE ME!
FORGIVE ME!
THESE THINGS FEED ON GUILT, MOLYB! THAT'S NOT YOUR HUSBAND! PLEASE!
IT'S NO USE. THIS PLACE IS DIRECTING ALL ITS FORCE AT HIM. AND HE'S BEEN IN HERE FOR DECADES.
THEY AIN'T REAL, OLD MAN! YOU GOTTA SNAP OUT OF IT!
!
NO!
AAARGH!
DO NOT TOUCH HIM!

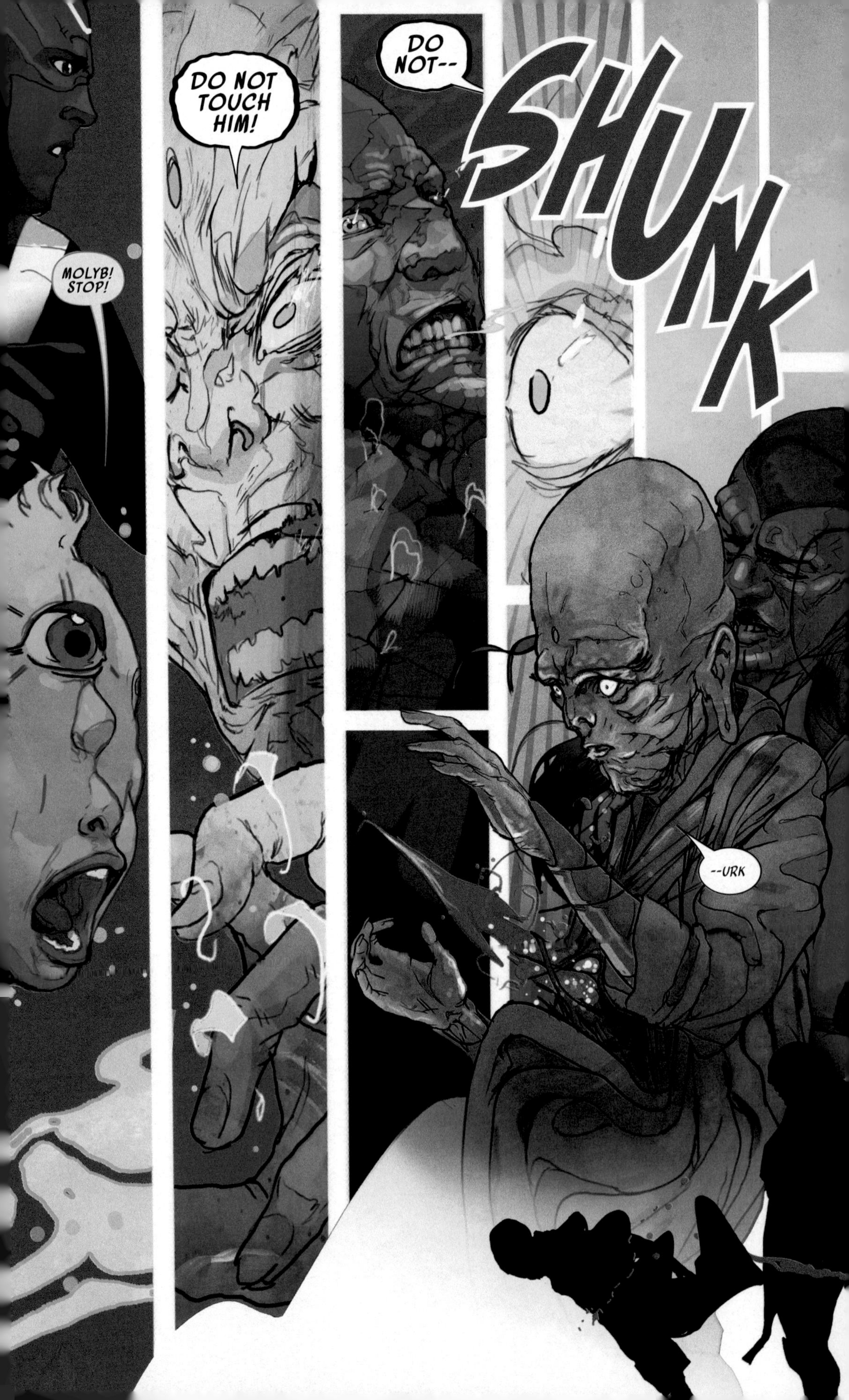
MOLYB! STOP!
DO NOT TOUCH HIM!
DO NOT--
SHUNK
--URK

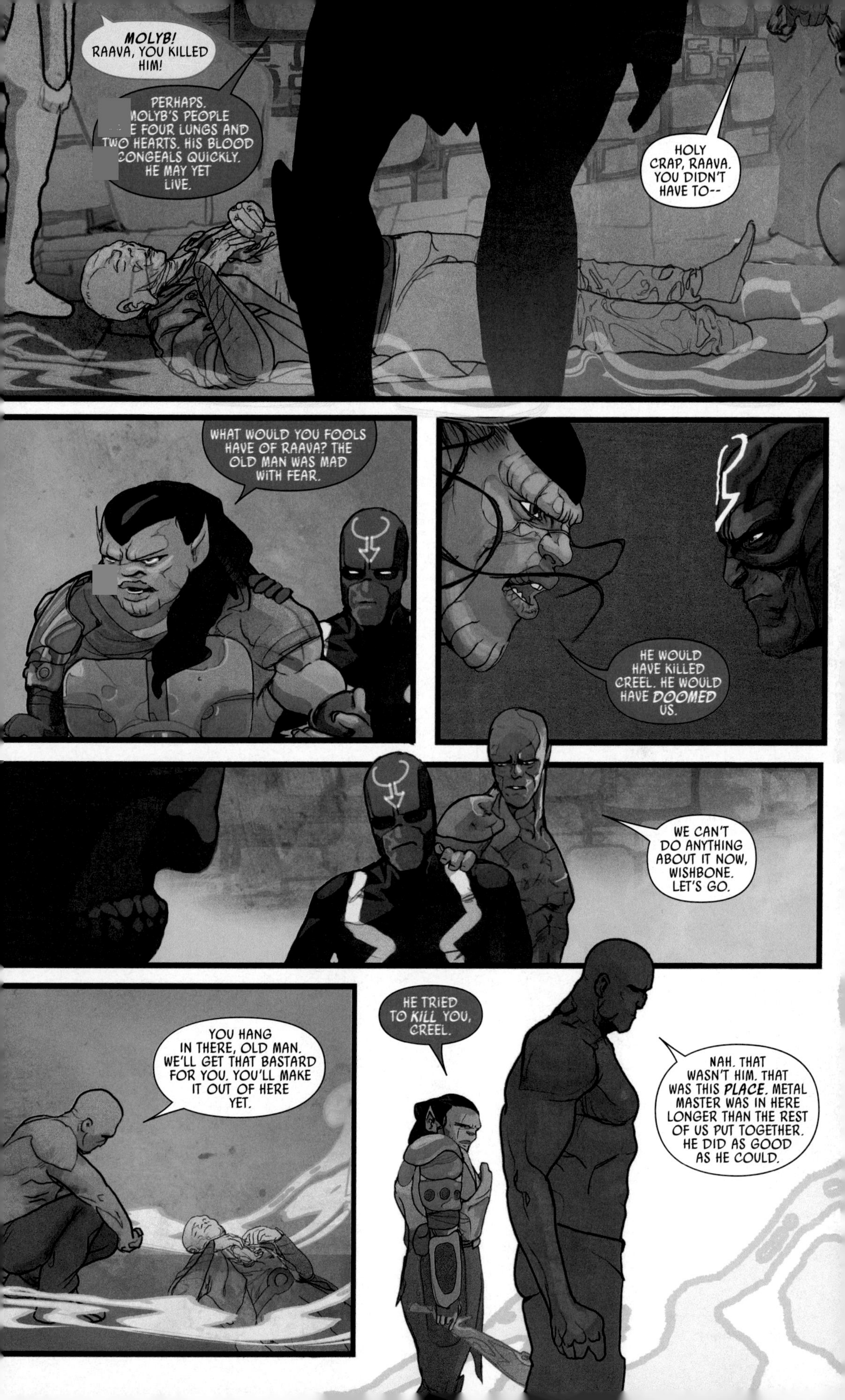
MOLYB! RAAVA, YOU KILLED HIM!
PERHAPS. MOLYB'S PEOPLE E FOUR LUNGS AND TWO HEARTS. HIS BLOOD CONGEALS QUICKLY. HE MAY YET LIVE.
HOLY CRAP, RAAVA. YOU DIDN'T HAVE TO--
WHAT WOULD YOU FOOLS HAVE OF RAAVA? THE OLD MAN WAS MAD WITH FEAR.
HE WOULD HAVE KILLED CREEL. HE WOULD HAVE DOOMED US.
WE CAN'T DO ANYTHING ABOUT IT NOW, WISHBONE. LET'S GO.
YOU HANG IN THERE, OLD MAN. WE'LL GET THAT BASTARD FOR YOU. YOU'LL MAKE IT OUT OF HERE YET.
HE TRIED TO KILL YOU, CREEL.
NAH. THAT WASN'T HIM. THAT WAS THIS PLACE. METAL MASTER WAS IN HERE LONGER THAN THE REST OF US PUT TOGETHER. HE DID AS GOOD AS HE COULD.

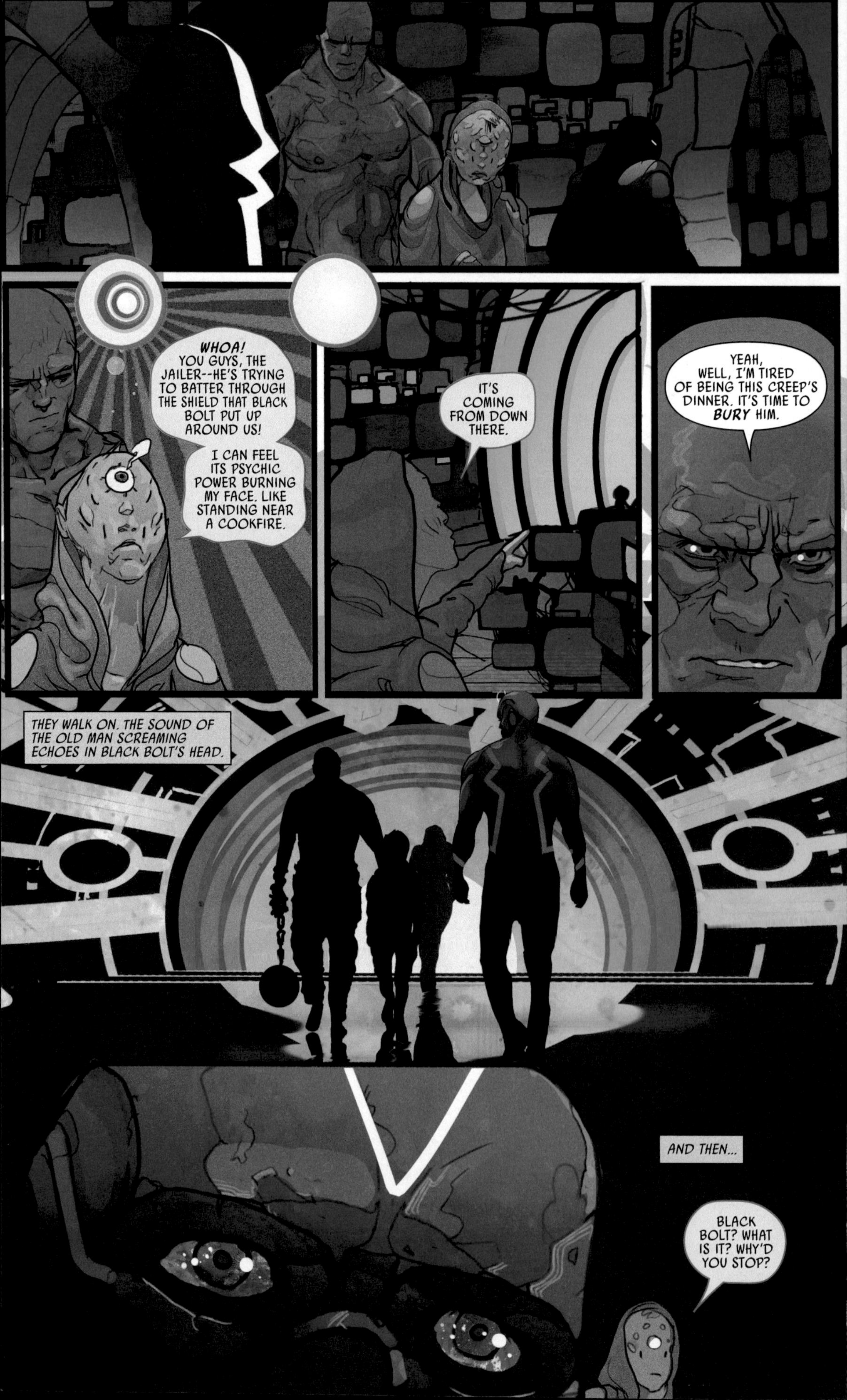
WHOA! YOU GUYS, THE JAILER--HE'S TRYING TO BATTER THROUGH THE SHIELD THAT BLACK BOLT PUT UP AROUND US!
I CAN FEEL ITS PSYCHIC POWER BURNING MY FACE. LIKE STANDING NEAR A COOKFIRE.
IT'S COMING FROM DOWN THERE.
YEAH, WELL, I'M TIRED OF BEING THIS CREEP'S DINNER. IT'S TIME TO BURY HIM.
THEY WALK ON. THE SOUND OF THE OLD MAN SCREAMING ECHOES IN BLACK BOLT'S HEAD.
AND THEN...
BLACK BOLT? WHAT IS IT? WHY'D YOU STOP?

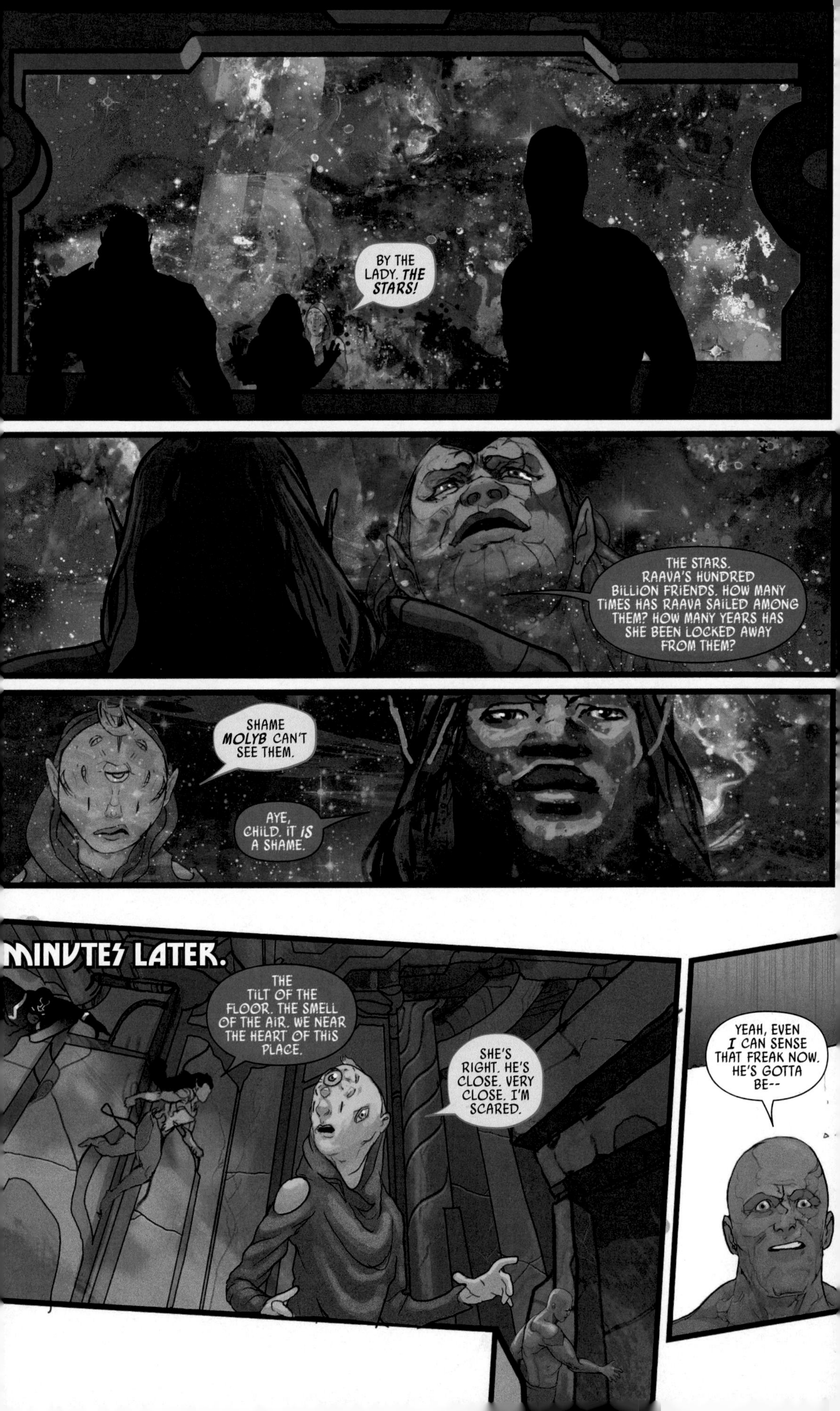
BY THE LADY. THE STARS!
THE STARS. RAAVA'S HUNDRED BILLION FRIENDS. HOW MANY TIMES HAS RAAVA SAILED AMONG THEM? HOW MANY YEARS HAS SHE BEEN LOCKED AWAY FROM THEM?
SHAME MOLYB CAN'T SEE THEM.
AYE, CHILD. IT IS A SHAME.
MINUTES LATER.
THE TILT OF THE FLOOR. THE SMELL OF THE AIR. WE NEAR THE HEART OF THIS PLACE.
SHE'S RIGHT. HE'S CLOSE. VERY CLOSE. I'M SCARED.
YEAH, EVEN I CAN SENSE THAT FREAK NOW. HE'S GOTTA BE--

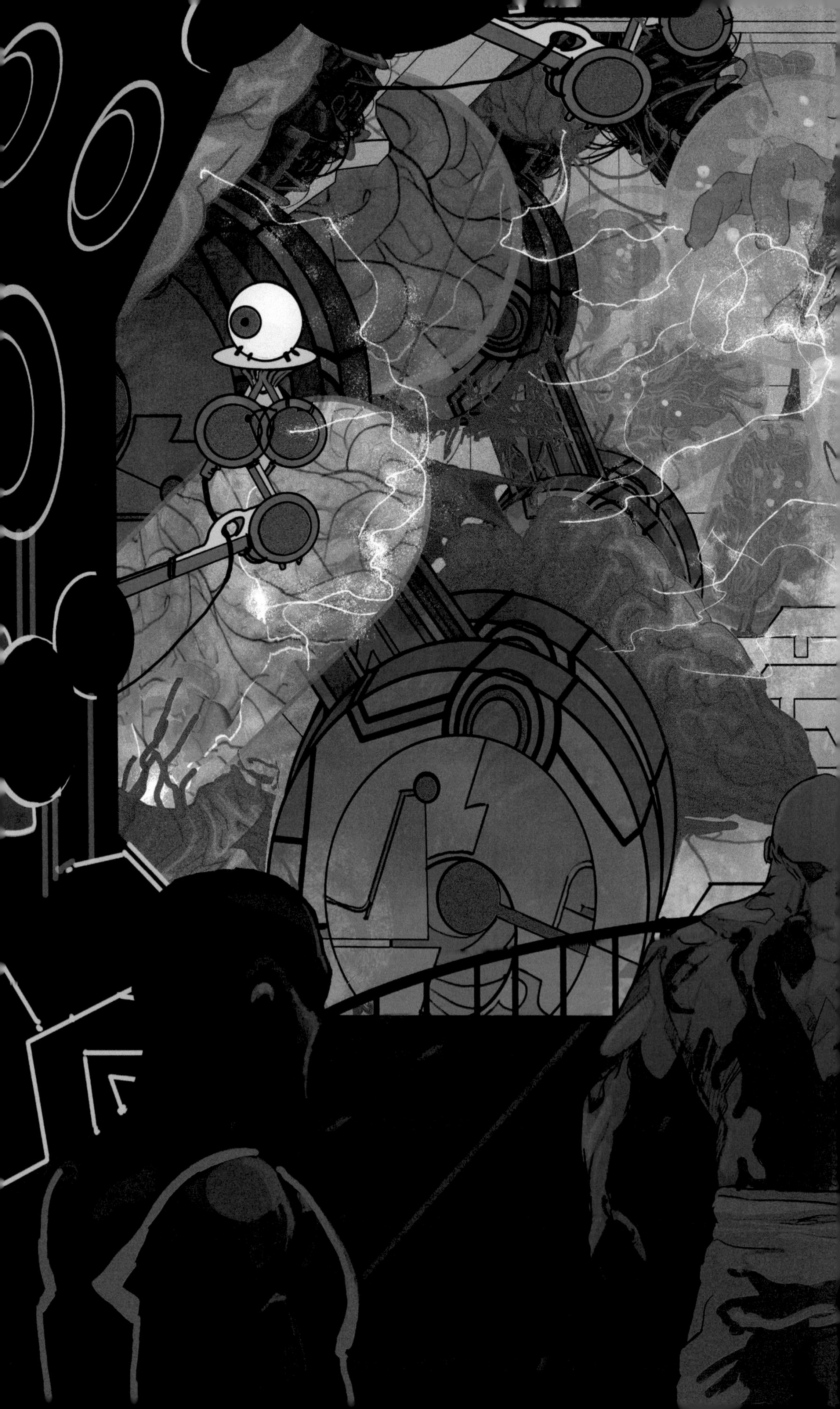

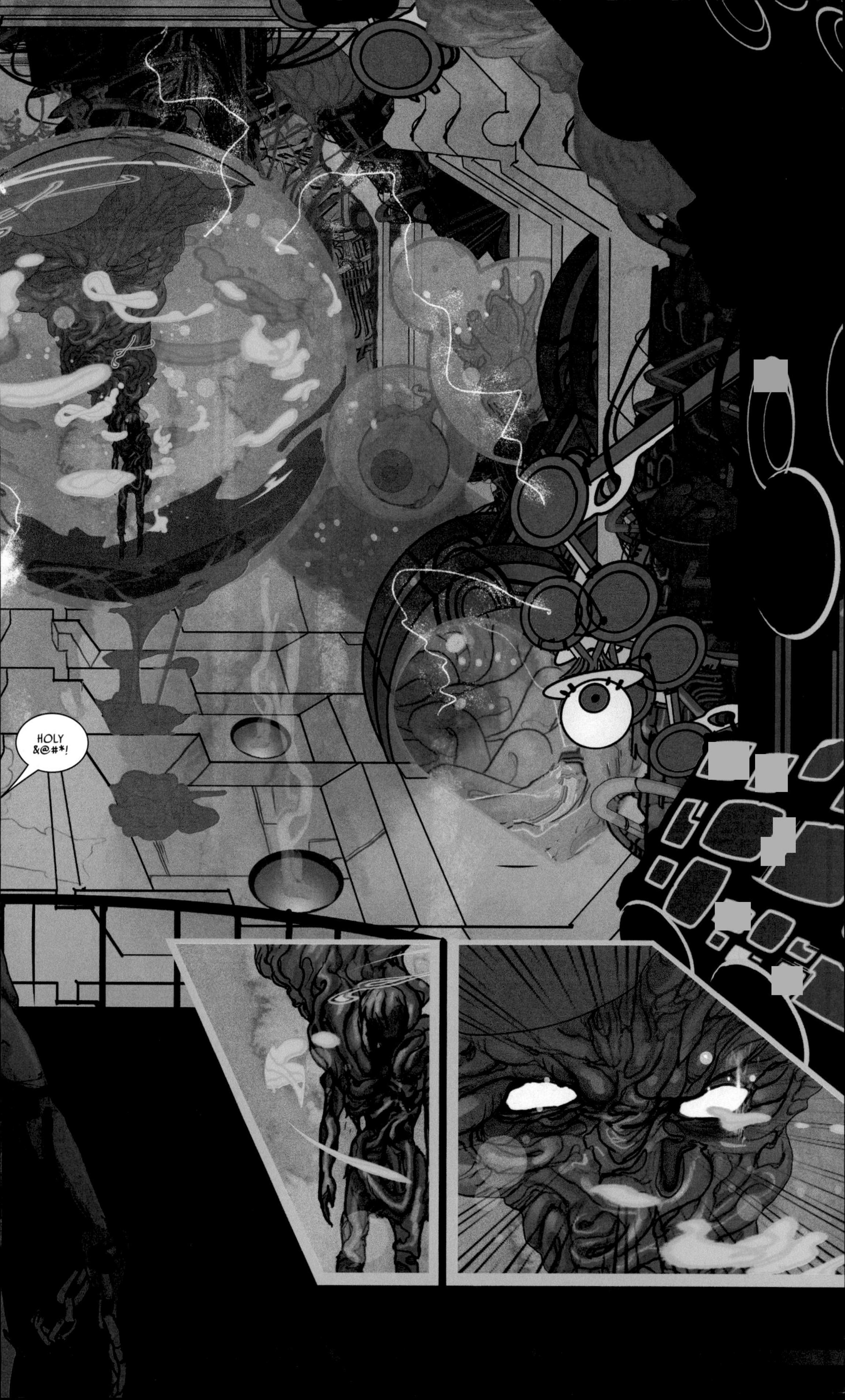
HOLY &@#*!

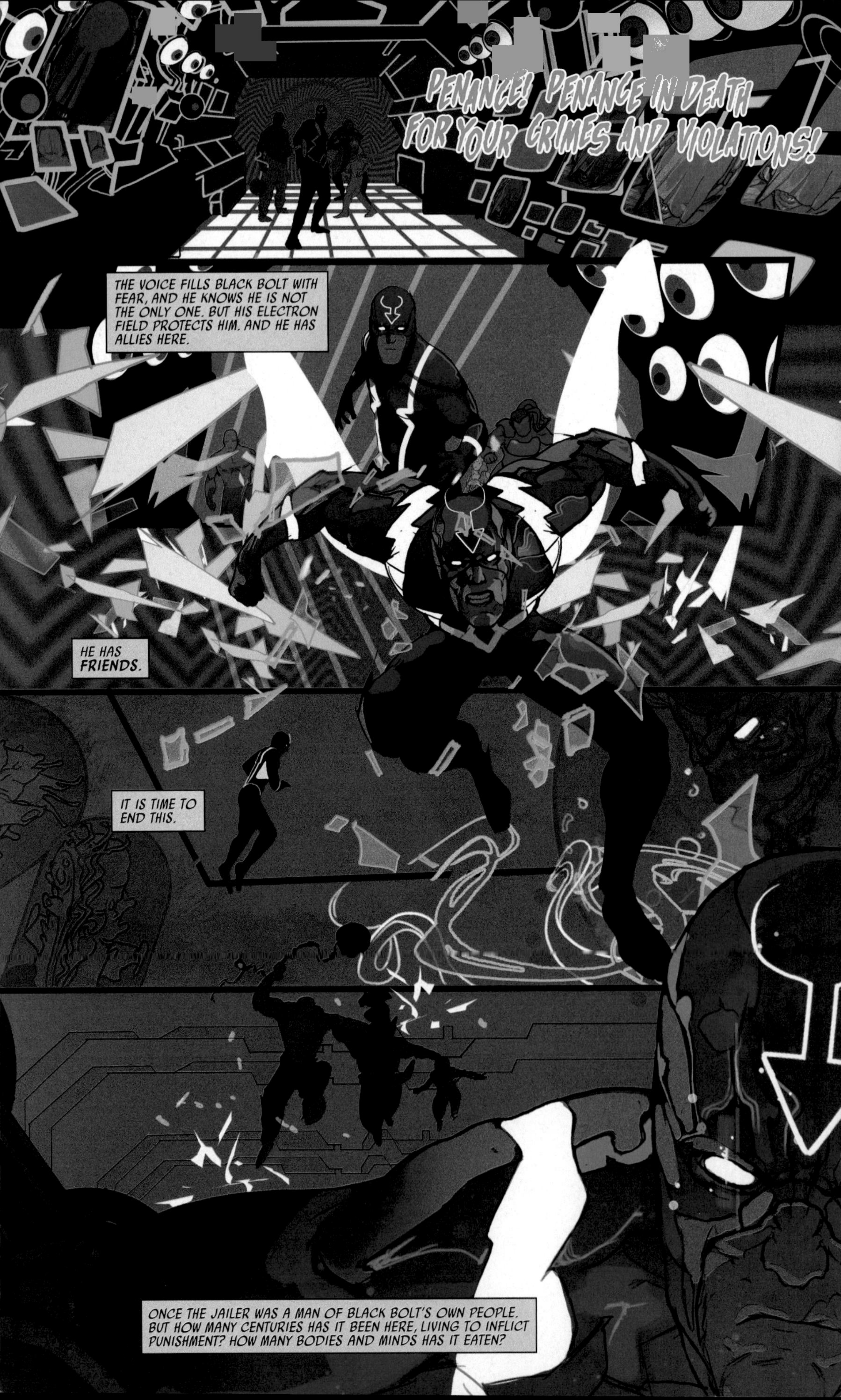
PENANCE! PENANCE IN DEATH FOR YOUR CRIMES AND VIOLATIONS!
THE VOICE FILLS BLACK BOLT WITH FEAR, AND HE KNOWS HE IS NOT THE ONLY ONE. BUT HIS ELECTRON FIELD PROTECTS HIM. AND HE HAS ALLIES HERE.
HE HAS FRIENDS.
IT IS TIME TO END THIS.
ONCE THE JAILER WAS A MAN OF BLACK BOLT'S OWN PEOPLE. BUT HOW MANY CENTURIES HAS IT BEEN HERE, LIVING TO INFLICT PUNISHMENT? HOW MANY BODIES AND MINDS HAS IT EATEN?

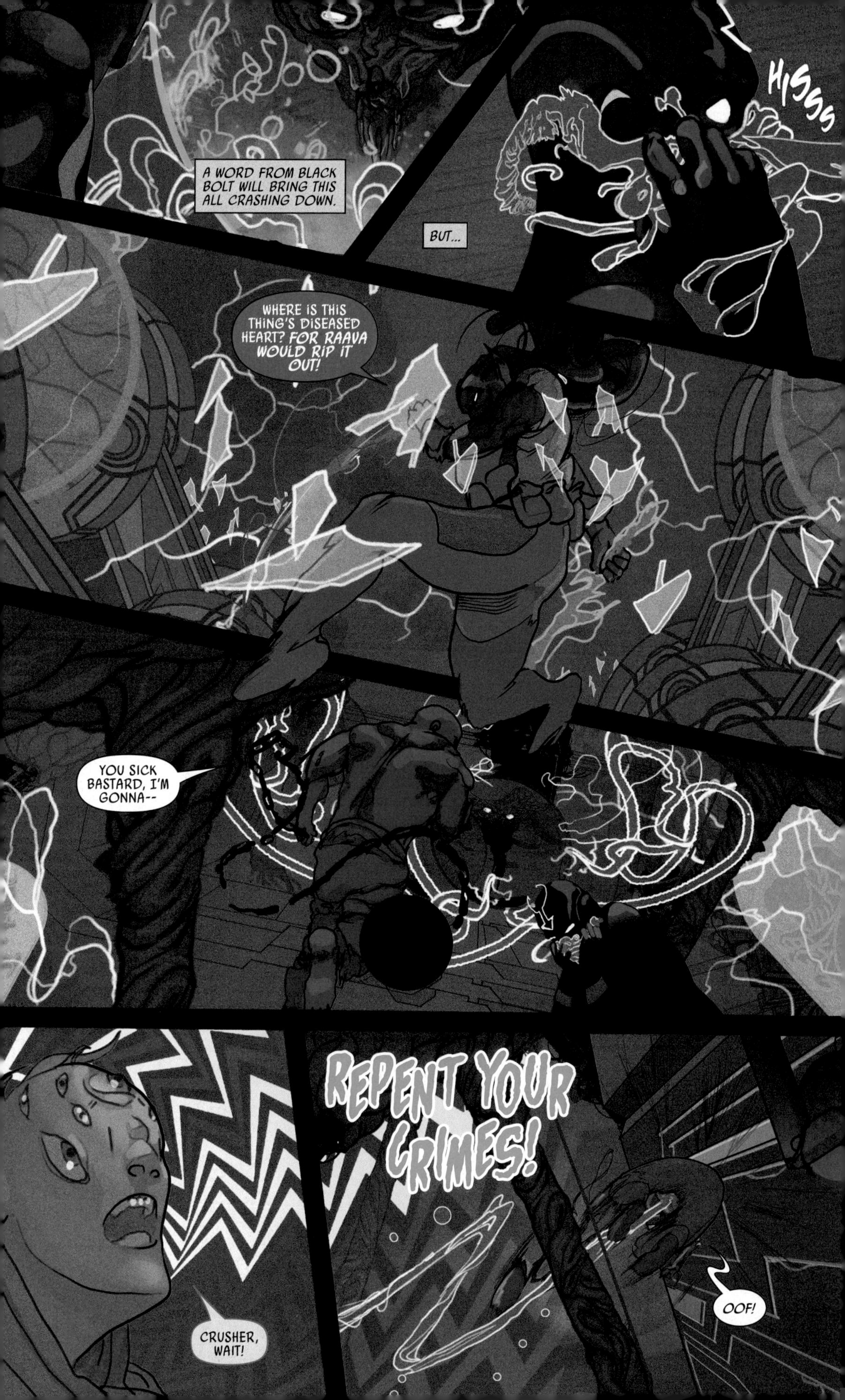
A WORD FROM BLACK BOLT WILL BRING THIS ALL CRASHING DOWN.
BUT...
HISSS
WHERE IS THIS THING'S DISEASED HEART? FOR RAAVA WOULD RIP IT OUT!
YOU SICK BASTARD, I'M GONNA--
REPENT YOUR CRIMES!
CRUSHER, WAIT!
OOF!

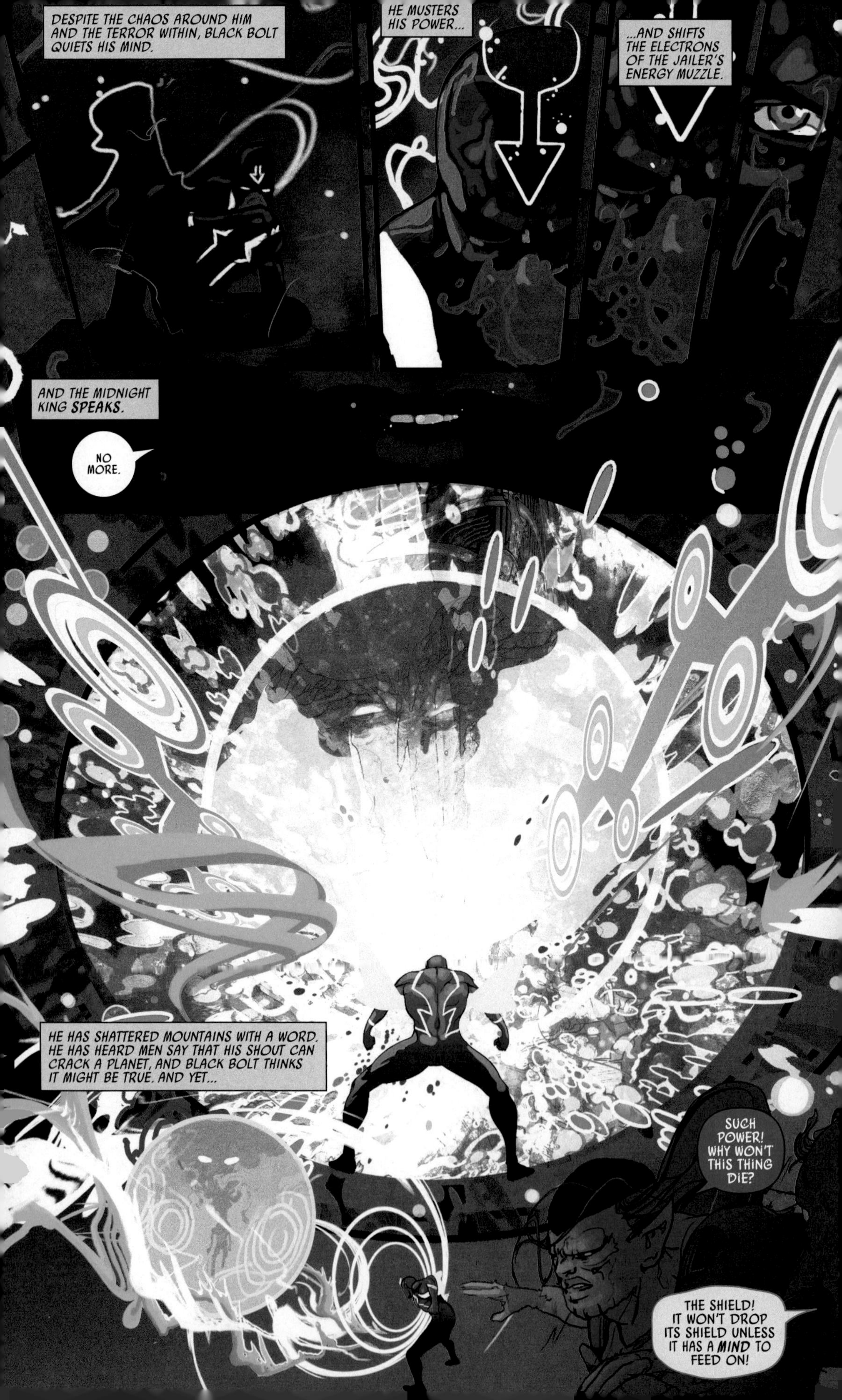

DESPITE THE CHAOS AROUND HIM AND THE TERROR WITHIN, BLACK BOLT QUIETS HIS MIND.
HE MUSTERS HIS POWER...
...AND SHIFTS THE ELECTRONS OF THE JAILER'S ENERGY MUZZLE.
AND THE MIDNIGHT KING SPEAKS.
NO MORE.
HE HAS SHATTERED MOUNTAINS WITH A WORD. HE HAS HEARD MEN SAY THAT HIS SHOUT CAN CRACK A PLANET, AND BLACK BOLT THINKS IT MIGHT BE TRUE. AND YET...
SUCH POWER! WHY WON'T THIS THING DIE?
THE SHIELD! IT WON'T DROP ITS SHIELD UNLESS IT HAS A MIND TO FEED ON!

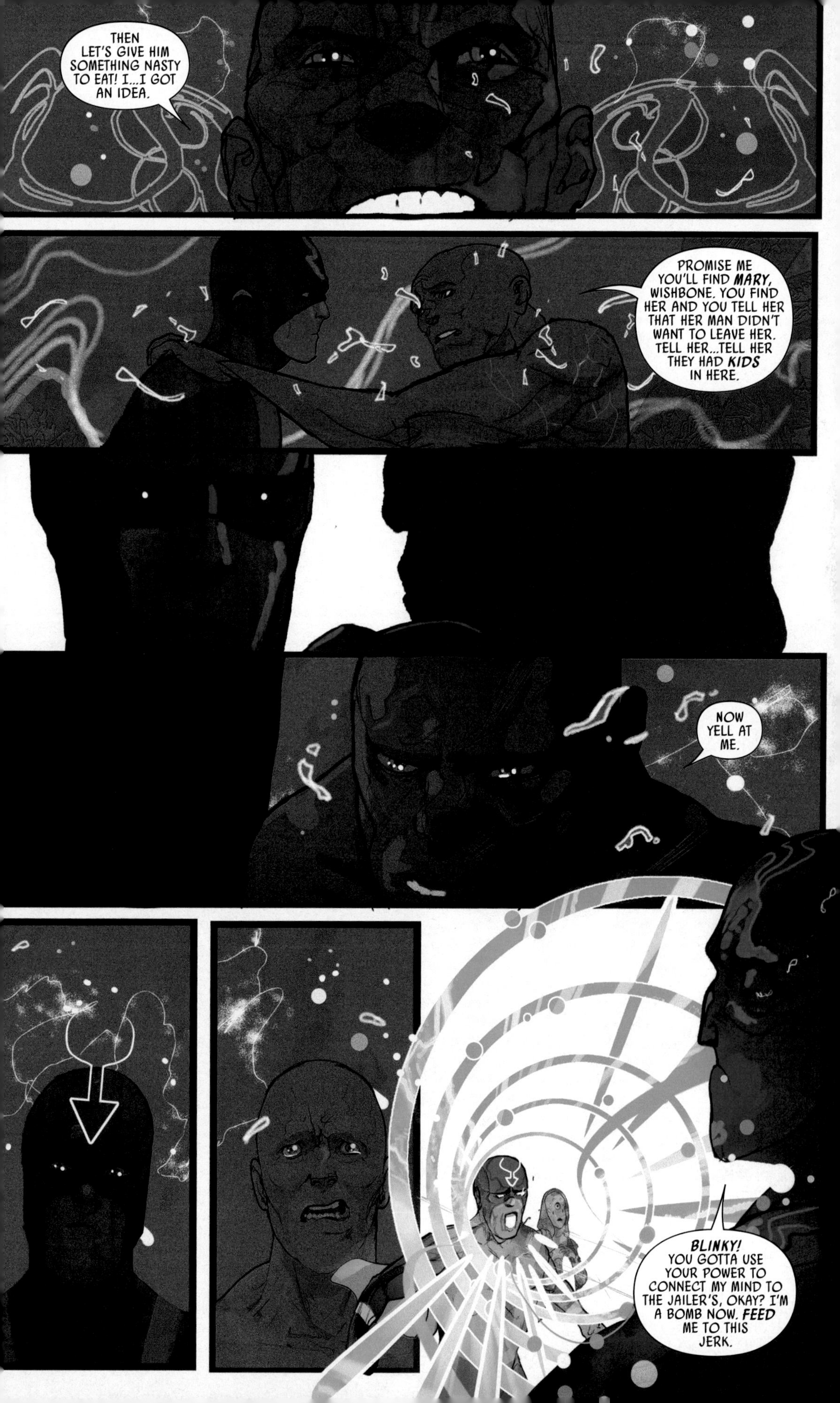
THEN LET'S GIVE HIM SOMETHING NASTY TO EAT! I...I GOT AN IDEA.
PROMISE ME YOU'LL FIND **MARY**, WISHBONE. YOU FIND HER AND YOU TELL HER THAT HER MAN DIDN'T WANT TO LEAVE HER. TELL HER...TELL HER THEY HAD **KIDS** IN HERE.
NOW YELL AT ME.
BLINKY! YOU GOTTA USE YOUR POWER TO CONNECT MY MIND TO THE JAILER'S, OKAY? I'M A BOMB NOW. **FEED** ME TO THIS JERK.

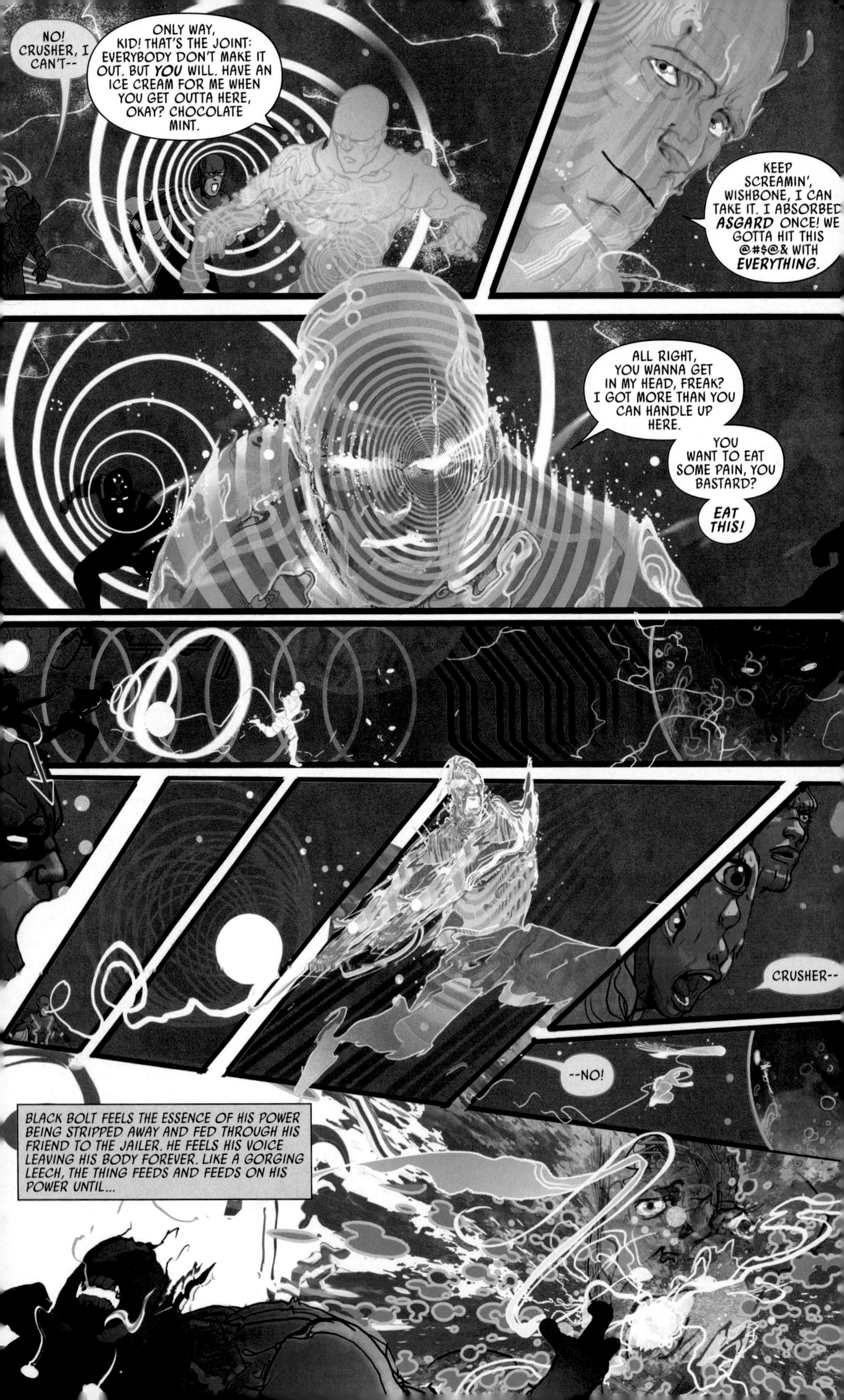
NO! CRUSHER, I CAN'T--
ONLY WAY, KID! THAT'S THE JOINT: EVERYBODY DON'T MAKE IT OUT. BUT *YOU* WILL. HAVE AN ICE CREAM FOR ME WHEN YOU GET OUTTA HERE, OKAY? CHOCOLATE MINT.
KEEP SCREAMIN', WISHBONE, I CAN TAKE IT. I ABSORBED *ASGARD* ONCE! WE GOTTA HIT THIS @#$@& WITH *EVERYTHING*.
ALL RIGHT, YOU WANNA GET IN MY HEAD, FREAK? I GOT MORE THAN YOU CAN HANDLE UP HERE.
YOU WANT TO EAT SOME PAIN, YOU BASTARD?
EAT THIS!
CRUSHER--
--NO!
BLACK BOLT FEELS THE ESSENCE OF HIS POWER BEING STRIPPED AWAY AND FED THROUGH HIS FRIEND TO THE JAILER. HE FEELS HIS VOICE LEAVING HIS BODY FOREVER. LIKE A GORGING LEECH, THE THING FEEDS AND FEEDS ON HIS POWER UNTIL...

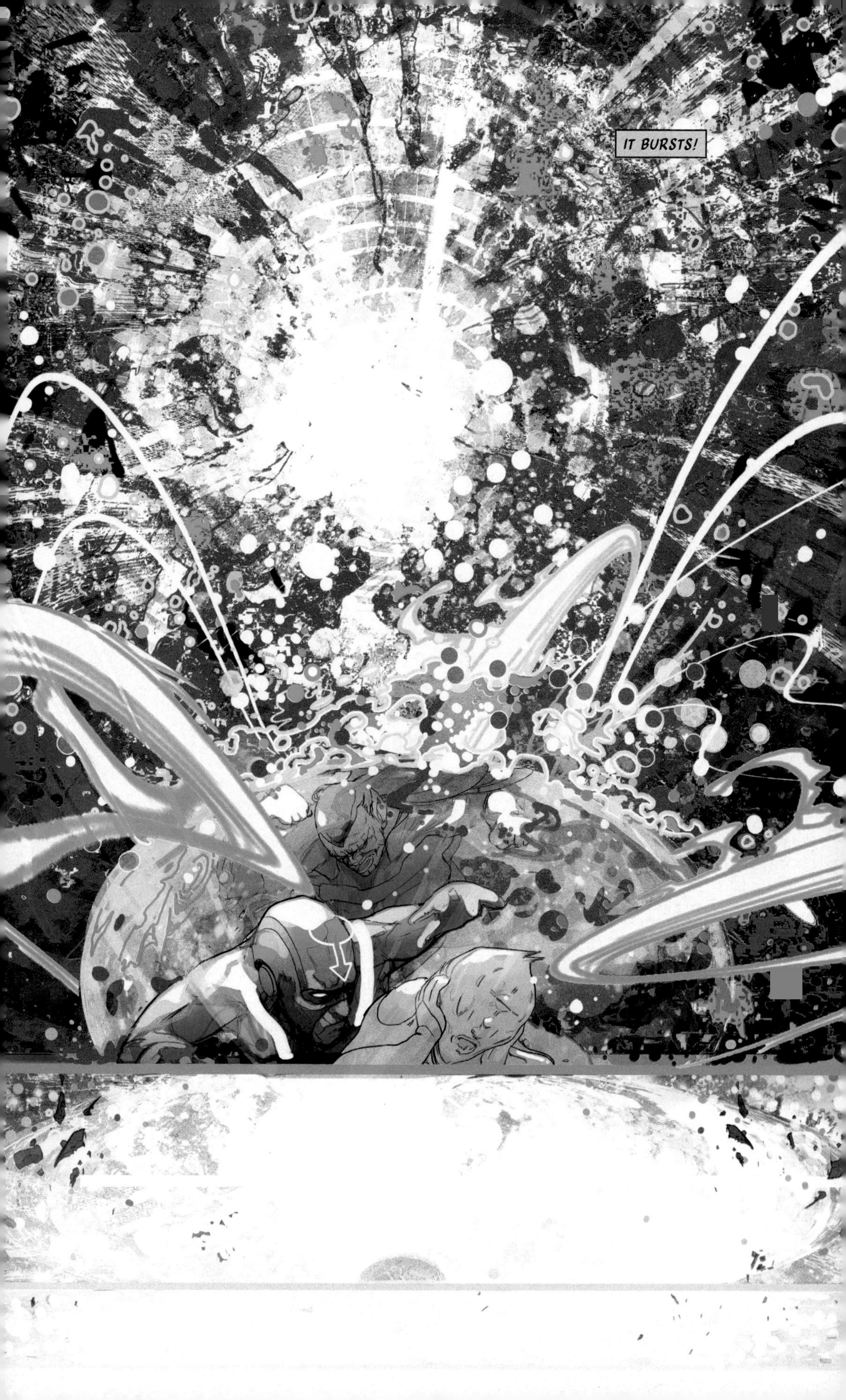
IT BURSTS!

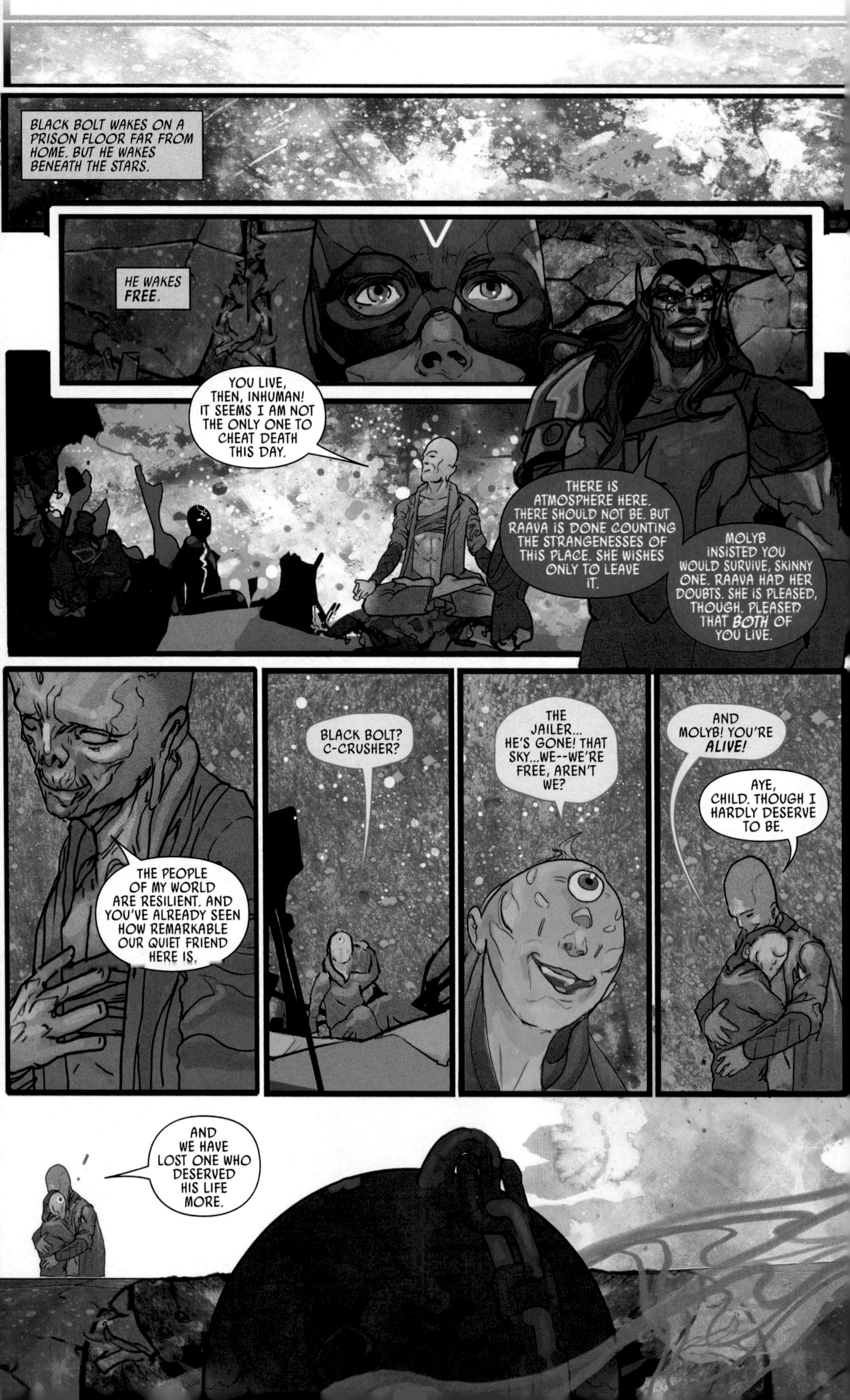

BLACK BOLT WAKES ON A PRISON FLOOR FAR FROM HOME. BUT HE WAKES BENEATH THE STARS.
HE WAKES FREE.
YOU LIVE, THEN, INHUMAN! IT SEEMS I AM NOT THE ONLY ONE TO CHEAT DEATH THIS DAY.
THERE IS ATMOSPHERE HERE. THERE SHOULD NOT BE. BUT RAAVA IS DONE COUNTING THE STRANGENESSES OF THIS PLACE. SHE WISHES ONLY TO LEAVE IT.
MOLYB INSISTED YOU WOULD SURVIVE, SKINNY ONE. RAAVA HAD HER DOUBTS. SHE IS PLEASED, THOUGH. PLEASED THAT BOTH OF YOU LIVE.
THE PEOPLE OF MY WORLD ARE RESILIENT. AND YOU'VE ALREADY SEEN HOW REMARKABLE OUR QUIET FRIEND HERE IS.
BLACK BOLT? C-CRUSHER?
THE JAILER... HE'S GONE! THAT SKY...WE--WE'RE FREE, AREN'T WE?
AND MOLYB! YOU'RE ALIVE!
AYE, CHILD. THOUGH I HARDLY DESERVE TO BE.
AND WE HAVE LOST ONE WHO DESERVED HIS LIFE MORE.

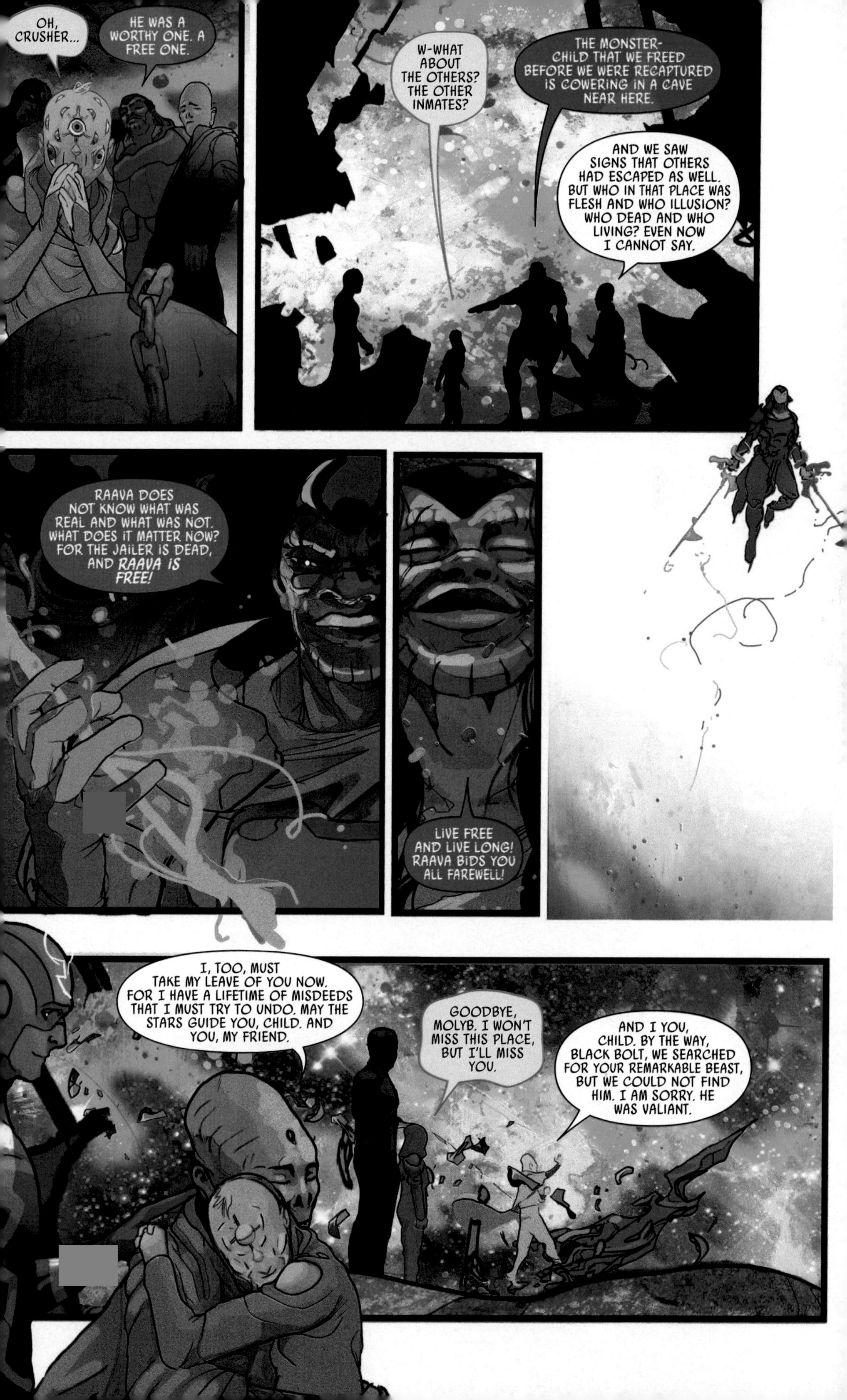
OH, CRUSHER...
HE WAS A WORTHY ONE. A FREE ONE.
W-WHAT ABOUT THE OTHERS? THE OTHER INMATES?
THE MONSTER-CHILD THAT WE FREED BEFORE WE WERE RECAPTURED IS COWERING IN A CAVE NEAR HERE.
AND WE SAW SIGNS THAT OTHERS HAD ESCAPED AS WELL. BUT WHO IN THAT PLACE WAS FLESH AND WHO ILLUSION? WHO DEAD AND WHO LIVING? EVEN NOW I CANNOT SAY.
RAAVA DOES NOT KNOW WHAT WAS REAL AND WHAT WAS NOT. WHAT DOES IT MATTER NOW? FOR THE JAILER IS DEAD, AND *RAAVA IS FREE!*
LIVE FREE AND LIVE LONG! RAAVA BIDS YOU ALL FAREWELL!
I, TOO, MUST TAKE MY LEAVE OF YOU NOW. FOR I HAVE A LIFETIME OF MISDEEDS THAT I MUST TRY TO UNDO. MAY THE STARS GUIDE YOU, CHILD. AND YOU, MY FRIEND.
GOODBYE, MOLYB. I WON'T MISS THIS PLACE, BUT I'LL MISS YOU.
AND I YOU, CHILD. BY THE WAY, BLACK BOLT, WE SEARCHED FOR YOUR REMARKABLE BEAST, BUT WE COULD NOT FIND HIM. I AM SORRY. HE WAS VALIANT.

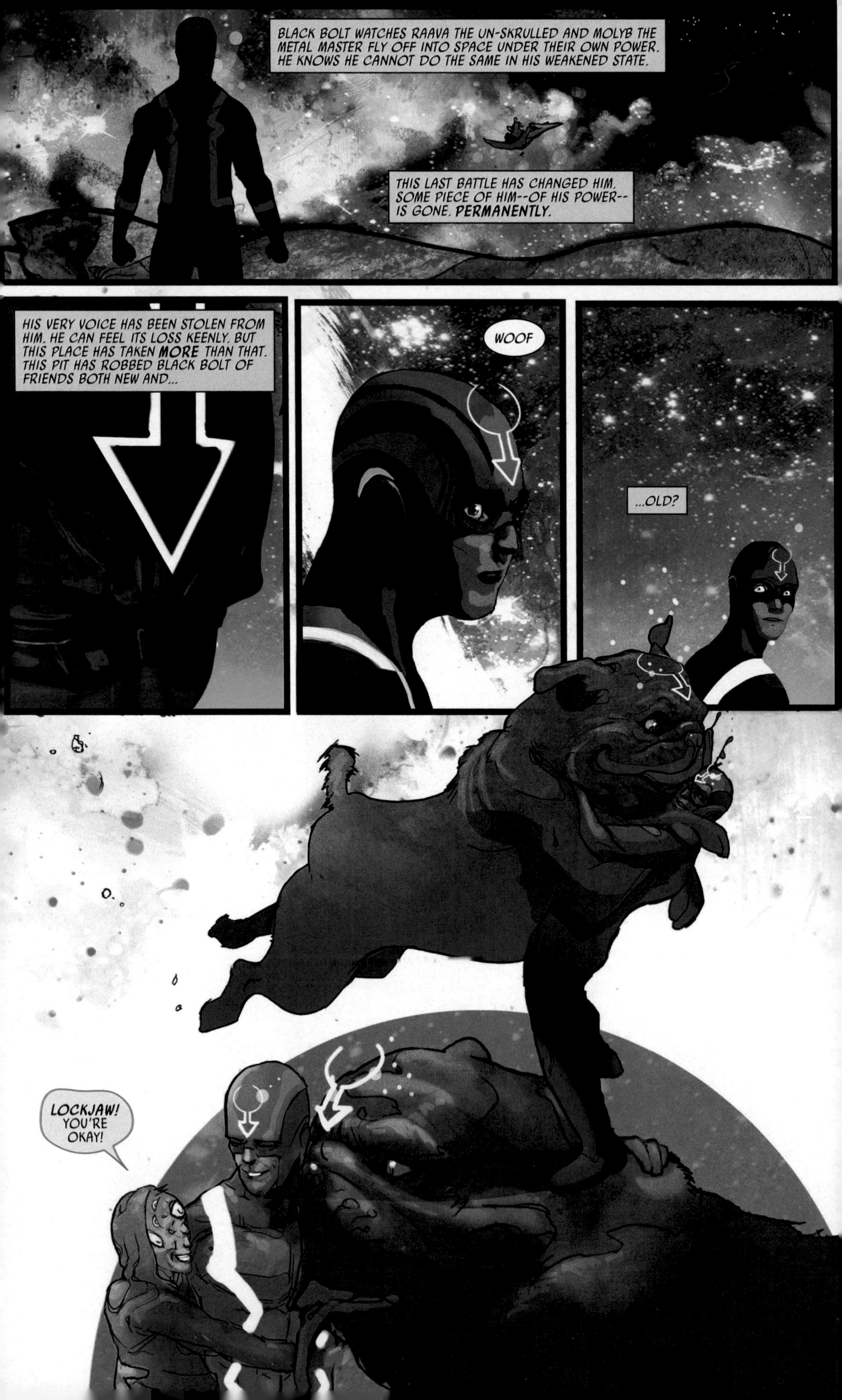
BLACK BOLT WATCHES RAAVA THE UN-SKRULLED AND MOLYB THE METAL MASTER FLY OFF INTO SPACE UNDER THEIR OWN POWER. HE KNOWS HE CANNOT DO THE SAME IN HIS WEAKENED STATE.
THIS LAST BATTLE HAS CHANGED HIM. SOME PIECE OF HIM--OF HIS POWER--IS GONE. PERMANENTLY.
HIS VERY VOICE HAS BEEN STOLEN FROM HIM. HE CAN FEEL ITS LOSS KEENLY. BUT THIS PLACE HAS TAKEN MORE THAN THAT. THIS PIT HAS ROBBED BLACK BOLT OF FRIENDS BOTH NEW AND...
WOOF
...OLD?
LOCKJAW! YOU'RE OKAY!

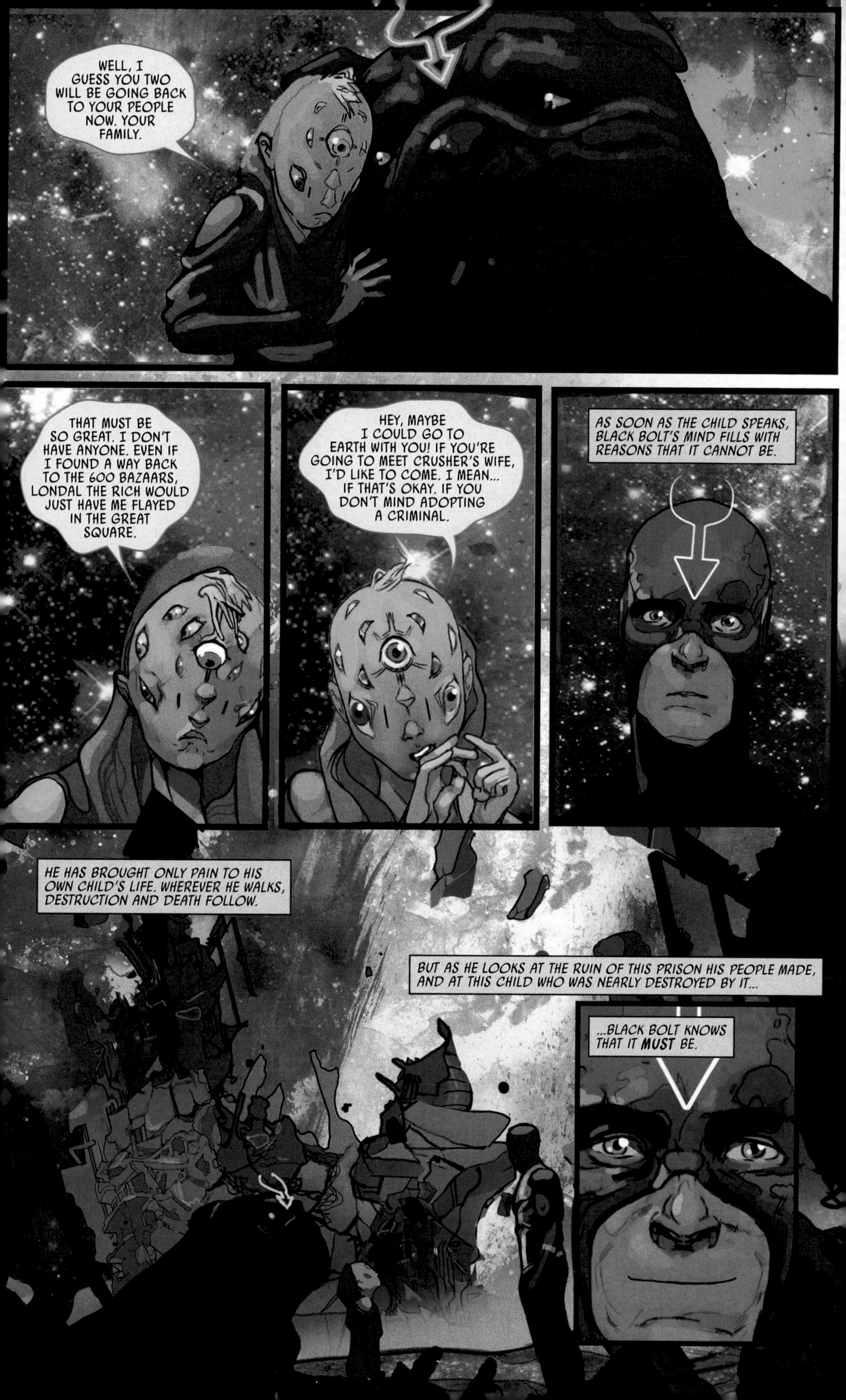
WELL, I GUESS YOU TWO WILL BE GOING BACK TO YOUR PEOPLE NOW. YOUR FAMILY.
THAT MUST BE SO GREAT. I DON'T HAVE ANYONE. EVEN IF I FOUND A WAY BACK TO THE 600 BAZAARS, LONDAL THE RICH WOULD JUST HAVE ME FLAYED IN THE GREAT SQUARE.
HEY, MAYBE I COULD GO TO EARTH WITH YOU! IF YOU'RE GOING TO MEET CRUSHER'S WIFE, I'D LIKE TO COME. I MEAN... IF THAT'S OKAY. IF YOU DON'T MIND ADOPTING A CRIMINAL.
AS SOON AS THE CHILD SPEAKS, BLACK BOLT'S MIND FILLS WITH REASONS THAT IT CANNOT BE.
HE HAS BROUGHT ONLY PAIN TO HIS OWN CHILD'S LIFE. WHEREVER HE WALKS, DESTRUCTION AND DEATH FOLLOW.
BUT AS HE LOOKS AT THE RUIN OF THIS PRISON HIS PEOPLE MADE, AND AT THIS CHILD WHO WAS NEARLY DESTROYED BY IT...
...BLACK BOLT KNOWS THAT IT **MUST** BE.

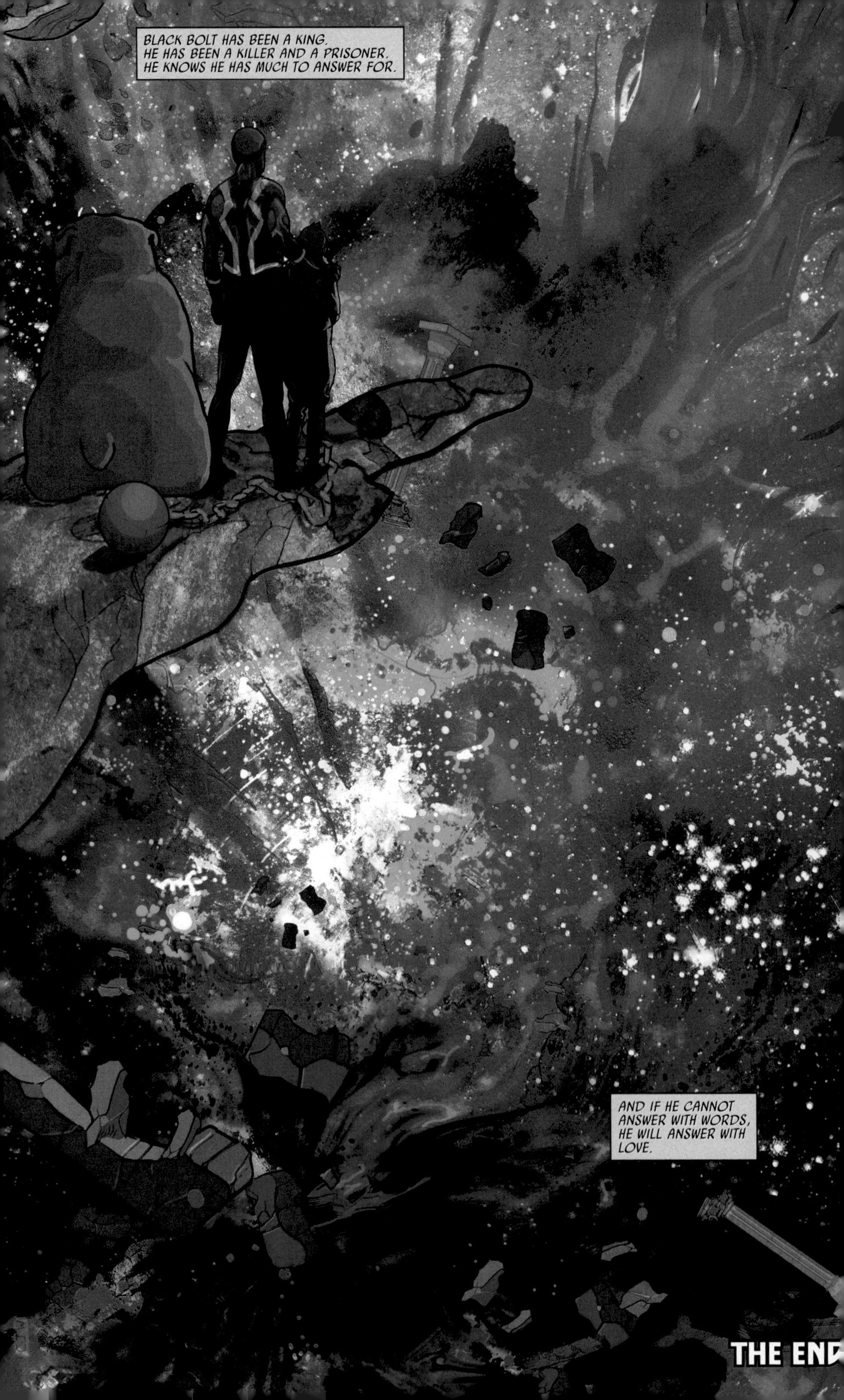
BLACK BOLT HAS BEEN A KING.
HE HAS BEEN A KILLER AND A PRISONER.
HE KNOWS HE HAS MUCH TO ANSWER FOR.
AND IF HE CANNOT ANSWER WITH WORDS, HE WILL ANSWER WITH LOVE.
THE END

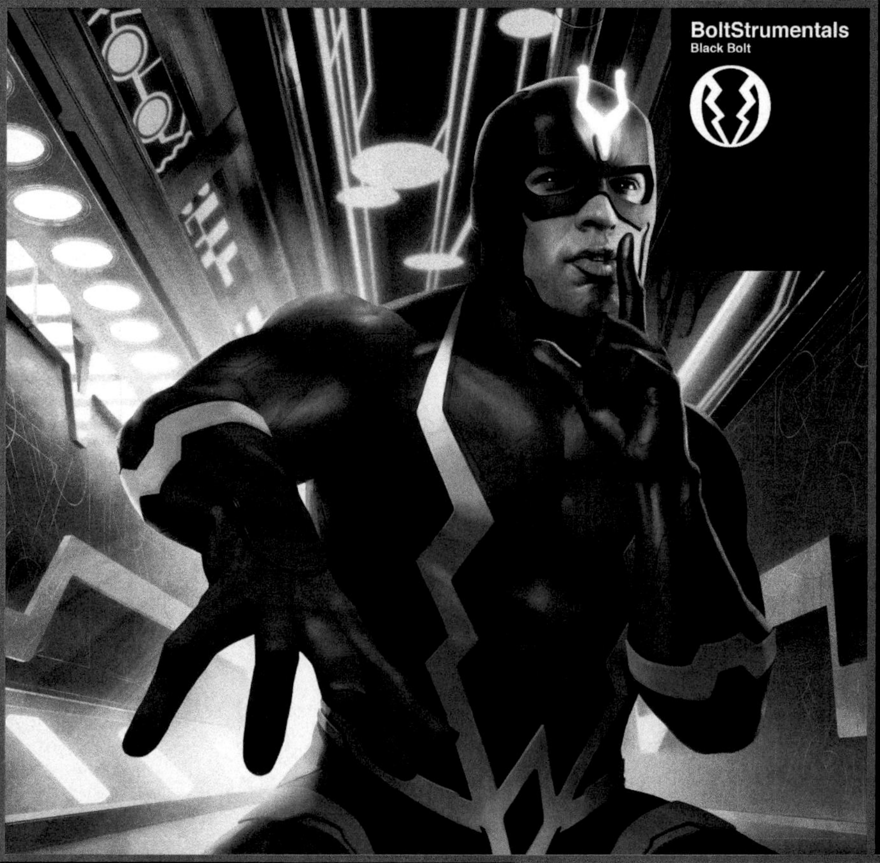
BoltStrumentals
Black Bolt

#1 HIP-HOP VARIANT BY RAHZZAH

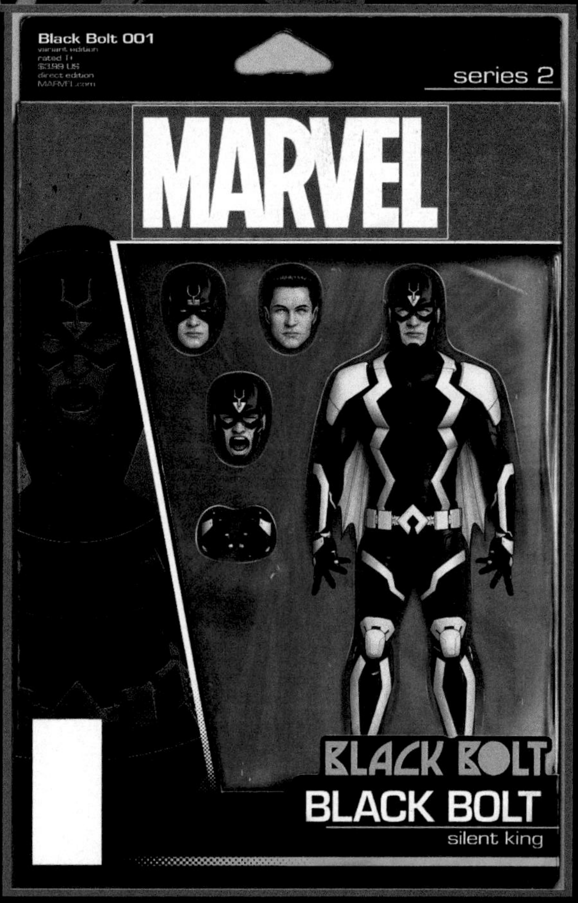
Black Bolt 001
variant edition
rated T+
$3.99 US
direct edition
MARVEL.com
series 2
MARVEL
BLACK BOLT
BLACK BOLT
silent king

#1 ACTION FIGURE VARIANT
BY JOHN TYLER CHRISTOPHER

#1 VARIANT BY BUTCH GUICE & ANDY TROY

#2 VARIANT
BY DECLAN SHALVEY & JORDIE BELLAIRE

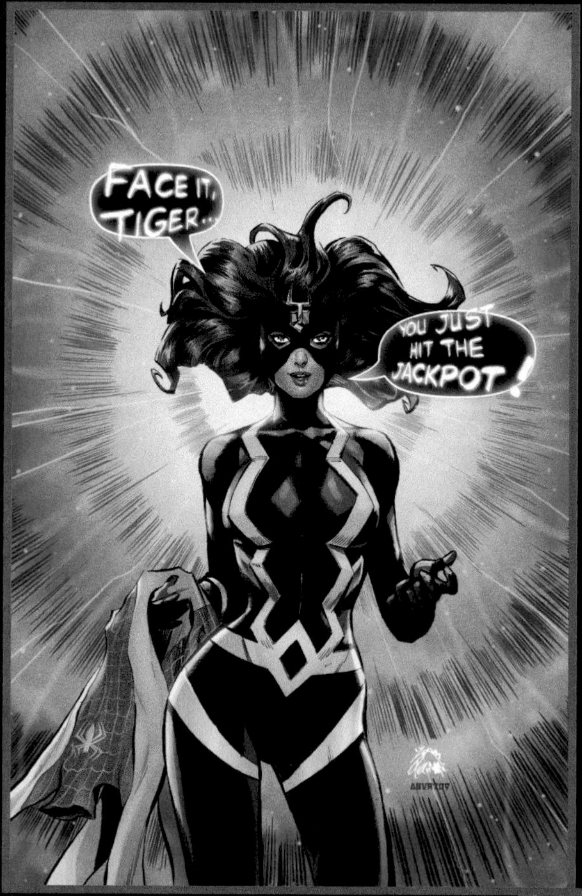
FACE IT, TIGER...
YOU JUST HIT THE JACKPOT!

#2 MARY JANE VARIANT
BY RYAN STEGMAN & JESUS ABURTOV

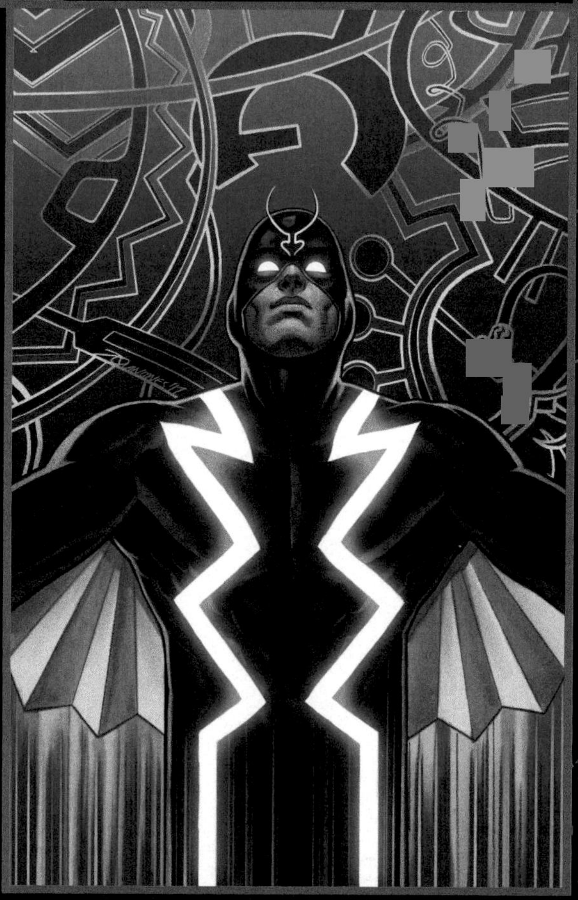

#3 VARIANT BY JOE QUINONES

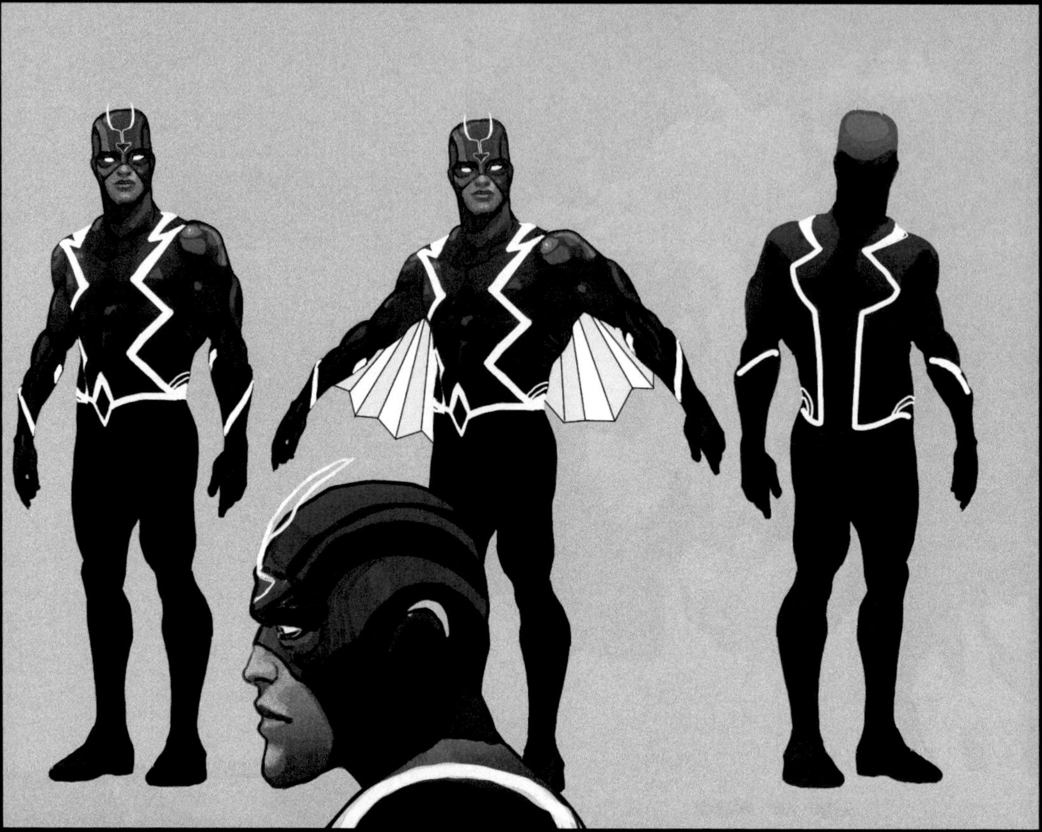

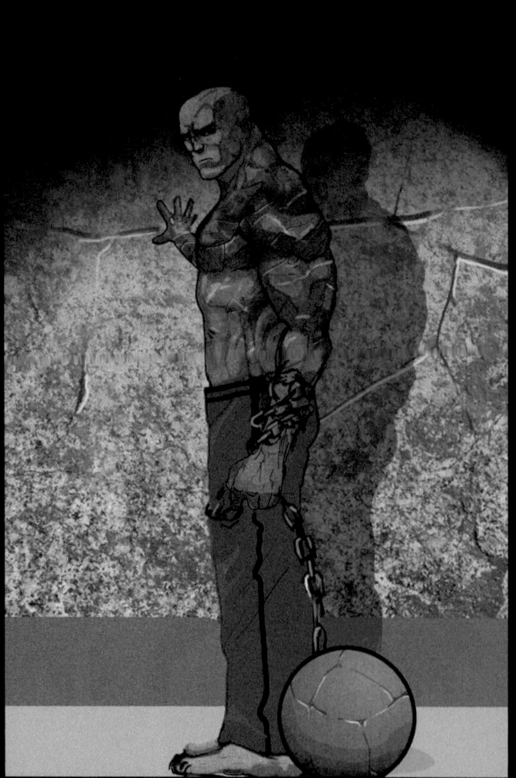

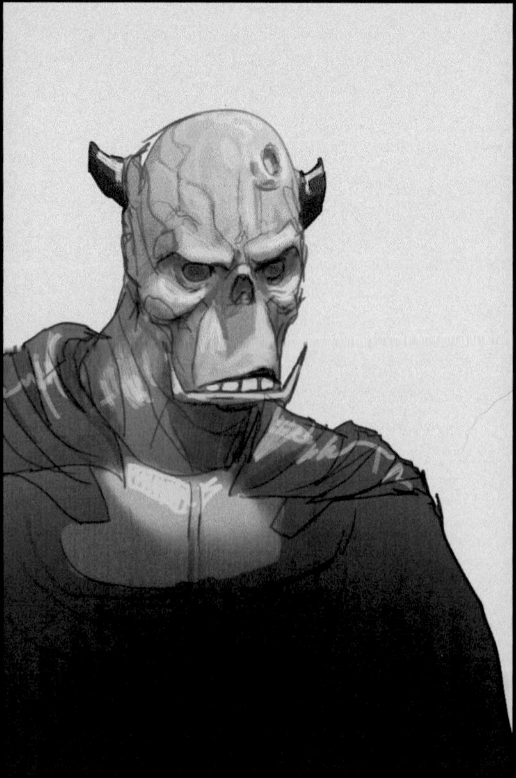

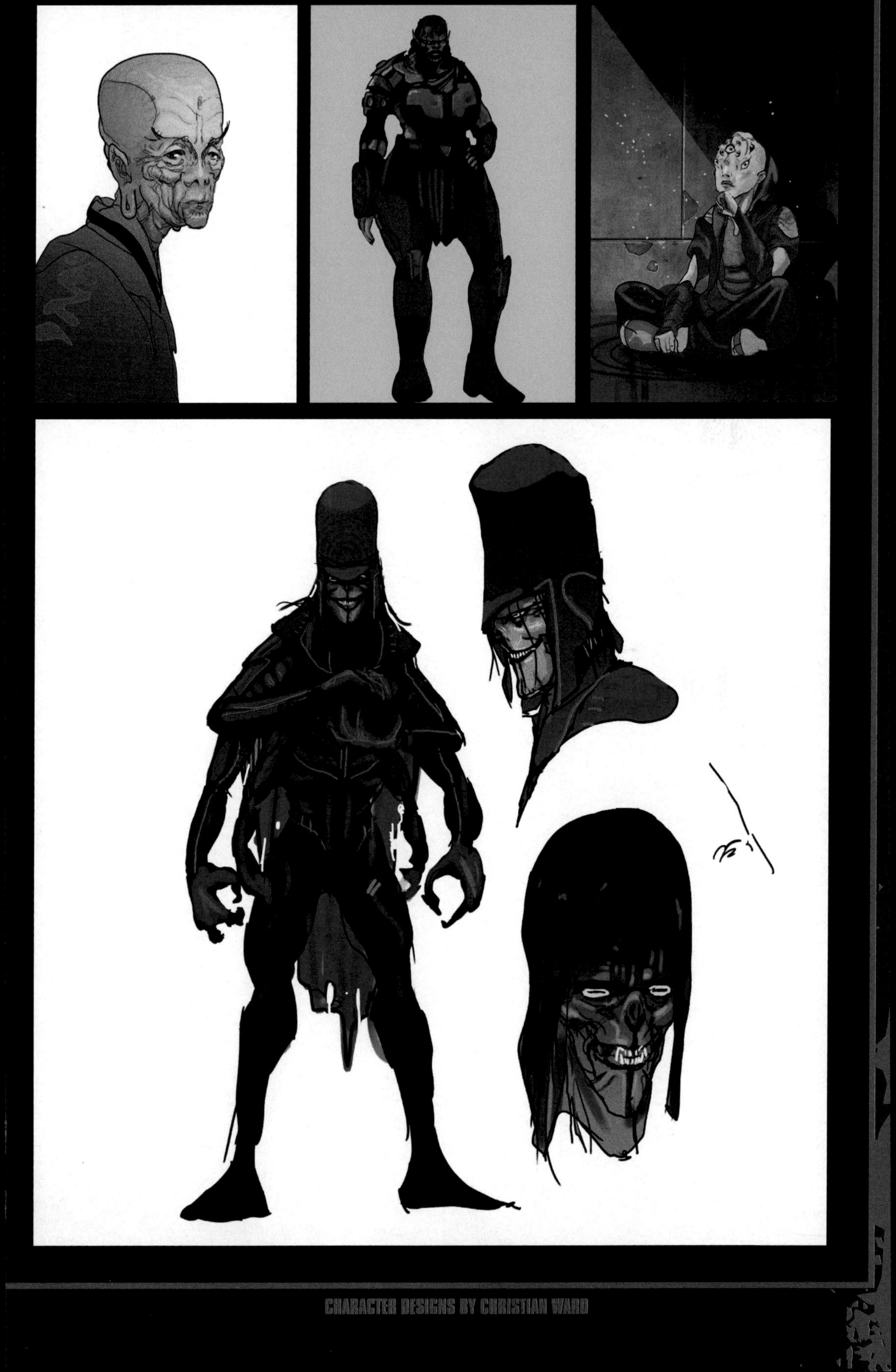

CHARACTER DESIGNS BY CHRISTIAN WARD

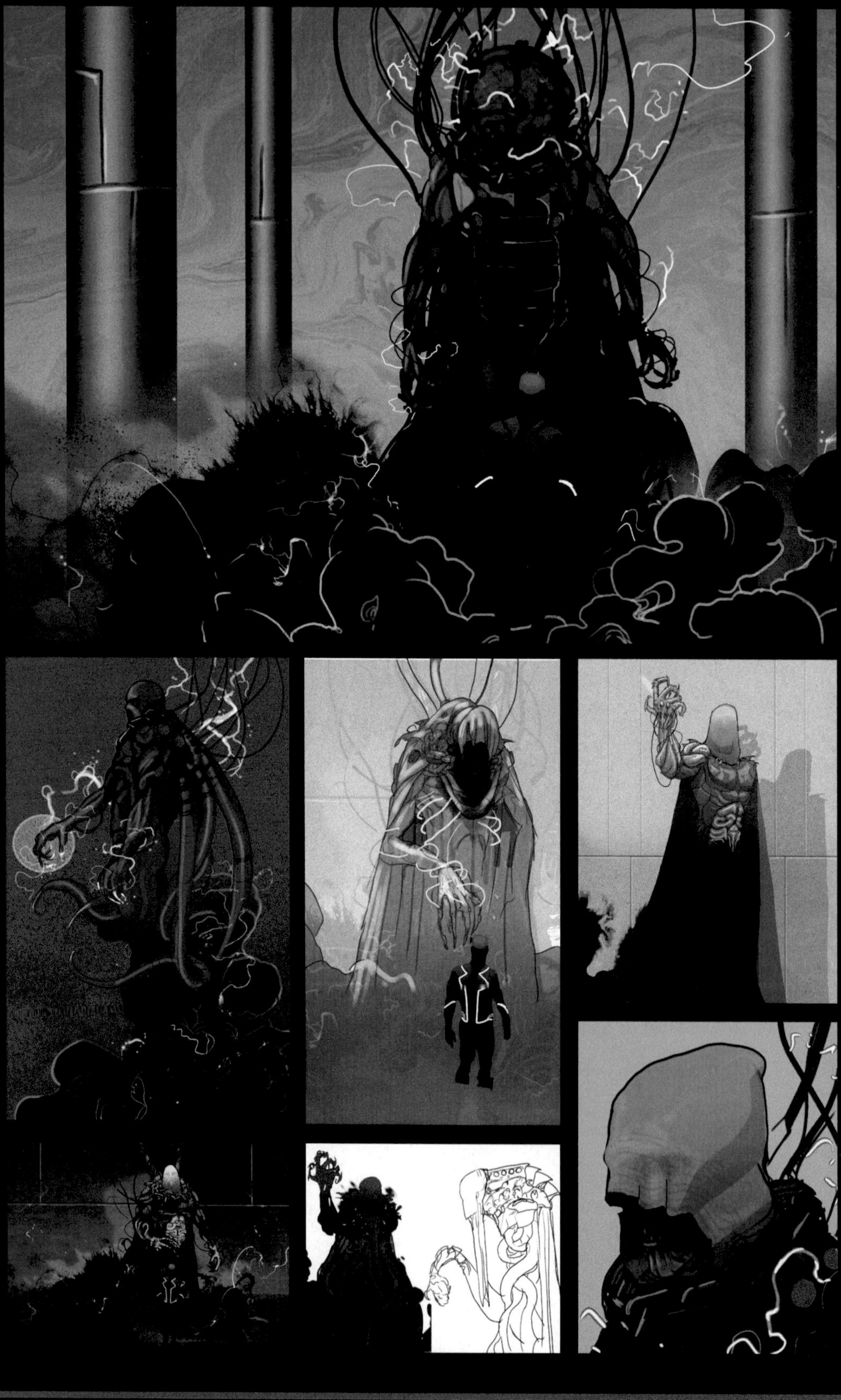

CHARACTER DESIGNS BY CHRISTIAN WARD